WAY *to the* WATER

**Quranic Truths,
Prophetic Teachings
and Sound Hearts**

WAY *to the* WATER

Quranic Truths, Prophetic Teachings and Sound Hearts

BASMA I. ABDELGAFAR

CLARITAS
BOOKS

1 2 3 4 5 6 7 8 9 10

CLARITAS BOOKS

Bernard Street, Swansea, United Kingdom
Milpitas, California, United States

CLARITAS
BOOKS

First Published in November 2025

Typeset in Minion Pro 14/11

Way to the Water
Quranic Truths, Prophetic Teachings and Sound Hearts
By Basma I. Abdelgafar

A CIP catalogue record for this book is available from the British Library

ISBN: 978-1-80011-950-5

بسم الله الرحمن الرحيم

To Gaza, that taught the world
the way to the water.

Basma I. Abdelgafar is a dedicated student of the Quran and Sunnah, deeply engaged in exploring their relevance to modern life. She currently serves as Vice President of Policy and Governance at the Maqasid Institute and as a Research Fellow at the Center for Islam in the Contemporary World at Shenandoah University. With a career spanning three decades across academia, government, and NGOs, she has played a pivotal role in shaping graduate and professional training programs worldwide. Her scholarly work addresses critical themes such as Quranic ethics, Muslim civic engagement in plural societies, public policy in Islam, and global governance and innovation.

CONTENTS

ACKNOWLEDGEMENTS

In the Name of Allah, the Merciful, the Giver of Mercy, all praise and thanks are due to Allah and prayers, peace and blessings upon Prophet Muhammad, the beloved, trustworthy, and pure. I thank endlessly for the blessing of the Quran and the Messenger who conveyed and embodied its teachings.

I owe a debt of gratitude to my parents Ibrahim Abdelgafar (d.2019), may Allah have mercy on him and admit him to the highest level of Jannah, and Afaf Abdelgafar who have given me lifelong love, support and encouragement to take the unconventional path. Thank you to my children Billal, Yasmeen and Hanna who gave the extra love that this journey needed and for becoming the young adults that afforded me the peace of mind to take on this project. Thank you to my sister, Shrouk Abdelgafar, without whom life would be so grim, and the sweetest brother-in-law, Garrett Rice, who always showed confidence in my ability to keep the course. To Elena Prutzerova, the kindest friend and sister, thank you for giving me a home away from home.

I have been blessed to share my life with a formidable scholar and prolific writer, Jasser Auda. Praise to the Lord of the Worlds who gifted me with someone who walks and talks the path of the Quran. Thank you for your encouragement, for having the patience to hear me talk about this project over the past few years, for never declining to help, and keeping me grounded in dreams of possibility.

Thank you to my family at the Maqasid Institute who gave me space and time to write. There is no more a dear brother than Zaid Barzinji, MI President, who has been a solid supporter over the years. You have taught me kindness and patience like no other. Thank you to my colleagues Idlus Rafikov and Heba Abduljawad for carrying the institutional burden during these intense years and for being first readers.

To my dearest friend and sister Rabia Naguib, thank you for the creative disruption of my academic journey. And to Sanja Bilic who dreamt with me about how we could serve our Ummah, for sharing your incredible talent and scholarship on this renewed path. Thank you to my lifelong sister and friend

Noha Attia for your ongoing support and enthusiasm. To the wonderful group of women, my students in Maahaduna, who convinced me that a book of this nature was overdue, Maryati, Siti Nurhaidah, Nurin Qaisara, Marisa, Normala, Nuruljannah, Surya Elyna, Nasirah, Nur Rizqin, Alia Fatin, Putri Suhana, Nur Fazliana, Azreen, Nur Filzah, Siti Nadia Yanti and the team at Hayaa Network, Maimouna, Liyana, Fajriah, Ameesha and our special friend Fiza O. For my friends all over the world that I cannot list by name but who dwell securely in my heart, thank you for enriching my life.

A special thanks to those who have sponsored this project. To my dearest friend and sister Mamak Shahbazi, may Allah grant you the highest level of Jannah. I miss you dearly. I pray that Allah rewards you beyond measure for your generosity, encouragement, and gentle presence in my life. It passed by so fast. Much appreciation to Ayman Abdelaal, a dear friend and brother, for your support and confidence. Thank you to the Maqasid Institute, the Barzinji Foundation, and the Mirza Foundation. Your financial generosity was indispensable.

Lastly but certainly not least, thank you to my publisher and editor, Sharif H. Banna, for believing in this project, and shepherding the process from draft to book.

It goes without saying that all views expressed in this book are my own and are not attributable to any of the individuals or organizations for whom I have expressed gratitude.

PREFACE

Read, is that not the word that unravels the most truthful and enduring revelation? Read and let me tell you about the beauty of a sound heart, calm and overflowing with mercy, filled from the water of a sacred source. Sensitive to the language of the universe, its person, and possessions in the service of The-One-God, Allah in Arabic, its Lord and Maker. Observe the ways in which it orders its life, governs its affairs and those of others, consistently calling to what is fair, just, and beneficial and barring what is mean, corrupt, and harmful. Recognize its honesty, loyalty, love and generosity and you understand the ultimate feature that will save its keeper on the Day of Judgement: a sound heart (Ash-Shu'ara 26:89). In Arabic, the language of the Quran, it is called *qalb salim*, the inner core that is pure, beautiful, and healthy. Connect with one of them and you've found a veritable treasure, connect with many and you can collectively change the world.

A sound, luminous, heart has graduated through multiple stages of purification. The tensions of life have softened and at the same time strengthened its resolve. As any keeper will tell you, it's all good. Like a firm tree its roots are deep, and its branches reach out to the sky. In the private, hidden, realm it continues to nourish everything surrounding it so that the darkness is nothing but a challenge to remain firm and patient. It signals peace and unity drawing kindred spirits into its field. Unified by an unspoken language, there is always some level of reciprocity with other hearts, unified by an unspoken language, all life is sacred. The ultimate stage in its development, which continues to its last beat, fuses the sound heart with the will of its Creator and all that is truthful, pure, and beautiful in His creation.

Read with an open heart. Put down your guard, set aside your biases, quiet the voices that will inevitably enter your mind, to engage the Book in your purest essence, simply as *'ebad Ar-Rahman* or servants of the Merciful. Recognize that when Allah speaks about or to certain individuals or groups, He does so in the presence of all, everyone is called to witnesses the Truth as *'ebad* before and above any other identity. If Allah addresses men more often than women, if He includes both in certain designations, if He provides specialized instructions regarding women, or likens both men and women and our relationships to each other to His other creation, we must strive to understand why. Allah is the most knowing of what He created. The beautiful surrender, *Islam*, can only be found in our respect of the boundaries of servitude (*'ubudiyah*).

Can we read the Book and follow our beloved Prophet Muhammad ﷺ – and the previous messengers – to carry the Trust (*Amanah*) with greater resilience, competence, and humility?

> *Verily, We presented the Trust to the skies, and the earth, and the mountains so they declined from carrying her and took caution from her and the human carried her. Verily, he was unjust, ignorant.*
>
> *So that Allah may punish the hypocritical men and the hypocritical women and the men and women who associate others with Him and that He may accept the repentance of the believing men and the believing women. And Allah is the Granter of Forgiveness, Giver of Mercy.* (Al-Ahzab 33:72-73)

I cannot fulfill the Trust, as complex and enormous as Allah's command not to sever what He has commanded to be joined (Al-Baqarah 2:27; Ar-Ra'd 13:25). Ultimately, we are all connected. But the Trust is not mine nor yours to fulfill, we are limited beings, to suggest fulfillment would only be due to arrogance and ignorance. The *Amanah* belongs to Allah. We can only carry the Trust, presented to us as it was that we may seek Allah's guidance, forgiveness, and mercy, that we may tread softly on His earth, on each other's paths, knowing that through our injustice and ignorance the universe's delicate balance is disturbed save for His Mercy.

To Allah we belong and to Allah we return, every man, woman, child, every living creature. We are guests on this earth, all of us. Prophet Muhammad ﷺ advised us to *be in the world as if we are strangers or wayfarers* (Sahih Bukhari). My hope is that this book will inspire a rethinking of our relationships to each other, to unify our hearts and in turn, our connection with Allah, ourselves, others, and His magnificent universe. That we will lay down our arms to embrace purpose, connection, and holism. It is an invitation to enter a symphony of glorification of our Creator, to position ourselves in relation to our closeness to Him rather than in perpetual struggle and conflict with each other. My narrative is comprised of three springs: Quranic truth, the teachings of Prophet Muhammad ﷺ, and the insights of a humble heart regarding what these sources tell us about the healing, light, and guidance that Islam holds for our contemporary moment and future.

PART 1

Basic Beginnings

Way to the Water

The *Shariah* is the divine law, the immutable way, it is the guidance upon which Prophet Muhammad ﷺ was set by Allah, a special path tailored for him and his followers, men and women, to guide and illuminate their hearts. "Then We put you upon an exemplary ordinance (*Shariah*) from the Command, so follow it and do not follow the whims of those who do not know" (Al-Jathiyah 45:18). It is possible to gain insight into it by studying his life and reflecting on the Quran of which he was the first and most perfect living embodiment. But if you want to live by it, to drink from it, you must first recognize a little-known fact - the *Shariah* literally is a source of water from which one draws without the aid of a rope as one would require for a water well. The *Shariah* is a blessed source of water, a source of life and revival. And although there is no physical rope, drawing from it demands grasping and holding on to the rope of Allah - the Quran. Prophet Muhammad ﷺ said: "The Book of Allah is the sturdy Rope of Allah, and it is His clear light…" (Jami' Al-Tirmidhi). The Shariah and the Rope to access it, are blessings provided by an all-merciful Lord for those who seek the bounties of this world and the next, who choose to live with the gentlest presence, doing the least harm and providing the greatest benefits to themselves and those around them.

Out of water Allah created a sentient being, *bashar* in Arabic, which was made to relate through kinship and marriage (Al-Furqan 25:54). If you look up the meaning of *bashar* you will find that it encompasses the attributes of contact, skin, connection, and physicality – a sentient being that connects. It is the term that Maryam ؑ uses in response to her Lord's messenger when he informs her that she will be gifted a boy: "My Lord, I will have a son and no human (*bashar*) has touched me?" (Al-'Imran 3:47). Water – *bashar* – combines, connects, and binds. Every male and female is part of a lineage of mixed or amalgamated, inseparable, fluid, literally water (As-Sajdah 32:7-8; Al-Mursalat 77:20). No human – no living creature for that matter – is created of anything else, nothing lesser or more superior.

All living creatures need water for survival and regeneration. It is the source of life in its origin. Water quenches our thirst, heals and purifies our bodies and souls. We drink it as do the earth's animals and plants (An-Nur 24:45). With the rains, gardens flourish and fruits grow for us to eat (Al-Mu'minun 23:19). Through water, Allah propagates for us plants, olives, palm trees, grapevines, and all kinds of produce (An-Nahl 16:10). It is Allah who drives water to parched lands, saving it, aiding in the production of vegetation, that is then consumed by animals and people (As-Sajdah 32:27). Water is therefore a common – a blessing to be shared by all living creatures (Al-Qamar 54:28). Prophet Muhammad ﷺ taught that the one who has access to water but withholds from those in need will not be spoken to by Allah on the Day of Judgement (Sahih Bukhari). He ﷺ stated that a Muslim partners in three things including pasture, water, fire, and another narration he added salt (Sunan Abi Dawud).

Is it not wonderous how this one pure fluid leads to the production of an incredible diversity of creation? It is Allah who brought down water from the sky to bring out from the earth plants of all kinds – greens that give seeds – and date palms, grape vines, olive groves, pomegranate orchards – plants that are similar and dissimilar, all from the same water source (Al-An'am 6:99). The Quran asks by way of challenge and astonishment at human arrogance, "Do you not see that Allah sends down water from the sky with which We bring forth produce of different colours? And of the mountains are streaks of white, and red, differing in colour, and raven black" (Fatir 35:27). "Do you not see that Allah sends down water from the sky directing it through channels in the earth to bring out by it plants of different colours then it dries up and you see them yellowing and He makes them deteriorate…" (Az-Zumar 39:21). Everything living, in all its diversity, is the outcome of one pure water source.

Water calms, heals, and purifies. It is a means for physical and spiritual purification (An-Nisa' 4:43; Al-Ma'idah 5:6). Indeed, Allah poured it in abundance on the believers who were participating in the battle of Badr to purify them and rid them of the taint of the devil, binding their hearts with peace and firming their step (Al-Anfal 8:11). Likewise, He sends it down to purify the earth and all that is in it. The Quran tells us that Allah sends down water from the sky so that valleys or basins in the earth flow to their measure. This flow carries with it contaminants the like of which is also the product of combustion used for making adornments and other things that we humans desire. We are told that this is how Allah demonstrates the difference between truth and falsehood. As for the contaminants they escape unseen and as for what benefits people it remains – settles – in the earth (Ar-Ra'd 13:17). Water needs to flow, to move, to be carried, for its ability to fulfill its mission to cleanse the earth, to revive it.

With water the earth is revived. Allah sends it down, pure, cool, refreshing, from the sky to revive dead regions and quench the thirst of creation – animals and humans (Al-Furqan 25:48). It is plain to see for anyone with vision how the earth comes to life when it receives the rains, how it moves and flourishes, this is how, we are told, Allah revives the dead (Fussilat 41:39). The bringing down of water from the sky to revive the earth after her death and enable other life forms (Al-Baqarah 2:164) is a great *ayah* – a truthful lesson, sign, proof.

Water and its necessity are *ayat* (sg. *ayah*) in our creation, continued survival, and our resurrection. Blessed water is released from the sky to propagate gardens and seeds for harvest and palms and fruit, for Allah's servants (*'ebad*) and to revive dead regions – it is as such that humans too will be revived (Qaf 50:9-11). Indeed, Allah sends down water from the sky to revive the earth after her death (An-Nahl 16:65; Al-'Ankabut 29:63) – yes, death. Reflect on this. We see the revival of the earth, of families, and communities, with the meeting of water and earth – we see them give and flourish. The earth, a beautiful *she* in the Quran – alive, conscious, responding to her Lord – cannot survive without the water that Allah replenishes her with. He brings her back to life with it, just as He brings us to life with water, with the *Shariah*.

"Oh you people if you are in doubt of the resurrection consider that We have created you from earth/dust, then from a drop of fluid, then from a matter that clings/attaches, then from a foetus created and not created (*mukhalaqa wa ghair mukhalaqa*), so that We may clarify for you, and allow to settle in the womb what We will for an appointed term, then We bring you out as children then you reach your strength and of you are those who will die and of you are those who will be sent back to the most pesky stage of life that one may know little compared to previous state of knowing. And you see the earth subdued but if we send down on her water, she moves, and swells and produces (*anbatat*) joyful happy pairs" (Al-Hajj 22:5). It is the abundance of water that enables the emergence of happy, bright, pairs (Luqman 31:10). It is clear. The Water. The Earth. Combined. Our birth in pairs, male and female. Life – propagation - and death. Life again.

The Quran tells us: "And give them an example of the life of this world [it is] as water that we sent down from the sky so that it mixed with the vegetation of the earth then it turns (literally awakens) brittle scattered by the wind and Allah is ever capable over all things" (Al-Kahf 18:45). When the water mixes with the earth's soils it produces diverse life forms but these are only temporary. They will eventually wither and die and yet the rains will bring forth new vegetation, varieties, perhaps in different locations. These too, very much like us, with flourish and decay – back to the earth where they originated. "...From this earth you were created and to her you are returned and from her you will be brought out another time" (Taha 20:55).

And again, we are reminded: "Indeed, the example of the life of this world is like water that We have sent down from the sky, that then mixes with the plants of the earth which is consumed by people and animals. To the extent that the earth takes her adornments and decorates herself, and her residents think that they can overcome her, she receives Our command by night or by day, so that We make her reaped as though she never prospered yesterday. It is as such that We detail the ayat for a folk that think" (Yunus 10:24). The water comes down by Allah's command, and the earth responds by Allah's command. Only the foolish come to believe that her beauty was of their doing – that they had to the power to overcome and subdue. It is an illusion. She ultimately responds only to her Lord.

Water, too, is under Allah's command in its abundance, purity, nature, and mission (Al-Qamar 54:11). What power do we have to grow beautiful gardens and trees without water and the source of water? (An-Naml 27:60). It is Allah, and only Allah, that has full control of it. "Do you not see the water you drink? Who brings it down from the sky?" (Al-Waqi'ah 56:68-69). "And if it were to disappear or sink into the earth, who could restore its flow?" (Al-Mulk 67:30). It is Allah who brings down water from the sky to quench our thirst, we are not the ones who have the stores or reserves of this water (Al-Hijr 15:22). Indeed, if the water of a land were to be swallowed up who could bring it back? (Al-Kahf 18:41).

The truth of water – pure water that quenches, sustains, revives – can only be associated with the truth of belief. The Quran tells us that the works of those who disbelieve is like a mirage, the thirsty will perceive it as water, but it is nothing other than illusion (An-Nur 24:39). Only belief can lead to the reality of water in its true meaning and material manifestations. To ask anything of any deity other than Allah, says the Quran, is like extending your palms to water with the hope that it reaches your mouth, which it certainly will not (Ar-Ra'd 13:14). Those who disbelieve can only reach its illusion not the real thing. Its physical or material form is only one dimension of its meaning and purpose. Its holistic meaning remains lost on the disbeliever, focused on the immediate, neglecting the lessons that water is intended to teach. Ignoring these lessons is perilous as the disbelievers find themselves with no access to it in the Hereafter (Al-A'raf 7:50). Yet had those who disbelieved taken a straight path, Allah would have quenched them with an abundance of water (Al-Jinn 72:16).

The *Shariah* invites believers, men and women, to seek Allah's special source of water, to set on the path of our beloved Prophet Muhammad ﷺ, where no rope, no instrument, other than a receptive and sound heart is required. It is this source that will lead to the pristine flowing waters of Paradise (Al-Waqi'ah 56:31), pure and unadulterated, mentioned before any other kind of river including milk, wine and honey (Muhammad 47:15).

The life of believers, men and women, is inextricably linked to water. Our faith leads us to water both physically and spiritually. We perform ablution several times a day using clean water to purify, soothe and calm us before approaching Allah in prayer. We must, with intention, clear away the impurities that make us unworthy of standing before Him. "Oh, you who believe, if you rise up for prayer, wash your faces and your hands up to the upper arm, and wipe your heads and your feet to the heels…" (Al-Ma'idah 5:6). We believe that this water is light, a purifying light that cleanses sins. Prophet Muhammad ﷺ said: "Know that if you place your hand in water and say, 'In the name of Allah, The Merciful, The Giver of Mercy', the sins your hands had earned are cast away. Then if you wash your face the sins that your eyes had earned by what they looked at and your mouth by what it said will be cast away. Then if you wash your arms the sins are cast away from you right and your left [arms]. Then if you wipe over your head and feet the sins that you walked toward with your feet will be cast away. That is what you gain from your ablution…" and then he ﷺ, went on to highlight the sin effacing impact of prayers that followed (Sahih Muslim). The water of ablution is a light that will illuminate the believer on the Day of Judgement. Prophet Muhammad ﷺ said: "On the Day of Judgment, Allah will resurrect my nation among other nations brightly lit from the remnants of ablution" (Sahih Bukhari).

Water reminds us of our vulnerability, without it we suffer. Its purposefulness allows us to achieve our purposefulness. Through it we connect to Allah, to the earth and to each other. We can see how this one element nourishes all living things. To understand its reach, to learn from it, we must think and experience life holistically. When we seek it, like we seek the *Shariah*, it is in extreme humility and gratitude for its mercies, for what it offers and teaches us so that we may lead dignified lives. The implications of water – and of the *Shariah* as the sacred source – for our lives are so serious that we simply cannot exist without it. It is for this reason that we must strive to understand the Shariah better. What was the path that Prophet Muhammad ﷺ was set on given the Truth of Allah's Command and His all-encompassing knowledge? The Shariah, as the water of revival, purity and illumination is so much more than a compendium of rules no matter how much effort has been exerted to detail it. Well before the extraction of any ruling, we must first have read the source of the Shariah – the Quran and the life of Prophet Muhammad – with open hearts. We must set aside prejudices, pre-conceived notions of mercy, equity, and justice. We must entrust ourselves to the journey.

The way to the water demands a comprehensive approach that engages all our beings and includes all creation, leading in the right direction from an infinite number of starting points, points that are already in complex overlapping, and in many cases contradictory motion. Picking and choosing rules is not a sufficient guide to the water and may even be misleading. The rules are bound by other elements including the truth of concepts, desired objectives, prioritization of values, unchangeability of universal laws, validity of proofs and parties involved in any given situation. Rules are only one dimension of this sacred water, and it is not possible to extract and benefit from them while greatly limiting them to human concerns or by ignoring other elements without altering its balance, impact and efficacy. It is often as such that our understanding of the Shariah strains rather than fortifies the health of our hearts.

Truth be told, and this is a difficult one for so many women and some men to accept, the Quran does address men more than women. Even Umm Salamah the Prophet's wife, questioned why women were not mentioned as often as men. In response to her concern Allah revealed the following *ayat*: "Indeed, the Muslim men and Muslim women, and the believing men and the believing women, and the obedient men and the obedient women, the truthful men and the truthful women, the patient men and the patient women, the humble men and the humble women, the charitable men and the charitable women, the fasting men and fasting women, the men who preserve their privates and the women preservers and the men who remember Allah plenty and the women who remember, Allah has prepared for them forgiveness and a great reward" (Al-Ahzab 33:35). The response, however, does not resolve her concern. Instead, it redirects the attention of believers to the mercifulness and generosity of Allah's plan towards men and women. This is not an equalization of any sort, rather it is an assurance that each will be rewarded in accordance with their unique specificities, with the soundness of their hearts. In accordance with their heedfulness of Allah. The fact that some scholars have taken this verse to mean that Quranic commands include both men and women, unless they specify otherwise, does not change the fact that men *are* addressed more extensively in the Quran. Even linguistically, we accept male and female inclusion in words that are essentially masculine like 'men' or pronouns like 'he'. The female or feminine is always a counterpart and a balance. And yet she stands as an individual, with full agency. So how can we understand this? We cannot make our way to the water if from the very start of the journey we reject Allah's prerogative to address His creation as He knows best.

When Allah told Adam to dwell in the garden with his mate, partner, spouse, pair – *zawjuka* – without naming Hawwa' or Eve it was not a diminution of her, but a reminder to him and the earliest demonstration to us that Adam bears that added degree of responsibility that his male progeny also shoulders till the end of time. She is his mate, and he is hers, an emphasis on union, love and mercy. She is of him, and he of her, *ba'dukum min ba'd* (Al-'Imran 3:195, An-Nisa' 4:25), guardians of one another, *ba'duhum awliya' ba'd* (At-Tawbah 9:71), created from the same *nafs*, self, being (An-Nisa' 4:1). *Zawjuka*, your pair, without whom the continuation of life is impossible. That the address is directed to Adam instills an immediate sense of responsibility.

Hawwa' is present, she is witness. She witnesses Allah's command to Adam that they are both to live in the garden and that they are both permitted to consume of what each desire. She also witnesses the prohibition to approach a specific tree. A tree whose fruit was detrimental to their continued innocence and felicity, representing everything in life that strips people of their inherent sense of dignity. Tasting of it – defying Allah's guidance – revealed their nakedness, instilled shame, neither of which would have been familiar to Adam and Hawwa' in their original state of divine obedience. It was the first instance of injustice against the self, *zulm an-nafs*, and it was perpetrated by both of them though the Quran presses the case more strictly against Adam.

Upon entering the garden, Allah had warned Adam that Iblis (Satan) was an enemy to him and to his mate. He cautioned Adam not to enable Iblis to expel them from the garden that they may fatigue. They were reminded that the garden had plenty for them not to go hungry or naked, nor to suffer from thirst or heat. But Iblis cajoled them, assuring that he was a sincere advisor. He utilized his knowledge of the human tendency to greed, the incessant desire to want more even when things seem perfect. Thus, he persuaded them that Allah had only forbidden them the tree to deny them becoming angels or immortal. The prospect was seductive, and they tasted of the tree. Together.

Iblis had succeeded in exposing to Adam and Hawwa' their immorality, the basest of their instincts. In that moment of defiance of their Lord, of listening to and trusting their enemy, they experienced vulnerability, shame, nakedness. What could have possibly been more alluring than the approval of Allah, the Lord who had provided for all their needs without demanding anything in return? They could no longer continue as they had before, they felt anxious and exposed. They reached out for cover, material and moral. Gathering leaves from the garden they cloaked their bodies, wanting once more to hide what had been previously hidden. Hidden by the cloak of heedfulness, *libas at-taqwa*, as the Quran refers to it. The innocence was gone and *libas at-taqwa* though better and more enduring would henceforth have to be accompanied with material coverings (Al-A'raf 7:26). "Our Lord," they both cried, "we have been unjust toward ourselves, and if You do not forgive us and have mercy on us, we will be of the losers," (Al-A'raf 7:23). Without the internal aspect, their external coverings did little to alleviate their anxieties. Their repentance was accepted by Allah, the Accepter of Repentance, the Giver of Mercy.

Only now were they prepared to descend to earth. They had been schooled in the essence of things, taught the value of faith, experienced the consequence of defiance, learned of their enemy, protected themselves from the elements externally and internally, and recognized the duties and responsibilities that they owed to each other and above all to their Creator. Humans, male and female, were now ready for their earthly sojourn. Earth would be a place of temporary settlement and pleasures. There they would live, die, and eventually return to their Maker. "We said: 'Descend, all of you collectively. Then when guidance comes to you from Me, whoever follows My guidance, there is no fear over them, nor shall they grieve,'" (Al-Baqarah 2:38). Guidance. The way to the water – the *Shariah* – would not be left ambiguous. A blessing from a Merciful Lord.

The *Shariah*, the source of sacred water, cultivates an ecology of compassion, quenching and nourishing those who immerse themselves in it. Like the water that produces all the diversity of plants and animals that we see in the earth, it likewise preserves our essence while recognizing our differences. It reminds us of our ultimate purpose, our connections, and the magnificent holism of which they are integral parts. It guides and illuminates our hearts. Everything in the universe is joined. It is a sad division that we have set for ourselves, between men and women, between human and non-human, between this earthly life and what is yet to come. Ignoring or misunderstanding the inseparable unity of our creation. We are all critical participants in the regeneration of life, men, women, human and non-human. Everyone without exception seeking some way to the water.

Homing to The Book

The History of Hayy Ibn Yaqzan, written by a twelfth century Muslim philosopher, Abu Bakr Ibn Al-Tufail (d.1185), presents the fictional story of an infant who is raised by a gazelle on an island. Hayy Ibn Yaqzan, whose name means Alive son of Awake, comes to know Allah without the aid of revelation. One day he is joined on the island by Asal, an ascetic who had left his people on another island in an attempt to reach higher levels of ascetism and self-discipline. The two eventually meet, learn about each other, and resolve to return to Asal's island to enlighten the people whose faith is based on rewards and punishments and who are therefore trapped in the sensual and mundane, unable to fathom let alone reach the felicity that these two were experiencing. It doesn't take long for Hayy to conclude that how the people of the island practiced their faith was indeed the most suitable for them. They could not be made to see the bliss inherent in unfettered belief and union with Allah. So, he apologizes to the people for his brief interruption, exhorts them to remain on the religion of their fathers, and takes leave back to his island with his friend Asal.

I have always felt that the acclaim that this story received was highly exaggerated, celebrating the expendability of Quranic guidance and Prophetic teachings. Ibn Al-Tufail either misunderstood the Quran or was unduly influenced by the shortcomings of his people and the attitude of the ruler toward them. Under a system of command and obey, no independent reasoning was permitted, and this is something that he would have been aware of given his proximity to political power. In bidding the people to continue to follow the ways of their forefathers, Ibn Al-Tufail disingenuously seeks to conflate the Quran and teachings of Prophet Muhammad ﷺ with the traditions and political oppression of his times. He would have been aware of the Quran's very stern warnings in that regard (Yunus 10:78; Az-Zukhruf 43:23-25). Those who believe do not have loyalties that betray Allah and the Prophet ﷺ (Al-Mujadilah 58:22; At-Tawbah 9:23).

Ibn Al-Tufail would have also known that the Quran does not base its guidance on hope and fear. These are emotions that the Quran utilizes – not to replace reason – but to marshal needed supports for its proper functioning. Allah has given every person the capacity to think critically and thereby to exercise choice. He has provided every one of us with an inherent code that enables us to make determinations about right and wrong. "And the self (*nafs*) and He who proportioned it [her]. So, He inspired it [her] as to what corrupts it [her] and what makes it [her] heedful" (Ash-Shams 91:7-8). Every one of us is a *nafs* – an essential and individual being distinguishable from all others, capable of self-reflection, direction and control.

By Allah's mercy we are aware of the good and bad that we do and yes, these are associated with emotional states in a healthy individual. Doing and being good makes us happy, calm, and content. Doing and being evil makes us agitated, fearful, and unstable. When they function properly, emotions are triggers, warning signs that enable us to be better monitors of our thoughts and behaviors. "Rather, the human is over themself watchful (*baseerah*)" (Al-Qiyamah 75:14). In other words, we have the capacity to take account of ourselves.

The Quran also marshals support for our reason by drawing our attention to the repercussions of our behavior in this life. Corruption arises in land and sea due to what the hands of people earn (Ar-Rum 30:41). The destruction and suffering resulting from misguidance and rejection of belief is reflected in this life. Likewise, the benefits of guidance are evident in this life, giving rewards in this life and the next. All the good, kindness, mercy, justice and equity that we give in this life are experienced by us and others in this life, in the here and now. We live in complex and connected communities, unlike the fictional world of Hayy who lives alone on an island. "Oh you people, truly We created you from male and female and made you ethnicities and tribes to know one another. Indeed, the most dignified of you with Allah is the most heedful. Indeed, Allah is Knowing, Proficient" (Al-Hujuraat 49:13). The guidance provided by the Creator, the One who made this knowing of each other a purpose of our earthly journey, is intended to manage our infinite and complex diversities so that we can get about this knowing while continuing to pursue our unique – both individual and collective – purposeful paths with as much harmony as possible.

As we question, adjust, accept, and assimilate Quranic guidance and Prophetic teachings in our lives we do so in accordance with our unique nature, resources, and conditions. We do not follow blindly nor are we commanded to do so. Instead, we are reminded of the limits of our reasoning in dealing with ourselves, others, and Allah's universe. We recall the lesson that our first father and mother learned when they disobeyed Allah's command. "And We have created the human and We know what his self (*nafs*) entices [him to], and We are closer to him than his circulatory rope (*habl al-wareed*)" (Qaf 50:16). Allah, our Creator, knows best. There are matters that we simply cannot encompass with our human limits. "It may be that you hate something when it is good for you and it may be that you love something that is bad for you and Allah knows and you do not know" (Al-Baqarah 2:216). And elsewhere in the Quran, it states, "...perhaps you may hate something and Allah places in it great benefit" (An-Nisa' 4:19). We must therefore humble ourselves and accept Allah's guidance as holistically expressed in the Quran and exemplified in the life of His beloved Prophet. Whether in our private or our public lives, we cannot do without Allah's guidance. Hayy's *discovery* of Allah without the aid of revelation may have worked on his solitary island. For the rest of us – connected in this life's journey with all other creation – homing to the Book is indispensable.

Homing to or toward something is the ability to return to a place after having journeyed quite a distance away from it. That, I believe, is our current state with the Quran. Yes, every believer owns a copy and many occasionally read it – Ramadan, funerals, births, weddings, sickness, pilgrimage, prayers – but few create the space within themselves for the Quran to settle and flourish. It has become a book for occasions, its *ayat* proudly displayed as art in homes and public spaces, rarely if ever to be read in its entirety for sound application to life and its events.

Many scholars rarely refer to it directly. They prefer the security of the volumes of *fiqh* (jurisprudence) that allegedly offer comprehensive coverage of all religious concerns if you dig deep and search wide enough – and if you are only concerned with a *legal* response. That, however, only represents a miniscule portion of the Quran that was produced in response to a unique historical moment. A select few see the need for new readings. Readings that challenge our perspectives on the past and offer us fresh insights for the present. Readings that can guide us toward a brighter future. This is something Prophet Muhammad ﷺ laments on the Day of Judgement: "Oh my Lord, indeed my folk have taken this Quran with abandonment" (Al-Furqan 25:30).

Though the Quran is intelligible to any reader – any receptive heart – it is nonetheless a "heavy discourse" (Al-Muzzammil 73:5). It is heavy in terms of actual content – notification of past, present, and future events, of the seen and unseen, of the subtleties of nature, and the nature of humans – that is provided in a straightforward manner. It is also heavy in terms of the text's connectivity to itself, to the world to which it refers, and to the infinite combinations of textual evidence that we can bring to bear on our attempts to resolve the multitude of life's concerns. The Quran resolves this seeming paradox of simplicity and complexity through its multiple layers, techniques, and references allowing it to penetrate all kinds of hearts and appeal to different intellectual capacities. The discerning heart will come to know the bigger Reality of simpler realities, the singular Truth of multiple truths, and the Unity of connected unities.

The Quran is the voice of Allah in our lives. It has 114 *surah's*, 30 parts, 6348 *ayat* counting the *basmallah*. All other writings about it are the voices of others, those who have strove to understand it. The Prophet ﷺ said: "The best among you [believers] are those who learn the Quran and teach it" (Sahih Bukhari). This isn't an exclusive call for a specialized group of people – though that is important – it is a call to every believer to study how the Quran guides the general and the specific, the private and the public, the personal and professional of each's life. Every individual has a duty to read the Quran for themselves and to internalize its meanings. The Quran was meant to reside in every believer and every believer was meant to seek its guidance, company, and illumination.

The word Quran comes from the root q-r-a meaning to read or recite. In the process we have the right to question, analyze, reflect, and synthesize the message in ways that uniquely combine with and respond to our uniqueness and our contexts. The Quran speaks to us as a collective while it also speaks to you and me as individuals.

The Quran is a reminder to people. It is an offering for which Prophet Muhammad ﷺ asked no reward or payment (Al-An'am 6:90; Yusuf 12:104; Al-Mu'minun 23:72; Saad 38:86; Al-Qalam 68:46). There is one exception to this, when he ﷺ asked that we become friends (*mawadata*) – that we keep good relations – with those who are close (Ash-Shura 42:23). That was his return – that we love and honour each other. Charity starts at home, but it also extends to neighbours and the broader community. Islam can be said to conform to the subsidiarity principle, which simply means that our issues whatever their nature are to be dealt with at the relational level closest to their resolution. When problems emerge between people, they are best resolved first among themselves, then family, community and finally, if all that fails, public authorities. The modern drive to resort to public authorities from the very start because we have neglected and destructed our lines of first defence has led to nothing but social and economic ruin. We only have to consider lengthy legal procedures and the costs of lawyers in modern divorce cases to realize how far we have strayed from these ideals.

The Quran is the light, gifted by Allah to receptive hearts (An-Nisa' 4:174; Al-Ma'idah 5:15). It provides insights that only Allah can reveal (Al-An'am 6:104; Al-A'raf 7:203). Prophet Muhammad ﷺ said: "The Book of Allah is the way, for it contains information of what happened before you, news of what will come after you and a decision regarding matters that will occur among you. It is decisive (*fasl*) and not jest (*hazl*). Whoever leaves it, is a tyrant and Allah will break him, and if anyone seeks guidance elsewhere, Allah will lead him astray. It is the rope of Allah, the wise reminder, the straight path, whims cannot deviate it nor the tongue become confused, and the scholars cannot be fully satisfied [due to its scope and depth]. It is not worn down by repetition nor do its wonders ever cease…He who knows its knowledge, is at the forefront, he who quotes it, speaks the truth, and he who judges according to it, is just, and he who acts according to it, is rewarded, and he who invites people to it is guided to the Straight Path" (Jami' Al-Tirmidhi). Is the one who has this light to walk among the people like the one who walks in darkness and is incapable of escaping it? (Al-An'am 6:122).

This straight path – the pure *deen* or way of life – is applicable today as it was in the past and will be to the Day of Judgement, there is no exchange in what Allah creates (Ar-Rum 30:30). Through the Quran, Allah shows us the truths of those before us, clarifying when they were faithful (An-Nisa' 4:26; As-Saffat 37:37) and when they were unjust (Al-Furqan 25:52). Distinguishing between *deen* and tradition, the Quran is clear that it stands outside history and must not be confused with any specific culture or social practice. Traditions may or may not be a manifestation of faith, but they are never the same thing.

The Quran is a guidance for believers, for the heedful (Al-Baqarah 2:215; Al-'Imran 3:138). In directing our faces and efforts toward Allah, taking His Book as our guide, we vindicate ourselves from misleading others, from contributing to injustice (Al-Baqarah 2:150). Whether male or female, we seek first to rectify ourselves, to exercise self-restraint, practice generosity, judge equitably and safeguard balance. By holding on to the Rope that He extends to us we learn how to cooperate, we see how this guidance brings us together. It is Allah that places love and friendship in our midst, saves us from ourselves (Al-'Imran 3:103).

The Quran guides to the stable and straight path (Al-Fatihah 1:6; Al-An'am 6:126) in which every believer can place their trust (Al-Baqarah 2:256) and do their utmost to carry the Trust (Al-Ahzab 33:72). It does this through the provision of a decisive discourse that clearly shows us what is good from what is evil, in a way that is gentle yet serious (At-Tariq 86:13-14). When studied in earnest, the Quran clarifies all matters. "And We have sent down on you [Muhammad] the Book, clarifying everything, and guidance and mercy and glad tidings for Muslims" (An-Nahl 16:89). Whoever holds firmly to Allah is guided to the straight path (Al-'Imran 3:101). Only Allah can place us on the path to righteousness and success in this world and the next (Al-An'am 6:39). Those who listen to the Quran with receptive hearts recognize that it is the truth and know that it guides to the straight path (Al-Ahqaf 46:30). There is no equality between those who seek and follow Allah's guidance and those who seek corruption in the earth and disbelieve (Saad 39:28).

The Quran is justice. There can be no exchange or alteration of Allah's words (Al-An'am 6:115). The Quran was revealed for all people for all time. Those who neglect it because it was not given to them or their people in the past are blinded by self-aggrandizement, rather than focussing on the truth of the message (Al-An'am 6:157). There are people who had previous guidance of the Book but still recognized the Quran as truth , they will have double the reward for their patience, warding of evil with good, and spending out of what Allah has provided for them (Al-Qasas 28:52-54). We seek the Quran when we call for justice (An-Nahl 16:76) because Truth is the heart of justice (Al-Baqarah 2:119; Al-'Imran 3:60) and is its only measure (Al-A'raf 7:8).

The Quran offers us a corrective lens with which to gain insights – *basa'ir* – to rectify our affairs. It is only by changing our ways, what is within us, that Allah changes our condition (Ar-Ra'd 13:11). The imposition of our prejudices or preconceived notions of truth and justice can never suffice. These false notions are damaging to our wellbeing and ability to reform and rejuvenate. Fortunately, falsehood does not have staying power (Al-Isra' 17:81). As believers, we accept that we are too limited in our human capacity to fully understand the implications of different courses of action on life and life systems. Truth is an indivisible reality. Only Allah can relate it in such a way that does not distort or disfigure it. He is the best separator (Al-An'am 6:57). "Do they reflect on the Quran? And if it had been from any other than Allah, they would have found in it much contradiction" (An-Nisa' 4:82). When we tell a story, convey a conversation, produce research in any subject, we are compelled to choose appropriate boundaries to make our effort intelligible. We know, however, that we are intentionally leaving things out, abbreviating others, or simply ignoring things either because we think they are unimportant, or we don't know enough or anything about them. As a result, our efforts may contradict those of others who have different considerations. The Quran offers us the truths that can help us avoid the most dangerous disagreements and pitfalls.

Every *ayah* of the Quran relays important truths in ways suited to our human capabilities. These verses or ayat are harmonized with each other, with the universe to which they often refer, and with our intellects as the recipients of the message. There is never any contradiction for those approaching the text holistically, not only in the sense of dealing with the entirety of the Quran but more important in exercising the height of our human potential when doing so. People of intellect recognize this (Ar-Ra'd 13:19) and it gives them assertiveness and stability in thought and action (An-Nahl 16:102).

Arabic and the Sultan of Names

Adam, the name of the first human that Allah announces to the angels who will be placed as a successor on the earth, was created of earth or soil. His name literally meaning tanned or darkened. We are told by Prophet Muhammad ﷺ that "Allah created Adam from a handful of soil taken from different lands [of the earth], so the children of Adam have been created according to the composition of the land. Thus, people are white, red, black, and yellow; we have good and evil, ease and sorrow, and what comes in between them" (Sahih Bukhari). The first few attempts of obtaining this soil, however, were not successful as the earth resisted being blemished. Jibril ﷺ, the archangel, is first sent to the earth on this mission to obtain soil for Allah. The earth said: "I seek refuge in Allah from your decreasing my quantity or disfiguring me." Jibril ﷺ thus returned without taking anything and told Allah: "My Lord, the earth sought refuge in You and was granted it." Allah then sent the archangel Michael ﷺ to do the same, and again the earth sought refuge with Allah and it was granted. He went back and said as Jibril ﷺ had said. So, Allah then sent the Angel of Death and again the earth sought refuge in Allah, but this time the angel responded: "I also seek refuge with Allah from returning without carrying out His command." He thus took soil from different places on the earth — white, red, and black — mixed it, and ascended to his Lord. And so, Allah portioned Adam from this soil and said to him "Be" and he was - a creature that could learn and teach, receive, and offer guidance.[1]

Adam was taught the names of all things by Allah. "And He taught Adam all the names (*asma'*), then He presented them to the angels and said, 'Apprise Me of the names of these, if you are truthful [what you said is true]?" (Al-Baqarah 2:31). "They said, 'Glory to You, we have no knowledge except what You have taught us. Indeed, You are the Knower, the Wise" (Al-Baqarah 2:32). These *asma'* (sg. *ism*) that Allah taught Adam represented the truth of all matters, the qualities and essence of all things and their purposefulness and connection in the universe. Through this knowledge Adam was made privy to something that the Angels had not been, he had been taught *the names*. Names that revealed truths, that governed reality, that showed Adam how and where he fit in the divine scheme, but most

1 The details of obtaining the soil for the creation of Adam are adapted from Al-Imam Ibn Kathir, *Stories of the Prophets*, Riyadh: Darussalam, translated by Muhammad Mustapha Gemeah.

important that Allah was Lord and Owner of the worlds. In not being able to name the things Allah had showed them, the angels immediately realized that their contention that humans would only corrupt the earth and shed blood (Al-Baqarah 2:30) was not the whole truth. They had no knowledge beyond what Allah had revealed to them. When Adam informs the angels of the names, Allah reiterates to the angels, "Did I not tell you that I know what is concealed of the skies and the earth, and I know what you express and what you suppress" (Al-Baqarah 2:33).

The names that Allah taught Adam have authoritative truth or *sultan* as designated by the Quran. A name (*ism*) is not something that we can just give to things though of course we do it all the time. We must for the sake of expediency. But there are people who give names to things out of defiance. "Indeed, those who do not believe in the Hereafter name the angels female names. And they have no knowledge of this. They only follow speculation. And speculation does not suffice at all against the truth" (An-Najm 53:27-28). "And they make the angels, who themselves are Allah's servants, females. Did they witness their creation? Their testimony will be written, and they will be questioned" (Az-Zhukhruf 43:19). "Or is it that We created the angels female and they are witness" (As-Saffat 37:150). "Did He choose girls over boys?" (As-Saffat 37:153). "What is wrong with you, how do you judge?" (As-Saffat 37:154). This is an example of naming something out of defiance, not having any clue as to the truth of the matter. This is not an offense to females, it is a mere rejection of falsehood.

But even when we give names to things out of pragmatism and necessity, we must accept that the names we give have no *sultan*. They just help us to identify things in different languages for practicality and other human purposes. The real names of things are known by their Creator. Whatever we come up with for necessity or otherwise – irrespective of importance – must be considered subsidiary to the names Allah has taught us. We are not permitted to invent false things attaching to them names as if they are real of truthful. The Quran reprimands the pagan Arabs for their idolatry and giving their goddesses names as if they had any truthful essence. Their exact form is disputed but some believe that the *Lat* was a human, the *Uzza* was a tree and *Manat* was a white stone. These are names, the Quran tells us, for which Allah has not sent down *sultan*; they have no authoritative truth in the world of truth (An-Najm 53:23).

The *asma'* are conveyed to the reader in Arabic. The Quran *is* Arabic; Arabic as a tongue (*lisan*) – a spoken language – and Arabic in its essential essence of eloquence, unambiguity, clarity, and expansiveness (*hukm*). It is the angel Jibril ﷺ, held in great honour in Islam, who delivered Allah's message to Prophet Muhammad ﷺ. This is something that the disbelievers doubted, accusing the Prophet ﷺ of forgery, while claiming that some man was teaching him. However, the man that they claimed was teaching him was not even an Arabic speaker. "Say: 'The Holy Spirit [Jibril] has brought it down from your Lord with the Truth to fortify those who believe and guidance and good harbinger for the *Muslimeen* [those who accept Islam]. And, indeed We know that they say, 'No one is teaching him [Muhammad] but a person (*bashar*).' [But the] tongue (*lisan*) for which they apostatize (*yalhiduna*) [literally losing faith over] is non-Arabic and this is a clear Arabic tongue" (An-Nahl 16:102-103). And although no criticism was leveled against Prophet Muhammad ﷺ that was not leveled at the messengers before him (Fussilat 41:43), the extent of persecution was astonishing given the fact that the Quran explicitly came to confirm what had come before it.

The Quran explicitly and repeatedly states that it was sent down to confirm the truth including those aspects of the revelations that came before it that would ease people's lives and unify them. "And this [Quran] is indeed sent down by the Lord of the Worlds; sent down with the Trustworthy Spirit [Jibril], upon your [Muhammad's] heart that you may be of the warners, with a clear Arabic tongue. And it is in the Psalms of the forebearers" (Ash-Shu'ara 20:192-196). Likewise, the Quran tells us, "And before it [Quran] the Book of Musa, a guidance and mercy and this Book is a confirmation, in Arabic tongue, to warn those who committed injustice and good harbinger for the doers of good" (Al-Ahqaf 46:12). In contrast to what had become of the true teachings of these previous messages, the Quranic message sought to cleanse the former of human distortions, ease people's lives, and unite diverse people by providing a unified word. This does not mean that we must all understand the Quran or Islam, more broadly, in the exact same way but it does establish a common core around which people could distinguish between right and wrong, understand basic truths, and hopefully live in harmony.

Arabic allows this diversity through its various qualities and particularly its clarity and expansiveness. "Indeed, We made it an unambiguous (*'arabeyyan*) Quran that you may understand" (Az-Zukhruf 43:3). Here the Quran is not referring to Arabic as a tongue, *lisan*, a spoken language, but rather the emphasis is on the quality of this choice. "And it is as such that We revealed to you an unambiguous (*'arabeyyan*) Quran that you [Muhammad] may warn the Mother of Cities [Makkah] and everyone around her, and warn of the Day of Gathering, no doubt therein, a group will be in Paradise and a group in the Blaze" (Ash-Shura 42:7). The main idea of the revelation being to encourage remembrance of Allah, truth, duty, responsibility, accountability, and ultimate felicity or misery. "And it is as such that We sent it [Quran] down, an unambiguous (*'arabeyyan*) Quran and We dispensed in it of warnings that they may heed or may be stirred with remembrance" (Taha 20:113).

The Quran is intended for those with receptive hearts, those who *know*. "Sent down [the Quran] from the Merciful, the Giver of Mercy. A Book whose *ayat* are detailed [tailored], an unambiguous (*'arabeyyan*) Quran for a folk that know" (Fussilat 41:2-3). It anticipates and responds to how some people might receive its exposition in Arabic, complaining that it was evidently not meant or tailored for them. "And had We made it [Quran] a non-Arabic Quran, they would have said, 'If only its *ayat* were detailed [tailored for us]. Non-Arab or Arab, say, 'It is for those who believe, a guidance and healing. And those who do not believe, in their ears is deafness and it [their disbelief] is on them blindness [prevents truthful vision]. It is these who are being called from a faraway place" (Fussilat 41:44). *Arabic is Allah's choice*. It is not the choice of people, nor does it continue to be hegemonic because of them.

We can never be the same once we come *to know* the Quran. I am not talking about casual or partialistic readings that involve close to no reflection on the words, on how they come together in the *ayat*, on the meanings and wisdoms of its teachings, on how it manifested in the life of Prophet Muhammad ﷺ and those whose prophethoods preceded him. I am not talking about the native Arabic speaker who by the way does not speak the Arabic of the Quran but who often assumes to understand the meaning of things based on common speech, is quick to refer to the interpretations of others when he does not, and neglects to question so as to delve deeper and establish a personal connection with the text. Instead, I am talking about those who come to know the Quran like they know themselves, or a close relative, or a favourite hobby, or an expert skill, those who invest time in their relationship with the word of Allah. This is "an unambiguous (*'arabeyyan*) Quran without any distortions that they may be heedful" (Az-Zumar 39:28). That heedfulness can only emanate from within; guiding those who seek the Quran to be an inseparable part of who they are and how they live. We are told that those who follow the Quran are like someone who resigns him or herself to one leader, one master, as opposed to he or she who chooses not to and so struggles, is torn, by the many conflicting partners that partake in his or her very existence; they are not equal in example but most people do not know (Az-Zumar 39:29).

To know the Quran is to live in peace and harmony, to be calm and balanced. It allows us to free ourselves from the whims of people and the tyranny of the unjust. It gives us the ability to distinguish truth from falsehood irrespective of how the world we live in distorts issues. "And it is as such that We sent it down, an unambiguous (*'arabeyyan*) judgement and if you were to follow their whims after the knowledge that has come to you, you have no guard or prevention from Allah" (Ar-Ra'd 13:37). That is the favour of Arabic on the believer.

I listen to the Quran regularly, silencing my thoughts in its melodic rhythm, to allow Allah's voice to reach the depths of my being. He calls in my ear "this is the Quran by which mountains can move and the earth can shake, even the dead made to speak but Allah commands the universe as He pleases" (Ar-Ra'd 13:31). I hear. I see. I sense. Arabic is a holistic experience. "And Allah Has brought you out of your mother's bellies not knowing anything and gave you hearing, sight, and heart-senses (*afi'dah*) that you may be thankful" (An-Nahl 16:78). These faculties are indispensable for learning the language of knowledge, truth, and mercy.

Before we can read the Quran, we are taught to listen to its recitation. And in that process our very nature changes, it responds to the sacred ingredients that Arabic is immersed in – knowledge, guidance, and mercy. All receptive hearts, even non-Arabic speakers, recognize this sacred quality. "Allah has sent down the best discourse, a consistent Book, giving goosebumps to those who hold their Lord in awe, then their skins and hearts become pliant to the remembrance of Allah, this is the guidance of Allah, He guides with it whom He pleases, and as for whom Allah misguides, there is no guide for him" (Az-Zumar 39:23). It is a quality that is lost in translation among so many other teachings.

Classical Arabic, known as *al-fusha*, is one of the wonders, miracles if you like of the Quran. *Fusha* means clear, unequivocal, pure, accurate, expressive, efficient, and free from error. In the words of the late distinguished Arab linguist, Tahia

Ismail, who spent a decade studying Classical Arabic as the ancestor of Latin and Old English, Arabic is "a huge language, of vast dimensions. This giant language was not conceived piecemeal, according to immediate needs nor built fortuitously. It was conceived and built on one master plan, on a grand scale, into one self-integrating, self-maintaining system".[2] She explains to us that Arabic is characterized by five interdependent levels which ensure that it is a highly integrated and well-regulated language. These five levels include the semantic or meaning in language or logic, phonological or sign system, morphological or how words are formed and how they relate to other words, syntactic or the arrangement of words and phrases to create sentences and the level of sound symbolism or the sense of words by their sound. I know that this is not easy stuff but bear with me because I want you to see, to come to appreciate, why a language like Arabic must be respected and preserved. The choice of Arabic as the language of revelation is not based on mere happenstance. A language used to express Truth in all its manifestations must itself display truthfulness. Allah's Word is Truth (Al-An'am 6:73) and so must be the language of its conveyance.

Arabic is a verb-based language in contrast to English which is noun based. A verb is like the nucleus around which electrons orbit. A root verb regulates and controls its family, while it is itself part of a larger paradigm that includes closely related verbs. Root verbs are only comprised of consonants, vowels are removed. Arabic has 27 consonants. These are stable and unchanging. Vowels possess the transformative quality for each word. They are mobile. Depending on which vowels and how we place them, we can achieve different sounds, meanings, numbers, categories and tenses using the same root.

Arabic dictionaries are arranged in accordance with root verbs. To understand the meaning of a word, we would have to know and look up its verb root. The root of my name is *b-s-m* which means to smile. The b or *baa* is a stop produced by opening the lips, the s or *seen* is a voiceless hissing sound and the m or *mim* is produced by closing the lips. Every letter has a sound and meaning. From that one root many words bloom. *Basma* (noun fem. sing.), means a smile. Its letter formation *baa-seen-mim-taa marbuta* brings together meanings of seeking knowledge, perception, water and breath or wind. *Baseema* (adj. fem. sing.) my grandmother's name whom I am named after, means always smiling. Bassam (adj. masc. sing.) means he's smiley. There are so many possibilities of this one root.

2 Tahia A. Ismail (1989). *Classical Arabic as the Ancestor of Indo-European Languages and Origin of Speech.* Cairo: Al-Ahram Press.

The verb-basis of the language therefore means that Arabic is action and condition oriented. *To be, to have been brought into existence by Allah, is to have purpose and in turn connection.* Purposefulness first and foremost to the Creator which includes purposefulness in the grand scheme of creation. Every letter, every sound, every atom, and all things of lesser or greater measure have purpose. "Those who remember Allah standing and sitting and, on their sides, and contemplate the creation of the skies and the earth, [saying], 'Our Lord, You did not create this aimlessly [or in falsehood]; Glory to You, so exempt us from the torment of the Fire" (Al-'Imran 3:191). In Arabic every letter, every sound, counts toward the expression of a truth that come together in different combinations to tell us something of the nature of what is being identified. To reveal purposefulness, connection and holism to us.

Arabic words that have been preserved for centuries have *sultan*. Ismail tells us that early Arab grammarians of the seventh century, "compiled with meticulous and conscientious care every word the Arabs have ever spoken or written".[3] The Quran of course does not include every possible Arabic word, nor does it need to. Arabic is not only a very expressive language, but also a very efficient one. The Quran tells us that if all the trees on earth were pens, and the ocean was ink, even if extended seven-fold, Allah's words would not be exhausted (Luqman 31:27). We would spend lifetimes upon lifetimes reading if that had been the case. It is out of Allah's mercy that Arabic is both expressive and efficient, offering infinite possibilities of learning and re-learning without burdening us with endless written text. What we have been given is more than sufficient to guarantee protection of the conventions of the Arabic language and the truths of the universe that it was intended to reveal.

We simply do not have the capacity to name things with such truthfulness. Our choices, especially in languages other than Arabic, do not sufficiently express the essence or purposefulness of things. That does not diminish the utility, beauty, cultural significance of other languages and indeed what we can and must learn from them, rather it emphasizes the important function of Arabic as the language of the Quran and in turn as the core of truth for other languages. The Quran recognizes the plurality of *tongues* among humanity as one of Allah's *ayat*. "And of His *ayat* is the creation of the skies and the earth and the diversity of your tongues [spoken languages] and colours. Indeed, in these are ayat for those of knowledge" (Ar-Rum 30:22). Note how the Quran does not say plurality of languages but rather of *tongues*. It is the

3 Ibid, XVI

tongues, like our colours, that gradually diversified indicating that in the beginning the language of our original parents was one. The Quran's revelation in Arabic is a purposeful choice that points to this oneness.

The language of the Quran expresses the oneness of Allah and the oneness of creation. *Tawhid* the most essential tenet of Islam. All the fields, not just language, emanating from this source must express this imperative of unicity. The Quranic Arabic supports and reveals the covenant that we have undertaken, as individuals and groups, with Allah, not to sever what He has commanded to be joined (Al-Baqarah 2:27). Connection is embedded in language.

I have spent countless hours translating the Quranic *ayat*, trying to better capture the meanings of the Arabic words for my personal understanding, lectures, writings and especially this book here. Trying to find the English equivalent, though there rarely are, that might better express the truths of a specific Arabic word. Any work of translation then is also necessarily one of interpretation. Those of us whose writings contain Quranic passages are often urged by our publishers, sometimes forced, to use an existing translation. I have and will continue to refuse to do this.

No doubt, there are several reputable translations of the Quran in English, but many do not capture the essence of certain critical Arabic words and their meanings. Reference to the interpretation (*tafsir*) of others, as opposed to the potential of the language itself, limits the accuracy of this approach for our lives today. When I translate Quranic words, I choose the most representative word in English given the Arabic word's meaning, not only in its immediate context, but given an extensive understanding of its usages throughout the text as well as its forms in the word family.

Taqwa Allah, for instance, is to be mindful or heedful of Allah. Taqwa is often translated as fear. But fear is *khawf* in Arabic, and it does have usage in the Quran just not when Allah intends for us to understand heedfulness as opposed to fearfulness. Our relationship with Him is premised on *taqwa* not *khawf.* Of course, heedfulness can result from fear, which is an emotion and thankfully not a constant state, but it can also result from love and hopefulness, which are also emotions. *Taqwa* is not an emotion, it is a state of being, a way of living, that is reinforced by our different emotions. It is something that we constantly strive to be in, to practice.

Similarly, *wahy* means revelation not inspiration. When the Quran informs us about Allah's favour to the mother of Musa, it states: "As We revealed (*awhayna*) to your mother what was revealable (*ma yuha*)" (Taha 20:38). Both *awhayna* and *yuha* are forms of the root *w-h-y*, meaning revelation. But translators often choose the word 'inspired' not revealed. Inspiration or *ilham*, in Arabic, is not revelation or *wahy*. Indeed, Musa's mother received revelation, albeit limited as qualified in the *ayah* by *what was revealable*. Nor is *wahy* confined to humans. The Quran informs us that animals and everything in nature may receive *wahy*. The seven skies each received their command by way of *wahy* (Fussilat 41:12). The bees also received *wahy* (An-Nahl 16:68). Allah communicates with His creation as He pleases, it is not for us to impose our limits, to unduly elevate some above others when Allah has not sanctioned it. In doing so we alter a truth and miss the wisdom of Allah's choice of words.

I also avoid simplifying the translation by choosing popular English words like many, especially contemporary, translators do. The Quran does not use simple Arabic, instead it uses truthful, efficient, and accurate words that may or may not be simple. Many Arabic speakers do not fully understand the meaning or import of Quranic Arabic, they too rely on understandings from common usage or on *tafsir*. When they are serious students of the Quran they go out and study, seek to understand meaning and to understand the distinction between words. The same should be expected of the English reader. I believe that the translator does an injustice to the English reader, and Arabic text, by substituting common words for those that may be more complex but also more reflective of their Arabic counterparts. The onus should be no less on the English reader, than the Arabic reader, to strive to understand the distinctions between words of similar but not identical import, of complex concepts, and of linguistic constructions that may not conform to convention but whose accuracy and ultimate truth are found in these nuances.

Perhaps one of the most difficult things to convey in translation is grammatical gender. No translation I know, not even mine can do justice to this fundamental reality. All the translations I know simply ignore this quality referring to anything other than Allah and humans as *it*. There is no *it* in reference to nouns in Arabic. *It* robs the subject of a critical attribute and denies us knowledge of his or her truths. *It* is always *he* or *she*, masculine or feminine in the Quran. This grammatical gender expresses an important dimension of meaning and presents us with an unsurpassed exhibition of balance in Allah's creation. When I read of the earth as a *she*, the rain a *he*, the sun a *she*, the moon a *he*, and so on, I learn of the attributes of other *hes* and *shes*. I learn about myself and others. I connect with creation. My psyche, largely without even realizing, internalizes an incredible balance of masculine and feminine. Of uniqueness of purpose and shared purpose.

The gender attributes of Quranic names, *asma'*, are not masculine and feminine classifications imposed or invented by humans, they are truthful dimensions of reality. It is Allah who has named them in accordance with their truthful attributes just as He has named us in accordance with ours. He created them with a gendered nature that we are informed of in the Quran. Our inability to fathom this dimension as it relates to all creation is due to our shortcomings, neglect, or disbelief.

We are not the ones doing the gendering, that is not within our power. Referring to and understanding other creation by acknowledging each's gender is not anthropomorphism. The creation of the skies, earth, rain, mountains, forests, stars, and all other elements in the universe that preceded our creation already expressed these attributes. Allah has ascribed something of their nature to us, not ours to them. This is a humbling thought. I will, where I can, therefore, include the gender of creation in the translation. Through it we can hopefully appreciate an important dimension of nature and ourselves, through a grammar that reveals the sacred balance of the universe.

In addition to equity, balance, and insight into the nature of things, the language of the Quran expresses moral propriety. When it speaks of the private affairs of people, and specifically of relations between men and women, its choice of words demonstrates refinement and decorum. Thus, the expression *lamastum an-nissa'* (An-Nisa' 4:43) literally meaning to touch women is used to denote a range of sexually intimate behaviours. This discretionary style safeguards and celebrates the modesty, *hayaa'*, of a believer who by nature and preference appreciates the avoidance of explicit and potentially vulgar expressions. Such moral propriety retains the language's clarity while ensuring accessibility and appropriateness for a wide range of sensibilities and levels of maturity.

All these and so many more features of Arabic make it especially suited for a message that not only aims to present and explain Reality and Truth, but that also – in conformance with this aim – fully utilizes the means to do so. Attempts to shift the linguistic centre of gravity in Islam from Arabic to any other language, is therefore misguided. Even when we consider learning Arabic a laborious task it cannot be written off as unnecessary. Nor can we reject its centrality in Quranic and Prophetic teachings because that reinforces conventional Islamic authority that is rooted in Arabic language proficiency. Instead, we must think that it is our lack of proficiency that weakens our comprehensive grasp and thereby denies us a credible opportunity to challenge that authority where it has fallen short of the beauty of Allah's message. Not being able to speak or read Arabic does not justify the negation of a solid Quranic truth. We must always recall that *Arabic is Allah's choice* for revelation of the Quran and not that of people.

As a final note, I would like to reiterate that it is perfectly fine to rely on translations as one develops needed capacities in Arabic and, even when that capacity is acquired, it is still fine to give lessons, sermons, lectures and write about Islam and the Quran in other languages. It is not fine, however, especially for those who claim an intimate relationship with the Quran to diminish the importance – the critical necessity – of preserving the Arabic tongue. Allah is aware of our struggles to acquire the language when we are not native speakers, and even for a native speaker to strive to understand the Arabic of the Quran, which differs markedly from how people speak today irrespective of their dialect. It is out of Allah's mercy that every letter of the Quran was given sultan, an authoritative truth, for this very purpose. Prophet Muhammad ﷺ explained, "Whoever recites a letter from the Book of Allah, he will receive one good deed and a good deed is multiplied by ten good deeds like it. I do not say that *Alif Lam Mim* is one letter, but rather *Alif* is a letter, *Lam* is a letter, and *Mim* is a letter" (Sunan Al-Tirmidhi). This underscores the importance of effort. Indeed, Allah facilitated the Quran for ease of remembrance (Al-Qamar 54:17).

Arabic will always be the language of truthful knowledge that is sourced from or related to the Quran, an assertion that is consistently and repeatedly stated in the Quran itself. Not recognizing and honouring this fundamental fact deprives believers, and humanity more broadly, of the expanse of Quranic truths, which can never be fully expressed in other languages despite our best efforts. Rejecting or diminishing the importance of Arabic to Quranic studies, especially seminal contributions, is not the proper response to our shortcomings or to authorities that we may legitimately challenge. A better, and more humble response is to find ways to learn and to reinstate Arabic language education, one that in its very fabric conveys beauty, connectivity, clarity, and yes, authoritative truth.

How the Quran Teaches through Ayat

We have within our grasp the most effective, comprehensive, and suitable knowledge source. The Quran not only provides guidance on how we can successfully navigate our lives, augmenting our ability to impact reality, it does so by simultaneously acting on our inner beings to ensure that this ability is deeply rooted within us. This provides stability and consistency in our behavior toward others and across times and settings. Deep study and continuous reflection on the Quran have major implications for our perception, meaning our ability to listen, envision, and heart-sense using our hearing, sight and hearts, all blessings granted by Allah, to become aware of actual realities and authentic truths. Internalizing the message of the Quran shifts our centre of gravity from revolving around our self or *nafs* to revolving around the Creator of that self, Allah, and His Reality and His Truth. In doing so it rectifies and disciplines the *nafs*, preparing and refining it for its true purpose, the subject matter of part two of this book.

The Quran is an indivisible whole that uses diverse methods and techniques to guide believers. Understanding any of its parts is not possible without having journeyed multiple times through its entirety. When I quote the works of other people, let alone the Word of Allah, I am always sure to have read the entirety of their thoughts to avoid misunderstandings as well as unsubstantiated agreement or disagreement. I sometimes see scholars, but mostly time pressed students, who barely scan a text for the quotes that they need for an essay without taking the time to engage with the author of the work. This is unacceptable for any serious scholar and when we are talking about the Quran it is completely rejected for believers. Not only does the Quran demand complete readings as well as multiple and ongoing rounds of reflection, before we can attempt to explain its teachings holistically, it also demands moral uprightness including the sincere practice of other rituals, like remembrance (*dhikr*), prayer (*salah*), fasting (*sawm*), giving (*infaq*) and charity (*zakah* and *sadaqah*), that purify the reader by bringing them in closer proximity to Allah. This is not an ordinary Book, and it cannot be approached in ordinary ways. I always tell my students that I can teach them what I have come to know but their journey will necessarily have to go beyond the classroom if they want to reap the knowledge and wisdom that this incredible Book has to offer.

The Quran is divided into two major units for ease of study – the *surah* and *ayah* – that are intended to shape our understandings of literally everything. The *surah*, commonly translated as chapter but whose literal translation is a step or degree is intended to elevate the believer. It is comprised of a definitive set of *ayat* (sg. *ayah*), narrowly translated and understood as verses, that present all the needed knowledge for a believer to be capable of correctly internalizing the key messages and meanings in a *surah*. In other words, the *surah* encapsulates or bounds all the *ayat* that ensure proper understanding of its key teachings. Rules or commands are not presented in a social or moral vacuum. They are always connected to important concepts, directed to certain objectives, couched in uncompromising values, supported by other rules, verified by universal laws, aimed at key parties, and explained through unfalsifiable proofs. We are always given a full picture to support our own decision-making processes.

Reflecting upon all the *suwar* (sg. *surah*), which include all the ayat of the Quran, is necessary for a comprehensive internalization of the message. This is how our autonomy is strengthened as believers, how our *fitra* or original state of Islam is fortified and extended so that we can deal with innumerable situations in ways that conform with Allah's guidance. The *ayah* or the building block of every *surah* and hence the Quran, plays *the* leading role in ensuring that Quranic guidance is universally applicable in time and place. The *ayah*, is so much more than a verse; it is an indivisible unit of knowledge or truth that expresses one or several ideas. It can be believed in, witnessed, heard, seen, sensed, observed, understood, and remembered. Alternatively, it can be rejected, manipulated, fragmented, neglected, forgotten, opposed, misunderstood, or purchased for a miserable price as is related repeatedly in the Quran.

Each *ayah* also forms part of larger sets of *ayat* that construct even larger and more complex ideas enabling the application of guidance to different contexts. The *ayat* regarding any specific subject, question or theme can be sequential or scattered throughout the Quran, embedded as they are in different places to show us that life is inevitably indivisible no matter what subject or theme we are considering. This fact that is reinforced by the presentation of *ayat* in written words as in the text of the Quran or real life as when the Quran draws attention to the life of an individual or group, a fact of nature, a historical phenomenon, a manifestation of divine intervention, and all other references that exhort the reader to go beyond the written provision.

"We will show them Our *ayat* in the horizons and in their selves until it becomes clear to them that this is the Truth. But is it not sufficient concerning your Lord that He is over all things witness?" (Fussilat 41:53). The ayat are available and evident no matter where we look. Only the discerning heart, however, can observes how the marvels of the universe and the intricacy of our own creation mirror each other demonstrating the incontrovertible Truth of one Author. And though our knowledge of both remains – and will remain – miniscule, those who study the Quran know that the source of the *ayat* in written and real form, in ourselves and the universe, is the same. Allah, the Originator. The written word and its extensions into the universe, into our lives and realities, explain and reinforce each other. The Quran expands our limits by augmenting our abilities to observe realities and truths related to ourselves, others, the worlds we live in and the worlds we will inevitably journey on to. It is the Quran that allows us to see beyond immediate manifestations of phenomena, giving us insight into important truths of past, present and future events.

The *ayat* construct the needed images, pictures, with all their connections in the mind of a believer so that we can properly understand their core lessons as they apply to our lives and to the world around us. As just noted, the collection of *ayat* presented in any *surah* serves to clarify the key messages of that *surah* while not limiting their transcendence beyond the *surah* thereby connecting the entirety of the Quran and the universe with which it is concerned. Occasional repetition of an *ayah* in different *suwar* or even in the same *surah*, whether with the exact wording or meaning, emphasizes the Quran's connectivity as well as the need to recall an *ayat* in different contexts.

Each *ayah*, even when repeated elsewhere, has its unique purpose and associations where it is located to evoke intended connections. This generates psychic effects in the human heart, transmitting meaning and eliciting response as needed. It propels us to think, understand and synthesize the Truth for the purpose of augmenting the images in our minds, so that we may strive to realign our realities and truths with actual Reality and Truth, which ultimately contributes to our authenticity as *'ebad* Allah and as good people in a more mundane sense.

Reflect on the following *ayah* as it describes the greatest relationship on earth. A beautiful depiction of the purpose and connection between men and women. "And of His *ayat* are that He created mates for you from yourselves (*anfusikum*) [of your likeness] that you may find tranquility [or dwell] within them and He placed between you both amity and mercy. Indeed, in this are *ayat* for people who are thoughtful" (Ar-Rum 30:21). How beautiful! Allah's indisputable truth that men and women are created from the same likeness. In all our diversity we remain compatible partners, providing each other with tranquility, security, but the *ayah* places emphasis on reminding men in particular of this divine favour. Women, we, are of you, *min anfusikum*, literally meaning, from your very selves, of your likeness, kind, breath. We are the other of a pair without which you are incomplete, only half. A pair, each one of which offers refuge for the other, a place where friendship and mercy have been placed to guarantee peace and harmony for the heedful.

Think of the essence of the *self*, created with the capacity to be a sanctuary for another being. This is profound. The expression *to dwell or find tranquility*, in Arabic *taskunu*, toward her, with her, in her, invokes consciousness of another space, another dimension where Allah willed man to find rest, release and residence. Only endless gratitude to Allah and the duty to honour, love, care, and reciprocate is in order. It is within the sacred accommodation of this space, its suitability, beauty, and upkeep, that the marital relationship expresses its divine glory. In this are *ayat*, not one *ayah*, but multiple *ayat*, images, lessons, truths, that the hearts of men may be softened, that women may witness, and that all may reflect.

In addition to direct and factual statements like that just mentioned, the *ayat* form the basis of different Quranic devices like stories, examples, and metaphors, among others, to support our ability to understand, make connections, prioritize, and apply key messages in different contexts. The use of all these devices ensures that the message of an *ayah* or set of *ayat*, a surah or group of *suwar*, and thereby the entirety of the Quran is deeply rooted and settled within our chests, ready for recollection, connection, and prioritization when needed. "We narrate to you the best of the stories in what We have revealed to you of this Quran, though you were previously among the unaware" (Yusuf 12:3). Stories in the Quran present us with common plots. Plots that were and that remain relevant to human life. But unlike the stories we tend to tell, the perfectly selected stories of the Quran reveal plots in their totality, not just the observable and explainable, but also that dimension of reality that only Allah, the All-Knowing, can expose. And it accomplishes this with extreme efficiency. Only the information needed to internalize the key messages of a story, to avoid the seductions that lead us to do wrong or harness the blessings that lead us to do right, are conveyed. Stories give us ideas on how to handle situations and on the values that we stand to lose if we act inappropriately or gain when we are heedful.

Think of this story. Imagine a woman granted a mighty throne. So great that it captures the attention of an officer of the court of a king of another mighty throne. "Indeed," says the officer, "I found a woman ruling them and she has been given of everything and she has a mighty throne" (An-Naml 27:23). Imagine what the officer must have observed, power, opulence, grandeur, so much so that it is the first thing that he describes to his king, who is famed for a kingdom and powers so great that they were not granted to anyone thereafter. To this king the winds and diverse creatures were subjected and he was taught the logic and language of birds. Surely all else paled in comparison, nothing could exist that warranted mention. All perhaps but this. Her dominion was notable. The narrative that unfolds with this fateful event reveals so many timeless lessons about power, leadership, wisdom, prosperity, decision making, war, peace, diplomacy, courage and above all faith. I am of course taking about the Quranic story of Sulaiman ﵇ and the Queen of Sheeba; an unparalleled exchange between a man and woman of great power.

What a delectable twist! The most powerful king on earth meets his match, and is tested through, the affairs of a female ruler. A woman. Intentionally not identified by her name, which incidentally was Bilqis. The Quran does not give proper names to individuals who potentially represent an archetype, a model, a replicable example whether in terms of the narrative that they are a part of or in terms of their persona. Only one-of-a-kind individuals are identified by their names. This allows us to distinguish between the elements that we can apply to our contexts and those that are in part or on whole beyond comparison.

So here we have a woman – *imra'ah* – identified first by her sex, then power, wealth, and magnificent throne. But that is not the only or even most important point. As a matter of fact, the part that she is female seems to be of no consequence to Sulaiman ﵇. The core concern of this narrative is that the queen and her people were disbelievers. "I found her and her folk (*qawm*) prostrating to the sun instead of Allah and the Shaytan has beautified for them their actions so obstructing them from the way [of Allah] so they are not guided" (An-Naml 27:24). Their submission to Allah is therefore Sulaiman's ultimate concern. The exchanges that happen during the course of the Queen's entry into Islam give us invaluable insight into the leadership qualities of women not the least of which are wisdom, consultation, and the avoidance of hostilities. They also show us how male leadership ought to perceive and deal with female counterparts – exactly as they would any other leader, with truth, justice and equity.

Sulaiman ﵇ had to recall that his ultimate aim was not to destroy her or her people or to take over her throne by force or otherwise, there was no issue with her rulership. Rather, the goal was to help guide her and her people, to direct them to the worship of Allah, a matter that she readily accepted when the Truth had been made manifest. She said, "My Lord, I have indeed committed an injustice against myself and submitted with Sulaiman to Allah, the Lord of the Worlds" (An-Naml 27:44). And with that her people also entered into Islam.

In addition to stories, the *ayat* also form and give us examples (*amthal*) Examples provide us with insights into outstanding cases, ideals, patterns, standards, or guides. They allow us to assess and compare an example with a situation in our own lives. The Quran is exceptionally comprehensive when it comes to the provision of examples. "And We have certainly dispensed in this Quran for people of every example and the human is more than anything argumentative" (Al-Kahf 18:54). "And We have indeed dispensed in this Quran of every example, yet most people rebel except [against] disbelief" (Al-Isra' 17:89). Similarly, we read, "And We have provided for people in this Quran of every example, perhaps they may remember" (Az-Zumar 39:27). Despite our argumentative nature, or perhaps due to it, Allah provides us with endless examples to educate, persuade and warn. We are equipped and expected to combine and adjust these examples to better understand modern manifestations of similar people, behaviours, places, and events.

The Quran draws *people's* attention to four specific women presented as exemplars for both disbelievers and believers. "Allah gives an example for those who disbelieve the wife of Noah and the wife of Lot. They were both under two of our righteous servants, but they betrayed them, so they were not availed anything of their [husbands] accounts and it was said: 'Enter the fire with those entering'" (At-Tahrim 66:10). The wives of Noah and Lot are given as examples to disbelievers, both men and women, of how affiliation to even the most righteous people in this world will mean nothing if the individual is not themselves righteous.

"And Allah gives an example for those who believe, the wife of Pharaoh as she said: 'My Lord build for me a home in Paradise near you and save me from Pharaoh and his doings and save me from an unjust people.' And Maryam, the daughter of 'Imran, who guarded her chastity, so We breathed into her of Our Spirit and she affirmed the words of her Lord and His Books and she was of the devout" (At-Tahrim 66:11-12). These exemplars are presented to all believers, men and women. Asiya, the wife of Pharaoh, despite being married to a tyrant maintained her dignity, compassion, and faith in Allah. She, along with Maryam bint 'Imran, Khadijah bint Khuwalid and Fatimah bint Muhammad ﷺ, are known as the most honoured women in Islam and dwellers of Paradise. Maryam is given as the example of chastity and devotion and although her life cannot be emulated by anyone else, she nevertheless sets the highest standards of purity and refinement for both men and women.

The examples of all four women demonstrate to disbeliever and believers that each individual is ultimately responsible for their own choices. No worldly affiliation no matter how excellent can be used to commit or excuse evil or to protect against accountability. Conversely, no amount of temptation or evil even by one's closest relations can prevent us from choosing to do what is moral or good or excuse us from not having chosen the right path. Moreover, even if we choose to remain single, we must respect the moral boundaries of that choice.

In addition to these general lessons, the choice of women as exemplars sends different messages to men and women. For men, it is a clear message that women have their own agency. A woman may choose to be defiant even if the men around her are pious and caring. Alternatively, she has every right, even a duty to be defiant when the men around her fall short of their duties toward Allah. We are individually accountable to Allah and therefore must ultimately take responsibility for our actions and do what will please Him and keep our hearts pure. For women it sends a clear message that the limits of our partnership with others, even though they be our closest partners, are determined by our heedfulness of Allah and our desire to maintain sound hearts. The goodness of those around us will not necessarily determine our goodness or save us from accountability. Conversely, the evil and nastiness of those around us is not an excuse for conformance or passivity. As individuals with full accountability to Allah, it is incumbent upon us to take all measures that allow us to live Islam in every way our capacities permit. And to both men and women, the message is clear that both have the right and are capable of making the choice to remain single while keeping pure and chaste.

The *ayat* also teach us through beautiful, truthful, and immensely insightful metaphors. "Do you not see how Allah gives the example of a good word which is like a good tree? Its trunk is firmly fixed and its branches [extend to] in the sky. It gives its edibles [consumables] in due time by the permission of its Lord. And Allah gives examples for the people, perhaps they may remember. And the example of a malignant word is like that of a malignant tree, cut from the surface of the earth, not having stability" (Ibrahim 14:24-26). A word, *kalimah*, also signifies an individual as when the angels tell Maryam ﷺ that Allah is "... giving her good tidings of a word (*kalimah*) from Him named the Messiah 'Issa ibn Maryam..." (Al-'Imran 3:45). This is a brilliant metaphor with almost endless lessons. How accurately we can understand the reality of words, people, events, and places through the study of trees. Reflect on how the metaphor situates us as dutiful and responsible individuals, never isolated observers looking from the outside in. Rather, part of an ecosystem whose flourishing above ground is reflective of what happens underground. Think of the power and stability of a solid trunk, of branches that extend into the sky, providing shade, shelter, nourishment, beauty. How leaves communicate using pheromones and other scent signals to warn each other of impending dangers among other messages. Trees in a forest do not compete for light as is commonly believed, they collectively reach for the light to secure the forest canopy in order to protect the natural balance that thrives beneath. They actually support each other in accessing the light by exchanging underground resources and nutrients to enable each member to flourish, to rise.

The surface of a forest can only be as strong as what is beneath. Root systems communicate and connect through chemical, low pulse electricity, and hormonal signals, not unlike our nervous system, which gift all kinds of creatures and is gifted by them. They behave as one community and are cognizant of their role in the preservation of all life. All in the dark, where there can be no show, no overt gratitude.

A good word, a good person, is like a healthy tree; capable and willing to fulfill its purpose in public and private because it is well established, rooted in belief, guidance, and goodness. "Allah firmly fixes those who believe with speech that is firmly fixed in the life of this world and in the Hereafter. And Allah sends astray the unjust and Allah does what He wills" (Ibrahim 14:27). An evil word, an evil person, in contrast, is cut off from the land, severed from its roots; incapable of settling, of making a useful contribution, of fulfilling its purpose and honouring its connections. A book can be written on this metaphor alone!

Clearly, the *ayat* must be cultivated within us. Cultivated as we would precious seeds, acquired, planted, fertilized, watered, sheltered, illuminated, and protected so that we can reap the benefits of their settlement within us. The Quran tells us about those who took their *deen* for distraction and play and were seduced by the life of this world, they will be forgotten as they forgot the day of reckoning and did not cultivate, *yajhadun*, the *ayat* (Al-A'raf 7:51). The word *yajhad* in Arabic is associated with the earth becoming parched and non-productive. It is not a simple rejection but rather a lack of cultivation even for those who may accept basic truths of the *ayat*. "And it is He who sends the winds, an exultation between the extensions of His mercy until it carries heavy clouds We drive them to a dead land, then by it We sent down water, so with it We brought out of every produce. It is as such that We bring out the dead that you may remember. And the land that is fertile/good, its vegetation comes out with its Lord's permission and that which is malignant, it does not come out except with distress. It is as such that We dispense the ayat for a people that thank" (Al-A'raf 7:57-58). Like the land, people are either receptive to mercy and guidance, and are capable of reproducing good in the world, or they are no-gooders causing distress to themselves and others by denying themselves the guidance, healing and success that comes with Allah's relief. Water to those who deny is a mere necessity for survival not a blessing for revival for themselves and others.

Only a believer's state of beautiful surrender allows the *ayat* to reform their internal and external aspects simultaneously. The *ayat* have the power to penetrate our depths enabling a recalibration and return to our original sense of dignity and giving us the courage to reflect divine truths in our worldly life. We do this, not through blind acceptance but through an active and continuous process of seeking, questioning, evaluating, mediating, and synthesizing the *ayat* so that their lessons can manifest in the different situations we face on a daily basis and throughout the course of our lives. This ongoing rectification process that consistently aims to guide to what is best is firmly settled in the chest of a believer.

"Rather, it [the Quran] is clear [demonstrative] *ayat* in the chests of those given knowledge and none neglects the cultivation Our *ayat* except the unjust" (Al-'Ankabut 29:49). Imagine the roots of a tree that are immersed in fertile, nourishing soil. The nutrients in the soil are needed to keep the tree healthy. When the nutrients are lacking or the roots are crowded the tree shows signs of distress, becoming vulnerable to the elements, prone to disease and stagnation. Now envision your lungs with their bronchi, root-like structures, much like the roots of a tree, delivering oxygen to your blood, without which you cannot survive. Envision the space within which your lungs and heart rest - the thoracic cavity in medical terms – so that your lungs can expand and contract, and your heart to beat. The quality of that space and the nutrients provided with every breath and heartbeat is reflective of your efforts to cultivate Allah's *ayat*. To cultivate mercy, truth, justice, wisdom, and love, crowding out injustice, harm and negativity. There, in the vicinity of your chest, you will find beliefs, emotions, intentions, motivations, commitments, and so on, that guide or misguide you.

Can you see that breathing or *nafas,* a defining dimension of your *nafs*, self or being, is not merely a mechanical exercise? Rather, it is a transcendental process that has the potential to give life, to revive. Every inhalation has the potential to deliver much more than oxygen to your blood, running through the circulatory rope that nourishes your entire body, it can deliver guidance, *huda*. Your breath is mediated by the quality of your *nafs*, the extent of its consciousness. Every breath is an opportunity, a chance at healing yourself and the world. You control the quality of the space and soil that supplies your lungs that then nourishes your heart that then instructs every organ and limb to direct itself to its Creator – to unite in the beautiful surrender.

The *ayat* are intended, custom-made if you wish, to dwell within us so that we can recall, recombine, and prioritize their lessons as needed. In doing so, they impress upon our conscience in such a way that alters our vision or worldview, shifting our awareness from our subjective realities and truths to the Reality and Truth. In other words, the *ayat* induce a process of objectivization of cognition, a process in which we replace or override our personal biases, prejudices, and inhibitions with truthful knowledge, with divine guidance. We become less self-centred, and more Allah and revelation centred, bringing us closer together with other believers. This not only strengthens our understanding and decision-making capacities but also greatly enhances the potential for collective or communal cooperation and agreement.

The *ayat* guarantee truth, consistency, expansiveness, and flexibility of the Quranic text. The envisioning of different patterns or arranging and rearranging the *ayat* allows us to prioritize some directives over others in any given context. This dynamic aspect of the Quran's presentation is necessary for its universal applicability, in my life and yours, at every point in time, and given all the diverse contexts within which we resort to it. I must emphasize, however, that dynamic interaction with the *ayat* cannot result from occasional, incomplete, or biased readings. Nor can it result from twisted minds who wish to profess Islam but refuse to accept its clear teachings. "It is He who sent down upon you [Muhammad] the Book, of it are well-defined *ayat*, these are the mother [core/unifiers] of the Book and others that are obscure (*mutashabihat*). So as for those in whose hearts is deviance, they follow what is obscure of it, seeking sedition (*fitna*) and seeking to spin it (*ta'weel*) and none except Allah knows its interpretation and those who are entrenched in knowledge say, 'We believe in it. All of it is from our Lord.' And none will be reminded except the possessors of intellect (*ulul-albab*)" (Al-'Imran 3:7). Thus, there are *ayat* that are clearly defined, which unify the text and form the core of the Quran. They can neither be misunderstood or spun to manipulate meanings. Other *ayat* are not clear in meaning inviting those in whose hearts is disease to use them for *fitna* or sedition, actions and speech that manipulate people into divisiveness and disbelief, to rebel against Allah and His *ayat*. People of intellect recognize their limitations even as they engage with all the *ayat*, and practice what they have come to know to the best of their abilities.

The way in which the *ayat* impact the human psyche while simultaneously providing guidance for worldly affairs over the course of history suggests that they cannot be produced by just anyone. Those who do not believe are asked to produce a *surah*, something no one is capable of doing (Al-Baqarah 2:23). If the Quran is fabricated, it challenges those making this accusation to produce ten fabricated suwar like it even while seeking all the reinforcements they could muster (Hud 11:13; Yunus 10:38). They would still be incapable. "Those who argue about Allah's *ayat* without authority (*sultan*) given to them, verily, in their chests is nothing but greatness that they will never reach. So, seek refuge with Allah. It is He who is the Hearer, the Seer" (Ghafir 40:56). Only Allah can produce an *ayah*. "Indeed, the *ayat* are with Allah" (Al-An'am 6:109). And only the believer can reap the benefits of their wonders and powers.

Only Allah can produce an *ayah* because every *ayah* is an ultimate truth. Even Prophet Muhammad ﷺ was told: "You can neither tunnel into the ground or set a ladder to the sky to bring an *ayah* so do not be of the ignorant" (Al-An'am 6:35). Not surprisingly, that is how the disbelievers challenged the Prophet in his mission. "They say if only an *ayah* was sent down on Him from His Lord. Say, 'Verily, Allah is able to send down an *ayah* but most of them do not know'" (Al-An'am 6:37). The *ayat* are not furnished at the whims of disbelievers. "And if you do not bring them an *ayah* they say, 'Why have you not contrived it?' Say, 'I only follow what is revealed to me from my Lord.' These are insights (*basa'ir*) from your Lord and guidance (*huda*) and mercy (*rahma*) for a people who believe" (Al-A'raf 7:203). *A people who believe.*

Ignorance of Worth

Not too long ago I was asked by a dear friend to contribute a chapter to a book that she was editing on women's empowerment. She suggested that I tackle the topic of the Convention on the Elimination of all forms of Discrimination against Women (CEDAW) from the perspective of the objectives of the shariah or *maqasid al-shariah*. This wasn't the first time that I had been asked to speak to women's rights and issues despite the fact that it was not my field of specialization. These repeated requests prompted me to challenge myself to study the Quran with this specific purpose in mind, something I had never done in earnest before. It was no longer sufficient to simply have a feel for what the text conveyed. I needed evidence for the views that I held, or thought that I held, before I took this deep dive. This book is partly the result of that journey. The chapter that I submitted to my friend opened a new world of understanding and challenged perspectives that I had until that point taken for granted or not considered at all, concepts like equality.

It is this journey, the one that resulted from the uncomfortable realization that the Quran presents no such thing as equality, that I wish to share here. Many of those who insist on this premise are reading their own desires into the Quran, neglecting or denying what the Quran is actually telling them. They are also uncritically accepting that the injustices that women face are a result of inequality with men. Such inequality is perceived and presented in many social spheres from family to the labour market. The main response has been to seek substantive justice or an *equalization* through the law or material conditions that create a facade of equality between men and women by discriminating in favour of women or taking account of their differences. The incessant drive to push women into the labour force, irrespective of the nature of work, and to monetize their contributions to family care are all part of this equalization process. Something about this perspective did not appeal to me and was certainly not in harmony with my observations of the lives of countless women over several decades from all over the world.

The demand for equality is an illusion that masks much deeper social disfunction and moral decay. The injustices suffered by women are not on account of their inequality with men because inequality is a universal law, a *sunnah* of Allah. It is part of a just and merciful scheme. The absence of equality is a pervasive state among all creation not just men and women. Equality is not a possible or preferable state. This is amply clear through observation and experience. Even as we say equal application of the law, we immediately consider individual differences and contexts to justify equitable not equal application. This is because even if the law is the same our duties and responsibilities differ in accordance with our personal circumstances, public office, and the contexts within which we act.

Thus, we do not treat the poor as we do the rich, the weak as we do the mighty, the public official as we do the private citizen, the brilliant as we do those with limited capacities. When a society equalizes – and more often than not treats the advantaged with even greater advantage – the entire system eventually decays. To be clear, this does not translate into men are superior to women, though we are not equals. Equality is an unjust and perverse condition given our differences, diversity, needs, duties and responsibilities. If we were equal or strove for equality, we would not be able to exercise important dimensions of our humanity like faith, dignity, charity, mercy, kindness and everything else that we do in response to our perception of differences.

The ayat of the Quran always inform us about the truthful concepts, objectives, values, rules, universal laws, parties and proofs of any question we may have. Through repetitive cycles of reflection on the text, layers upon layers of meaning are continuously added as we connect these elements into meaningful wholes. This gradual and seamless process of knowledge acquisition ensures receptivity, connectivity and consistency in an ever-expanding and changing universe. Let us consider each element as it applies to equality.

The concepts, names, or designations (*asma'*) are the key Arabic words in the Quran and Sunnah that have authoritative truth or *sultan*. This authority places Quranic concepts above concepts that we may conceive for whatever purposes we have in mind. The concept of equality despite its popularity when it comes to male/female relations is not a thing – mention or concern – in the Quran. The word *musawah* or equality does occur even once, not between men and women or between any form of creation for that matter. *Musawah*, like its English counterpart, means to be equal in status, rights and opportunities. It is true that not all Arabic words are in the Quran but the relationship between men and women is so extensively covered that it would be incredibly unlikely for such a concept to have been overlooked.

Musawah has a kind of horizontal impact where men and women compare themselves to each other while attempting to downplay, neglect or reject any differences. Accepting this concept makes it difficult if not impossible to understand the vast majority of directives that men were given in relation to women. Directives that mitigate potentially negative masculinities that are associated with the natural disposition of men. Even those who insist on equality know that there are clear and significant differences between men and women. Where differences are impossible to ignore, the proponents of equality have striven to change mindsets and alter material conditions that would allow women to do exactly what men do and be treated exactly as men are treated – including to carry the same burdens. This has led to unfortunate confusion in people's minds and in social interactions and institutions.

The clearest statement in the Quran that men and women are not the same or equal is found in the birth of Maryam. When the wife of 'Imran, Maryam's mother, observes that she has given birth to a girl, perhaps something she was not expecting, the Quran states "...and Allah was more knowing of what she delivered, and *the male is not like the female*" (Al-'Imran 3:36). To be clear there is no suggestion of superiority in this statement. If anything, we must accept that Allah intended for this gift to be a girl. A female who was chosen by Allah to precede and to produce the male. It is disingenuous to claim that difference and inequality are two different things. By definition if two things are different, they are not equal. Simple. But what are the objectives of inequality?

The objectives or *maqasid* are the purposes or the 'why' things are as they are. Purpose responds to our quest for meaning and the *ayat* are the foundation of the Quran's revelation of purpose. The ultimate purpose of humanity is to worship Allah (Adh-Dhariyat 51:56) with everything else either fulfilling such worship or yielding to it. Purpose is not only expressed through the rituals of Islam, but perhaps even more so, in the way people are guided, inspired, to behave. It follows that all truths, objectives, values, rules, universal laws, and proofs derived from the Quran guide to this ultimate purpose. Understanding the absence of equality between men and women demands intuition, observation and investigation. Some purposes of inequality are clear, others demand much more reflection. Some are general in nature and tacit while others are specific and explicit. For example, the Quran affirms that some people are raised above others in ranks so that we can commission each other in various ways. We need each other in our full diversity. "Do they divide-up the mercy of your Lord? It is We who have distributed between them their livelihoods in the life of this world and raise some of them above others by degrees so that some may take others in service. And the mercy of your Lord is better than whatever they accumulate" (Az-Zukhruf 43:32). Men and women employ and benefit from each other because of this diverse and unequal distribution of capabilities, resources, and talents.

Zaynab, the wife of Abdullah ibn Mas'ud, was a kind woman with several orphans under her care. She was an artisan who made a decent income by selling her goods while her husband was a man of limited means. She once related that the Prophet ﷺ had gave a speech to the women, telling them to give charity, even if it meant giving up some of their jewelry. As the family's main breadwinner, Zaynab wondered as to whether her spending on her family constituted charity. She questioned the Prophet ﷺ about this and he responded by telling her (and others in her situation) that for them there was a double reward, one for the sustenance of family relations and the other for giving charity (Sahih Bukhari).

Clearly this is not a matter of equality, but about directing our focus toward serving Allah. Whether man or woman, our capabilities, merit, resources and provision – all due to Allah's mercy and generosity – must be directed to serving His *'ebad*. Men and women need each other to build families, communities, and nations. The quest for equality obscures the truths of Allah's providence. Who is more amply endowed? Who has greater merit? In any particular context it may be the man or it may be the woman but this changes nothing of the expectations and directives that Allah has instituted to guide each toward a harmonious life. To fulfill this purposefulness, however, the Quran couches these objectives in certain values.

Values (*qiyam*) are the standards and worth that the Quran attaches to everything. In addition to teaching us the purposefulness of things – which in itself is a value – the Quran helps us to see importance, urgency, priority. Through the association of all thoughts and actions with positive, negative, and neutral values, we are aided in our decision making and self-correction processes. "Not equal are the blind and those with vision; nor are the darkness and the light; nor the shade and the heat; nor the alive and the dead. Indeed, [it is] Allah who makes who He wills to hear, and you [Muhammad] cannot make to hear those who are in their graves" (Fatir 35:19-22). This *ayah* draws our attention to the inequality that is found among people and nature. It encourages us to value vision, light, shade and *being* alive, which is not the act of merely living. To internalize these values, we must have the capacity to listen, to be receptive to the message that educates us about values.

It is not our positioning in relation to each other, that I am equal to you or you to me, rather it is the status of both of us to Allah given our unique creation and potential. A beautiful life is not based on the equality of women with men, or men with men or women with women. It is based on our relationship to Allah, and how we reflect that in our relations with each other, which is only possible when we are able to value things properly – when we have illuminated and sound hearts.

I value my womanhood and everything feminine with which I share characteristics. It is Allah who determined that I be born and live female. It is Allah, who way before my existence, determined that the earth and the sun are feminine forms of creation. I am bound to them in ways I cannot fathom and ways that I can. I am woman. I was created with a womb, the *rahim* that binds humanity, that shelters and nourishes the seeds of the future. I am illuminating and my warmth and light are reflected in the lives of those around me. These values are rooted in the Quran and teachings of Prophet Muhammad ﷺ and they are unique to my being a woman. I also value my father's, husband's, son's, uncles' and nephew's manhood, who Allah also determined should be born male. It is Allah who determined that the rain and moon are masculine forms way before humanity was a thing. Think about it, what happens when there is a drought, or when the rain becomes acidic and polluted, does not the earth suffer?

It is not equality that we should value but rather the potential of everything that Allah created to have the greatest possible chance at fulfilling purpose and in doing so enabling others – both human and non-human – to do the same. "It is not suitable for her, the sun, to catchup with the moon, nor the night to overtake the day and each is swimming in an orbit" (Ya Sin 36:40). Whether sun or moon, night or day, male or female, they are not equals. Nor should they strive to be. Rather their value is found in their responsiveness to their Lord, in the purposeful paths they pursue, sometimes unique yet in many instances overlapping, by His command so that other creation may pursue their purposeful paths. Our value is determined by Allah in accordance with our heedfulness of Him, not in terms of our equality with each other. Both the sun and moon are luminous and provide direction. The rules in the Quran that deal with male/female relations have to be read, interpreted, and understood in this light.

The rules (*ahkam/awamer*), that specifically govern our behaviour play a great role in mitigating the differences that are inherent in the creation of men and women. With the absence of equality woven into the very fabric of what this universe is made of, including in our own creation, how must we behave so that this predicament is a mercy and not a curse? A first step is to recognize that the rules in the Quran are first and foremost about *self-regulation*. When the Quran speaks to men about women, its aim is to regulate male behavior not to offer men a pretext or justification for regulating women. Whether speaking to or about women, or to or about men, or other groups, the Quran calls all believers to witness its guidance and urges each to practice it individually and collectively. Prophet Muhammad ﷺ said: "A believer to another believer is like a building whose different parts reinforce each other" and he clasped his hands with the fingers interlaced to demonstrate (Sahih Bukhari).

Believers, men and women, are literally members one of another, *ba'dukum min ba'd* (Al-'Imran 3: 195; An-Nisa' 4:25) or guardians of one another, *ba'duhum awliya' ba'd* (At-Tawbah 9:71). This is not a conflictual relationship based on the struggle for sameness. Rather, it is a call for men and women to support each other in every way that enables, empowers, the other to fulfill their purpose as *'ebad*. This includes all facilitations associated with Islamic rituals as well as worldly affairs that individually and collectively strengthen the Ummah and enable it to direct its energies in the service of Allah. "And it is He who has created you as successors of the earth and raised some above others in degrees to test you with what He has granted you. Indeed, your Lord is swift in account and verily He is the forgiving the merciful" (Al-An'am 6:165).

The members of this Ummah, every male and female, is commanded to have the best interest of the other at heart – that interest is to support each other in serving Allah. In doing so, we not only elevate our brothers and sisters and facilitate for them a dignified life, but we also increase our value in this life and the next. We must know and acknowledge how we have been mercifully endowed by Allah and to share in all those blessings with others – all others. Goodness is not limited to those who profess Islam. Thus, we also must understand what Allah tells us about others, all kinds of others. In our example, we have to understand what Allah tells us about men and women, their status, nature, needs, aspirations, abilities, duties, responsibilities and rights. There are important differences in the rules directed at men and women in the Quran and teachings of Prophet Muhammad ﷺ.

If Allah has directed much of the Quran's commands to men, it is likely because the self and mutual regulation of men by other men and women is most significant to the welfare of this Ummah, its members, women, families, communities, and nations. This emphasis is not meant to restrict women – who are expected to actively participate in the success of this order – but rather to guarantee opportunities for them to fulfill personal, familial, communal and social aspirations. It warns that if the men are rogue, if they misunderstand this basic point, if they misinterpret the rules, the entire Ummah suffers more proportionately than if its other members faltered. Likewise, if they are reformed and righteous many other things are concomitantly taken care of. In other words, the rules support us in respecting universal laws.

Universal laws (*sunan*) are Allah's unchanging ways and directives in the universe. The *sunan* govern all life. Those like the ones just mentioned regarding the sun and moon, night and day thankfully are not amenable to our impact, they cannot be altered or distorted in any way. While others like male/female relations and other social phenomena are subject to human will. This does not mean that the *sunan* of human nature and social communities are changeable, it simply means that Allah gave us the choice to respect or reject them to our benefit or detriment respectively. "The *sunnah* of Allah regarding those who passed (*khalaw*) [literally vacated] from before, and you will not find in the *sunnah* of Allah any exchange" (Al-Ahzab 33:62). All social phenomena are subject to divine or universal laws or *sunan.* If this was not the case, we would not be compelled to maintain some semblance of social order and all manner of behavior would be possible without causing corruption or injustice. That inner compulsion, the sense of duty, is instilled in us by Allah so that we can, even in the presence of such moral diversity, live together.

The Quran and teachings of Prophet Muhammad ﷺ carry us way beyond this basic understanding of how to live together with those who may not share our beliefs. While the disbelievers are turned off by any such warning and guidance, the believer recognizes through observing reality, that the end of misguidance can only be loss. A sunnah that will never change. For many this discussion of equality will be uncomfortable, a turnoff that challenges a dominant discourse. They will be repulsed, choosing to continue their impossible quest. Recognizing that equality is not a divine *sunnah*, challenges our thoughts and actions, it elicits a gut reaction. The Quran teaches us about this *sunnah* not so that we can ignore, reinforce, or futilely try to change it but rather so that we can understand it and understand our true nature as human beings, as women and men; so that we can appreciate diversity; and finally, so that we can consistently challenge ourselves through giving and gratitude.

The idea is not to seek equality with each other but to build our value in the sight of Allah, to turn our faces towards Him and support others in their desire to do the same. Rejecting divine guidance ultimately leads to corruption and demise because the social, not like but as an inseparable dimension of the natural world, works by universal laws or Allah's *sunan.* We do not have the capacity to see or understand how our behaviour impacts everything in the universe, how every action has a ripple effect from the time of its occurrence to the Last Day. Allah's guidance guarantees a respect for universal laws if only by intention.

This brings us to the element of parties (*fi'at*) which are the individuals or groups, human and otherwise, to which the Quran gives names while ascribing to those names specific characteristics, traits, behaviors, histories, duties and rights. Human parties are identified by proper name, association (family and followership), behaviors, beliefs, intellect, and sex (male, female, men, women, boys, girls). There is no equality within or among any of these parties. Rather, each is valued in accordance with their proximity to Allah or how hard they try to understand and follow His guidance. Male and female are not equals but that does not translate into the superiority of one over the other since superiority is not a function of sex but of heedfulness to Allah. That heedfulness demands the acceptance of different duties and rights on the part of men and women based on the acknowledgement of mutual support and divine blessings and provisions for the fulfillment of divinely determined purpose – the worship of Allah. Thus, the nature of injustice suffered by women today and historically is not on account of their lack of equality with men. Rather equality is the illusion, a disguise of much deeper social ills – diseases of the heart – that are more intractable but patently obvious in their impact on the dignity and welfare of both sexes.

Allah's guidance is tailored to the nature, abilities, endowments, provisions, and self-determined paths of men and women. The Quran is expressive of Allah's Knowledge of His creation. "And He who created the male and female. Indeed, your strivings are diverse. As for he who gives and heeds and confirms what is best/beautiful (*husna*), We will [as a result] facilitate him toward ease. And as for he who withholds and considers himself sufficient and denies the *husna*, We will facilitate him toward difficulty" (Al-Layl 92:3-10). The different dispositions and aims of men and women do not conflict when Allah's guidance is respected. The emphasis on practicing generosity, heedfulness, and substantiating what is most beautiful in moral and material affairs ensures harmony between the sexes. There is no rigid determination of roles in this regard, just that each is to give what they can to support the dignified life of the other.

There are no strict divisions in the Quran regarding what men and women can do beyond their biological role in procreation and the duties they owe each other, particularly men to women, on account of the differences, broadly speaking, in their creation. These differences have social implications as is amply clear from male dominance in many public and private domains.

Acknowledging this fact allows us to read and understand Quranic guidance correctly, ensuring that people, and especially men and women, do not mistreat each other on account of a divine law that is intended to facilitate life and test those who are of ample means. Any advantage, whether wielded by men or women, does not translate into freedom to do as one pleases though men are more restricted by the Quran in terms of their duties toward women. Rather, any advantage or provision is an added responsibility on the possessor.

The final element that we must consider are the proofs (*hujaj*). These are the evidence and correct argumentation presented in the Quran and teachings of Prophet Muhammad ﷺ that support the clarification of truths. To demonstrate that equalization is beyond human capacity no matter how generous we are, the Quran states: "And Allah has favoured some of you above others in provision. Those more favoured are not going to redistribute their provision over those held-by-oath (*ma malakat aymanuhum*) so that they are equal in this. Do they then deny (*yajhadun*) Allah's blessings?" (An-Nahl 16:71). I often pose this question to my students. If you had, whether by earning or winning, a hundred thousand dollars, would you give your employee or neighbour the required portion to make them your equal? I have not yet encountered anyone who would do this. Would you? The Quran tells us that if we owned *all* of Allah's blessings and provisions we would still withhold. "Say [Muhammad], 'If you owned the stores of the mercy of my Lord, you would [still] restrain [from giving] out of fear of spending'. And ever is the human a miser (*qatura*)" (Al-Isra' 17:100). People simply do not have it in them to equalize. And it is by Allah's mercy that we do not need people to equalize wealth or any other blessing for that matter, for us to live well. There is of course a minimum threshold of sharing and wealth distribution that is necessary to provide ease for all people and enable them to live meaningful lives, but that is far from a demand for equality. It is as such that the Quran offers proofs for the truths it puts forward for us to ponder.

There is no, nor can there ever be, a certainty of equality between any of us but there is certainty in the notion that we are ignorant of each other's worth in the sight of our Creator.

The Quran presents us with noble idea that people – all people – are to be dignified, treated not in accordance with false notions of equality, but a truthful belief in ignorance of worth. It may just be that those whom we are quick to judge may be better than us. It is on this basis, that a believer is commanded to dignify – to apply the Islamic moral code – to every individual and group.

> *Oh you who believe, let not one people belittle another people, perhaps they may be better than them or women toward women, that perhaps they are better than them. And do not insult one another and do not offend each other with labels. Horrible is the designation of immorality after belief, and whoever does not repent then they are the unjust.*
>
> *Oh you who believe, avoid most assumption, truly some of it is sin. And do not spy and do not backbite each other. Would one of you like to eat the flesh of his dead brother? You would hate it. And heed Allah, indeed, Allah is accepting of repentance and giver of mercy.*
>
> *Oh you people, truly We created you from male and female and made you ethnicities and tribes to know one another. Indeed, the most dignified of you with Allah is the most heedful. Indeed, Allah is Knowing, Proficient.* (Al-Hujuraat 49:11-13)

It is the lack of knowledge of a person's or group's worth in Allah's estimation that ought to motivate the believer in their worldly dealings. No matter who I am dealing with, there is always a latent, if not explicit, thought that this person may well be better than me. They may be more beloved to Allah. There is also a thought that my treatment of them for the sake of this possibility will hopefully increase my value with Allah. I choose to dignify people, to humble myself based on my ignorance of their worth, not my certainty of their equality. In the first instance I direct my energies toward attaining Allah's approval, in the second I would merely be establishing myself as the standard of comparison incapable of ascertaining equality or even my own worth.

Equality is neither pre-ordained nor is it the foundation for action. Whether man or woman, there is no way for us to know divine worth. The Prophet ﷺ once asked his companions, "What do you say about this man?" They replied, "If he asks for a lady's hand, he ought to be given her in marriage; and if he intercedes (for someone) his intercessor should be accepted; and if he speaks, he should be listened to." The Prophet ﷺ kept silent, and then a poor Muslim man passed by, and the Prophet ﷺ asked them again, "What do you say about this man?" They replied, "If he asks for a lady's hand in marriage he does not deserve to be married, and if he intercedes for someone, his intercession should not be accepted; and if he speaks, he should not be listened to," to which the Prophet ﷺ responded, "This poor man is better than so many of the first filling the earth" (Sahih Bukhari). It is in this state of ignorance that we must fear overstepping our limits, that we must make the choice to dignify each and every person we encounter.

The onus, the responsibility, is on the believer. A believer does not wait for someone to demand their dignity as we have become accustomed to because of secular thinking. Sure, someone can demand their rights but the priority – the first initiative – is for the believer to provide without being asked. At the very least, these *ayat* command people to refrain from insults, from hurting each other, and labeling each other. These acts only degrade the perpetrator and dimmish their worth. We are told to avoid assumptions about each other and not to pursue acts that would in any way compromise mutual respect or at the very least, neutrality. Then a reminder that we emanate from the same source of male and female. Our differences, our inequalities, are not reason for discrimination. Rather, they are an invitation to knowledge and exchange. This is binding on men, women, and the communities we collectively form.

The Quran does not take an unequivocal position on equality, except to negate its possibility. Inequality is not only a condition that characterizes differences between and among men and women, but it is also a condition evident in all creation. Inequality has *sultan* or is an authoritative truth that has purpose. The key is to understand why and in turn to address reality, not to negate it and then strive with futility to change it. Just as the *ayat* have led us to see this truth, they also lead us to understand why and present us with what is a more truthful understanding of reality.

The wisdom of *inequality* can be found in three other universal truths, including: (1) the necessity of balance; (2) the mutual benefit and interdependence of all created matter; and (3) the measure of worth of all creation in relation to its responsiveness, whether voluntarily or by decree, to its Creator and not in relation to the mutual equivalence of any of its dimensions. Inequality is neither negative nor discriminatory in the divine scheme. In its infinite manifestations, it is a mercy that permits balance and allows creation to exist in synergy. Every element and dimension of creation is purposeful. Everything counts toward a moral and material order that potentially contributes to the welfare of all living things. In this scheme, it is unproductive to keep talking about equality. Instead, we must understand and respect the guidance that supports our abilities to address Reality.

The Divine Hue

Mercy is a dye, a colourant, penetrating everything that responds to Allah. It is an inseparable dimension of all created matter, having its, her, own authoritative truth, demanding a knowledge of purpose, connection, and holism. Mercy saturates the beautiful life. Love is meaningless without mercy. To understand this, is to experience the ubiquity of the divine hue.

When Prophet Muhammad ﷺ, the messenger of Allah and seal of prophets, our exemplary teacher, *bashar* (sentient being), man, was sent to deliver the message of Allah, he was aware of who was heedful of Allah and who wasn't. He was disappointed when he saw the Kaaba filled with idols, where people came to worship multiple gods and had lost touch with their true purpose – to worship Allah and only Allah. Makkah had become a town of prosperity and revelry, where trade flourished, and tribal leaders competed for honorific titles. Instead of showing gratitude to the source of all blessings, Prophet Muhammad ﷺ saw pilgrims to the Kaaba giving thanks to statues of wood, metal, and stone. They had forgotten Allah, forgotten the purpose for which Ibrahim عليه السلام and Ismail عليه السلام had built the foundations of the Kaaba, the reason that Zamzam flowed, the guarantee of refuge and security in this sacred place.

The Makkans were for the most part polytheists, insisting on their paganism. They loved wine and women, often losing their senses under the intoxicating influence of the unlimited supply of both. And now, a Prophet has come, a man from among them, calling to the One True God, disturbing the lies that people often propagate to live lives of heedlessness. The vehemence with which they would reject his message was expected but he only had one consideration in mind – to dutifully serve Allah. And so, when his people turned away from his calling, he was commanded to say, "Sufficient for me is Allah, there is no deity except Him and on Him I rely and He is the Lord of the Throne, The Great" (At-Tawbah 9:129). It is in this complete resignation to Allah, that unwavering focus on what ultimately mattered, Allah and Allah alone, that the message could be conveyed gradually, courageously, and foremost, with mercy, *RAHMA*.

Rahma, the most beautiful word, the gentlest of approaches, the most magnanimous of meanings, and definitely the best of ends, characterises Allah, His Messenger, the message, and the very fabric of our own creation. Allah, the Merciful, who possesses mercy (Al-An'am 6:133), who owns the stores of mercy (Al-Isra' 17:100), and even then, has decreed mercy upon Himself (Al-An'am 6:54), extends that mercy to all things, *wa Rahmati wasi'at kulla shay'* (Al-A'raf 7:156). We are in dire need of this mercy not only as it relates to forgiveness, suffering, and patience but as it manifests in every facilitation, all the beauty, that we experience in this life.

Have you not pondered on provisions like the day in which we seek livelihoods, the night in which we seek rest, the winds with which we generate electricity and that disperse pollution, the ships that generate commerce, the earth that gives us refuge, joy and nutritious produce of every kind, the water that gives us life, the stars that help us navigate and beautify the sky, the animals that contribute to our wellbeing and extend our capacities, the design of our bodies, the strength of our spirit, the diversity of creation, the moral and social laws that dignify human beings? Are these not all proofs of a Merciful Creator? Not experiencing this mercy is not due to a lack of it. Allah has provided in abundance for all creation. It is the ugliness of some humans that prevents fair and equitable enjoyment of such mercies among all living things.

No one exemplified mercy more beautifully than Prophet Muhammad ﷺ. In the Quran, Allah tells us that the Prophet was not sent except as a mercy to the worlds. "We have not sent you except as a mercy (*rahmatan*) to the worlds (*li'l-'alamin*)" (Al-Anbiya' 21:107). In its plural form, *worlds* implies that Allah's mercy is boundless. It extends to the entirety of humanity and even beyond to the animal and plant worlds and to all the other worlds of which we have little or no knowledge. The Prophet was, in everything he said and did, the embodiment of mercy. And this was reflected in the highest standards of moral conduct (Al-Qalam 68:4). He told us to show mercy to everything on earth so that He in the heavens will have mercy on us. He also stated: "May the mercy of Allah be on one who is kind and forbearing when he sells, kind and forbearing when he buys, and kind and forbearing when he makes a demand"(Sahih Bukhari). Those around him did not need to verbalize their troubles for him to perceive them. He always asked about family and friends and even honoured the dead. Perhaps, one of his most magnanimous displays of mercy can be found in the incident of *Ta'if*.

When Prophet Muhammad ﷺ was eventually commanded by Allah to spread the message of Islam, he started with those closest to him of family and friends – those who could be trusted. This covert operation lasted for approximately three years until the conversion of 'Umar Ibn Al-Khattab who insisted that there was no reason for the truth to be kept secret any longer. Despite having gained a strong and important following, the nascent Muslim community was still very vulnerable as there were still significant factions outside of Islam who could wield great destruction upon it. The potential threat of the new faith to conventional hierarchies and social structures of control were greatly worrying to the leaders of Quraish. The weak were especially vulnerable because it was then, as it is now, that the social and economic system thrived on their continued oppression and subjugation. The liberation of the slaves, poor, women, orphans, and generally those without social connection or consequence by a faith that did not strive to equalize but rather to elevate the believer through his or her piety was revolutionary. And the prevailing powers would have none of it.

Sumayyah, the first martyr in Muslim history. The first among men and women to insist on her faith, her choice, until her last breath. Formerly a slave, she was heinously tortured along with her son and husband to force their renunciation of Islam. She refused to abandon the faith despite the verbal and physical abuse of her captors, despite witnessing the torture of her loved ones. Such was her knowledge of Allah and belief in the message that Prophet Muhammad ﷺ had brought. Stabbed multiple times and finally impaled with a spear, she became the first martyr of Islam.

I write these words against the most painful backdrop of the genocide being perpetrated against the Palestinian people by the Israeli occupier and its corrupt allies around the world including the so-called western secular democracies and corrupt regimes of predominantly Muslim societies. Countless innocent lives, *Sumayyahs*, are being tortured and killed, tens of thousands injured, homes, hospitals, schools, mosques, and churches completely destructed. Humanity is forever changed. New alliances are being formed as a new global consciousness is emerging. Non-Muslims from around the world, many turning to the Quran, others just relying on their innate sense of morality are protesting in the millions. Israel has spun its own demise.

Quraish knew that they were losing ground. The conversion of Umar and then Hamza, the Prophet's uncle, along with the nobles who refused to give up the Prophet's protection sent a chilling message to the disbelievers that Muhammad's faith – and the changes it came to effect for a better world

– were secure. And so, in addition to the hostilities, they resolved to lying, cheating, propaganda, false accusations and finally an extreme siege that cut off all relations, family, and business, to suffocate the Muslims. No mercy.

This intensification of violence against the Muslims began in the seventh year of prophethood and lasted for three years – the last three of Khadijah's ﷺ life, the Prophet's beloved wife and first to believe. The first among men and women to believe in the message of Prophet Muhammad ﷺ. The boycott was lifted in the tenth year of prophethood as Quraysh realized that it had actually galvanized attention and support for the Muslims rather than turning the tides against them as the perpetrators had planned. It is clear from global reaction, the clear stand of the common citizen, that the Israeli genocide has achieved pretty much the same result regarding the Palestinian cause. This, despite the support that Israel continues to receive from the morally corrupt leaderships and political regimes, democracy and dictatorship alike, from around the world.

Leaders around the world have demonstrated complete disregard for the millions upon millions of people from all walks of life who have poured into the streets of all major cities to protest the genocide, injustice, and blatant violation of basic humanity. How clear it is for all to see that "corruption has appeared on land and sea due to what the hands of people have earned, so that He may give them a taste of some of what they did, perchance to return [to the right path, to Him]" (Ar-Rum 30:41). But there is something deeply sinister about what we are witnessing, about our perceived helplessness. There is something clearly unsettling about the impotence of the voice of the people, and the power of politicians, the hypocrites, to ignore every cry for mercy. Those who when they speak lie, when they give their word they break it, and when they are given a trust they are unfaithful, exactly how Prophet Muhammad had described the behavior of hypocrites (Sahih Bukhari). In this world where evil colludes so efficiently, social media followership is nothing more than delusions of grandeur and influence, so dispersed in its reality that even in the millions it is susceptible to eradication by the mere closure of one individual account. Resorts to human rights, humanitarian law, institutions of global governance, have not been effective.

We must question the crisis of leadership across the world, a crisis that has leveled and exposed a lack of humanity, of minimal levels of mercy. A crisis that has erased differences between democracy and dictatorship. Loss of mercy has rarely been exhibited with greater obscenity.

Seeking refuge for the small but growing Muslim community from the intense persecution of the pagan Arabs, Prophet Muhammad ﷺ set out for Ta'if after the death of Khadijah ؓ. He invited several tribes to Islam on the way there, but no one heeded his call. He found the same reaction in Ta'if, a small town just southeast of Makkah, and was harassed on his way out as people jeered and threw stones at him and his companion, Zayd ibn Haritha. He and Zayd took cover in a garden, saddened and injured. There he made his famous prayer: "Oh Allah, I complain to you of my weakness, and my limited capabilities and my dispensability among people. Oh Most Merciful of the merciful, You are the Lord of the weak and you are my Lord. To whom are you entrusting me? To someone distant who frowns upon me? Or someone close to whom you have given control over my affair? If You are not angry with me, then I do not care, as Your pardon is much more encompassing for me. I seek refuge in the Light of Your Countenance for which the darkness lights up and the affairs of this world and the next are rectified, from the coming down on me of Your anger or the manifestation on me of Your condescension. For You is to reproach until You are pleased and there is no effort or power except through you." How beautiful a supplication under these dire conditions.

On their way back from Ta'if to Makkah, Allah sent the archangel Jibril ؑ with the Angel of the Mountains to propose to Prophet Muhammad ﷺ the possibility of destroying Ta'if for what its residents had done. "No," responded Prophet Muhammad ﷺ in his beautiful mercy, "I do not want it. I pray to Allah to give them descendants who will worship Allah alone without associating partners with Him." Can you imagine that being the outcome of Israel's aggression? A progeny that worshiped Allah with mercy, gratitude, and humility.

Imagine having been through everything that Prophet Muhammad ﷺ had been through, witnessing the killing and torture of innocent people, their displacement, migration, starvation, all for want of witnessing that there was One God. One God, and a faith that would unite humanity, allowing for diversity, but insisting that all live in peace and harmony together and with the rest of creation. Imagine being given the opportunity to avenge such injustice but instead wishing that the perpetrators of such violence produce offspring that worshiped Allah and established that peace and justice. That was Prophet Muhammad ﷺ, *a mercy to the worlds*, a man who commanded people according to the Quran to dispense mercy (Al-Baqarah 2:219), a healing for the ailing human collective.

Every *surah* in the Quran with exception to At-Tawbah opens with *Bism Allah Ar-Rahman Ar-Rahim*, in the Name of Allah The Merciful The Giver of Mercy, setting the tone for everything that is to follow, demanding that the believer enter a peaceful and generous state of mind as they set to engage with the Word of Allah. It calls on us, all of us, Muslim and non-Muslim, to recognize that wise counsel has come from our Lord, and a healing for what is in the chests, and a guidance and a mercy (*rahmatun*) for the believers (Yunus 10:57). Mercy is woven into the very fabric of the Quranic text. "And We have indeed brought to them a Book that we tailored (*fasalnahu*) upon knowledge, guidance, and mercy for a folk who believe" (Al-A'raf 7:52). Such mercy is manifested in its explicit confirmation of what came before it, only distilling previous messages from human innovations, introducing moderation, integrating diversity and infusing the entirety of the text with an indomitable spirit. It urges every believer to follow the best of what has been revealed; the best only being possible when followership is saturated with the divine hue, with Mercy.

It is important to recognize that we are inherently equipped to be merciful beings both in our moral and physical dispositions. In surah *Ar-Rahman*, the Quran states: "The Merciful; [Who] taught the Quran; created the human; taught him evidential verification," (Ar-Rahman 55:1-4). Allah chose for Himself the attribute of Mercy in this context. The Merciful. Taught the Quran. Created the human. Showed him how to seek and identify Truth. In that order. Essentially, we are being told that we were created in a way that is suited for reception of the Quranic message whose teaching preceded our creation. It is a mercy that our constitution of heart-mind, body, breath, attachment, family, community, purpose and need to worship, to call upon, to seek succor, not only ensures that we can receive, internalize and make use of Quranic guidance, but that we have an innate attraction to the undertaking. To be human is to be merciful, to have heart. To be an *exceptional human* is to be a mercy, to dispense it in every way possible.

We were all the dwellers of the *Rahim*, the womb in English, a word that scarcely captures any real meaning. Here we all settled for a time and then exited having been, in our first instance, secured by its layers of mercy – refuge, quiet, protection, nourishment, seclusion. It is Allah, *Ar-Rahman*, who named *the* womb *ar-Rahim* drawing our attention to the physical and moral imperative of mercy that defines our common source. In a sacred narration or hadith *qudsi*, Allah declares: "I am The Merciful (*Ar-Rahman*), I created the

Rahim and cleaved her a name from my name, so whoever keeps connected with her, I will connect with him and whoever severs ties with her, I will sever My ties with him" (Musnad Ahmad). It is as such that we are consistently reminded of the inextricability of mercy from our very fabric, our place of origin. So significant is this truth that Allah premises our relationship with Him on our relationship to *her*. Our heedfulness, *taqwa*, of Him is connected to our heedfulness of the wombs, *al-arham*, that bore us and that ultimately connect us to every other human being. "Oh people," calls the Quran, "be cognizant of your Lord who created you from one *nafs* and from her created her mate and propagated from them many men and women and be heedful of Allah by whom you entreat [each other], and the wombs (*al-arham*), surely Allah is your overseer" (An-Nisa' 4:1). It is through our immediate uterine ties that we first anticipate our rights and to whom we first owe duties. It is in these relations of blood and marriage that we first find our dignity and exercise our humanity.

It is no wonder that Allah placed mercy between men and women and especially between married couples. "And of His *ayat* are that He created mates for you from yourselves [of your likeness] that you may find tranquility [or dwell] within them and He placed between you both amity [friendship, love] and mercy. Indeed, in this are *ayat* for people who are thoughtful" (Ar-Rum 30:21). Not only do we emanate from a merciful source, but we are also gifted friendship and mercy from our Most Generous Lord so that we may live with each other in peace and harmony. Through this added mercy, moderation and kindness in speech and behavior is impressed upon us in our interactions with each other, but specifically on men who, generally speaking, might exhibit more forceful tendencies. When a man genuinely cares for a woman, whether his mother, wife, daughter, relative, or other divinely sanctioned relation, he tends to be gentle, merciful, loving. This natural instinct is strengthened by Quranic guidance and the teachings of Prophet Muhammad ﷺ.

It is the overriding value of mercy that ensures that Quranic truths are well understood and prophetic teachings properly emulated. Prophet Muhammad ﷺ said, "The believers who show the perfect faith are the ones with the best morals, and the best of you are those who are best to their women," and in other narrations he said, "their wives and daughters" or "their families" (Jami' Al-Tirmidhi). In his farewell sermon, he warned men to heed Allah in the treatment of women, that their relationship with them was a sacred trust, and that it was based on Allah's guidance. No aspect of Revelation can be understood or applied in any relationship between people or between people and other living creatures in the absence of mercy.

Mercy is that value that brings the best of who we are as humans to everything we think and do. It is the attribute that Allah has elevated for Himself and for Prophet Muhammad ﷺ above all other attributes. It is the moral and physical imperative that connects humanity with each other and with nature, more broadly, in its infinite diversity. The search for knowledge and wisdom in the Quran is inseparable from the mercy that accompanies them. To engage with the Quran without experiencing this indivisible feature of its fabric, is like missing the radiance of a blue sky on a clear summer day. Indeed, there is no better hue that evenly and consistently saturates the Word and worlds of Allah than Mercy. It is with this spirit that we must approach Quranic guidance and teachings of Prophet Muhammad ﷺ regarding ourselves, others, and all of Allah's creation. It is with this heart that the rest of this book is written.

PART 2

Purposefulness

Brilliant Stars Rising

> At night, when the velvet sky envelops the earth in a blanket of calm slumber, this is the time to rise. Brilliant stars emerge from the darkness to worship the very source of Light. In that silence, stillness, the path to Him is crystal clear. The homes in which they rise, in which Allah has permitted His name to be glorified, twinkle like a reflection of the luminous lanterns in the sky above. On earth as in the sky, these brilliant stars emerge to beautify the world and guide its inhabitants.

He was wrapped up in a blanket, resting peacefully when the command came to stand in prayer, in worship, during the night. Half of the night, or less, or more, to recite the Quran. The tranquillity of night offered the best conditions for focusing the mind and articulating the words - the weighty words that Allah would deliver to Prophet Muhammad ﷺ.

The day was plentifully long to see to other concerns, even then he was commanded to remember the name of Allah and devote himself wholeheartedly. Lord of the east and the west, his guarantor, protector, disposer of affairs, *wakil*, fully aware of what the deniers were saying and how it saddened him. Even so, the Messenger – he who was set on the path of the highest morals – was commanded to patience and to abandon them with beautiful abandonment. It is Allah who would deal with them in due course. Those with blessings in this life and reprieve, nothing of which would defend against Allah, their Creator, the One who despite their denial still granted.

Soon he would not be alone. The believers, that select group who had given themselves to the beautiful surrender, woke too, for half or a third of the night to pray and worship, to glorify the Lord of the worlds. Oh, to be in this company, to be of that group. To enter the court of all courts and prostrate to the King of kings. Allah appreciates the qualities of the night and the day and knows that we cannot compass the entirety of the Quran. "So, recite what is facilitated of it" (Al-Muzzammil 73:20). He knows our circumstances, those who are sick, must work, travel and defend, so He turns to us in forgiveness. Every good put forward will be found with Him. No, a better and greater reward. So, get up, stand in prayer and read what you can. Affirm your devotion to your Creator, to the Light of the skies and the earth. Recite the Quran that you may illuminate your heart and repel the darkness, that you may join in the company of the beloved. Prophet Muhammad ﷺ said, "the house in which the Quran is recited is seen by the inhabitants of the heavens like the people on earth see the stars." We were created to rise.

The meaning of life, human purpose. How many books, articles, seminars, and discussions have taken up this topic? How many people spend their lives in search of meaning? How many suffer as they struggle to understand why? Why are we here? How many individuals and communities have succumbed to 'deaths of despair' due to hopelessness, loneliness, sadness, and self-destruction due to a general lack of purposefulness in life? Many who have taken up this man-made dilemma have not provided adequate answers. Instead, they differ and contradict each other. For some there is meaning, for others there is none. For some meaning is to be found within us, for others it is outside. Meaning becomes a purely subjective exercise, each according to their capacity to figure it out and live it out, or to follow the suggestions of someone who has claimed to have done so. Such a wishy-washy approach, celebrated as a hallmark of human freedom, simply cannot be. Allah tells us in the Quran, "And We did not create the sky and the earth and what is between them as play" (Al-Anbiya' 21:16). Purpose is so fundamental to our well-being and that of other creation that it is not something we can reduce to a human guessing game and invention. Indeed, the Quran settles the matter with one simple question: "Did you think that We created you purposelessly and that to Us you would not be returned?" (Al-Mu'minun 23:115).

Purpose is embedded in the very fabric of every self or *nafs*. It is a basic and indispensable dimension of being human, of being a created thing, and as such having a Creator toward whom a believer is compelled to draw near through ritual and other forms of worship. "And I did not create the *jinn* and *ins* [human], expect to worship Me" (Adh-Dhariyyat 51:56). A simple yet encompassing *ayah*. We were created with a clear purpose, to worship Allah. All of us, no one is excepted from this divine imperative. It is *the* timeless and universal meaning of human life.

To worship Allah is a two-fold imperative. Belief (*iman*) and action that aims to rectify, to set things right, beautify, ease, improve, advance and all else that is good and beneficial (*al-'amal al-salih*). The first is an admission that there is no deity except Allah, the One. It is a state of heart-mind, of being, defined and shaped by *tawhid*. It is a commitment to live with intention -a consciousness of Allah in everything that we think and do. In the Quran, belief always precedes action because it is the light that guides, rectifies, and justifies what we do. My belief in Allah, His Books, Messengers, Angels, the Day of Judgement, After-life, and Divine decree whether good or bad and in turn my promise through that belief to listen, obey, and exercise patience define and shape my life. It gives me meaning. A meaning that is not dependent on any external factors or vulnerable to any worldly pressures.

I have meaning – I matter – by virtue of my faith. I know what is right and what is wrong, and what is in between. I can attach meaning to other things because of this. I recognize and respect the purposefulness of all creation. "Those who remember Allah standing and sitting and [lying] on their sides, and they think about the creation of the skies and the earth. 'Our Lord, You did not create this falsely; glory to You so protect us from the Fire'" (Al-'Imran 3:191). I am not lost, confused, or doubtful. Without even a single physical, outward, expression of belief, the very fact that I know beyond a shadow of a doubt that I am here to worship my Creator, gives my life purpose. I am a meaningful creature.

The second imperative of worshiping Allah is the translation of belief into what we do in this world. It is an application of faith. There are two possible and simultaneous outlets for this. The first is the expression of belief through rituals while the second involves literally everything else we do on a daily basis. Both expressions have minimal, obligatory, thresholds of performance, while increments in quantity and quality are left to the ever-expanding aspirations of a believing heart. Thus, to establish prayer means to fulfill the five daily obligations, to fast means to complete the month of Ramadan, to pay the annual zakat is to donate certain percentages of your wealth based on types of assets held, and to perform *hajj* means to perform the pilgrimage at least once in your lifetime if feasible physically and financially. You can do more than this, but you cannot do less, keeping in mind possible adjustments in response to unique or disabling circumstances.

Similarly, believers are required to undertake certain duties toward themselves and others throughout their lives. Although many of these acts are seamlessly woven in the routine of everyday life, they cannot be taken for granted or neglected. These acts involve being good to parents, family, neighbours, strangers; being just and honest when giving testimony and in all other dealings; speaking with kindness and respect; seeking knowledge; defending the weak; and so on. Whether associated with rituals or daily dealings, minimal, obligatory, thresholds of performance are intended to supply life with stability. In performing these basic requirements, we, each one of us, demonstrate a respect not only for our purposefulness but for that of Allah's other's creations. It is an existence of cooperation and harmony.

Beyond these minimal duties we are at liberty to contribute to worldly life as we wish so long as it does not contravene Allah's guidance. This dynamic dimension of action encourages us to leverage all the blessings that Allah has bestowed upon us in terms of personal traits, strengths, capacities, skills, knowledge, aptitudes, and wealth with our interests. There is nothing in the Quran or Sunnah that told me I must be a professor or writer. Just like there is nothing to guide others to be what they choose to become. Rather, that is what I chose to do with the abilities and blessings that Allah gave me. Everyone works according to their specificities, and Allah knows who is guided (Al-Isra' 17:84). Beyond the basic rituals and duties, we are at liberty to determine what we would like to do with our lives, how would we like to contribute. This is not to say that a believer's life is all work. There are times when we rest and times of leisure. Even then, we can direct our attention to Allah. "So, if you become free/unoccupied so rise up and long for your Lord" (Al-Inshirah 94:7-8). Rituals, basic duties, dynamic contributions, even leisure, all are different expressions of one purpose – to worship Allah.

Whether I am performing my prayers, fasting, giving charity, undertaking the 'umrah or hajj in terms of rituals, or whether I am preparing breakfast, exercising, working, feeding my cat, even smiling at someone, my intention to obey and please Allah turns all of these acts into worship. Prophet Muhammad ﷺ informed us that actions are judged by Allah in accordance with the intentions that we have when we undertake them. He explained that "he who migrates for Allah and His Messenger, then his migration is for Allah and His Messenger; whereas he who migrates for a worldly gain or to marry a woman, so his migration is for what he migrated for" (Sahih Bukhari). The beauty of Islam is that everything can be transformed into an act of worship if we know how to discipline our intentions. My intention when I got married, for instance, was to preserve my chastity and find a partner with whom I could compete to serve Allah. In doing so, I hope through Allah's Mercy, that He would accept my actions as forms of worship and that He would bless our union with His Grace and Generosity, not to mention reward in the Hereafter.

Without pure intention directed toward Allah's Countenance, even the rituals lose their meaning and may even be detrimental. Thus, the Quran states, "Oh you who believe, do not void your charities by harping and harming, like the one who spends his wealth to be seen of people and does not [actually] believe in Allah and the Last Day. His example is like that of a smooth stone on which there is soil that is hit by a downpour leaving it desolate. They are incapable of [reaping the benefits of] anything of what they have earned. And Allah does not guide the disbelieving folk" (Al-Baqarah 2:264). And elsewhere we are told of the hypocrites who believe that they are deceiving Allah when they stand in prayer, only to do so lazily, to show off among others, and truly remembering Allah very little, conforming neither to belief or disbelief, they are those who have gone astray (An-Nisa' 4: 142-143). Similarly, Prophet Muhammad ﷺ affirmed that among the first to go to Hell are a person of knowledge who studies by night and day so that people say what a great scholar they are; a rich person who gives charity so that people say how generous they are; and a soldier who sacrifices their life so that people say how brave they were (Sahih Muslim).

It is amazing how so many people today have difficulty accepting their divinely ordained purpose, while they are fully capable and willing to accept a similar notion on a worldly scale. Someone starting in an entry level position will know their relationship to the organization's owner or leader. Even though they may never see or meet that person in reality, they have no doubt of their existence. They know that in order for the organization to achieve its goals, for the owners to be happy, and therefore to keep their job and receive compensation and other rewards, they must perform in certain ways. In other words, they must accept organizational values and undertake the duties and responsibilities that will allow others to carry out their functions as well. If they are weak or falter in their role, they must rectify their performance. If they persist in their wrongdoing or incompetence others are bound to suffer to the extent that they depend on them. The ambitious among them will strive, through harder work, longer hours, and voluntary initiatives, to reach a level that secures them promotions, higher earnings, and perhaps a place among the organization's leaders. They may even manage their personal life in a way that does not compromise these ambitions. Throughout this journey they believe that they are either living the good life or working towards it. They know their purpose.

But purposefulness that is largely based on satisfying material desires turns out to be rather empty. There is no more a wasted and sad life than that based on short-lived hedonic pleasures. The aging process itself is an *ayah* to recognize the transitory nature of all things worldly. "And he to whom we grant long life, We deteriorate in creation, so will they not comprehend?" (Ya Sin 36:68). Only through the suppression or temporary numbing of our sense of createdness can we live mostly or purely hedonic lives. Only through the active denial of our divine essence, of the power and boundlessness of Allah's insufflation of His Spirit, *Ruh*, into us can we be oblivious to our purposefulness and in turn, divinely inspired dignity. "And when your Lord said to the angels, 'I am creating a sentient being (*bashar*) from putty of fine silt. So, when I have formed him, and blown into him of My Spirit (*Ruh*), so fall to him in prostration'" (Al-Hijr 15:28-29). Do you now understand how Allah is closer to you than your own circulatory rope (Qaf 50:16) and mediates between you and your heart (Al-Anfal 8:24)? Those who choose to reject their purpose are in denial of the very Breath that gives them life – the very Breath that they could only separate from if they chose to die even while living.

We carry within us the Divine Breath that warranted the prostration of the angels. We are entrusted to guard it, to recognize its sanctity, by disciplining the self in accordance with the purpose that Allah has set for us. To worship Him, and Him alone. It is the only purpose that admits His essence, and thereby directs the self to live according to the values and virtues of His guidance keeping us mentally, emotionally and physically balanced. And that more significantly can secure the life to come, with its promise of felicity, in no small part a contributor to earthly wellness.

The Divine Breath or Spark as it has been called, however, is only one, albeit the greatest favour, that Allah has bestowed upon us to recognize and fulfill our purpose. There are three other favours granted to each and every one of us that drive us toward Him. We have testified that Allah is our Lord and as such we cannot claim on the Day of Resurrection that we were unaware (Al-A'raf 7:172). You may respond with 'I certainly do not remember that' but then again if I asked you to recall your birth or something that happened on a precise day five years ago or even two months ago you would not likely recall either. It is highly unlikely, however, that you would deny that you were born or the details of your mother's account of the event. In fact, if you heard the story often enough you would likely have visions of it in your mind. You would be able to recall it if someone were to ask you.

Our inability to recall is not proof that we didn't witness, that we were not present. It is not a coincidence that those who remember are those with the deepest intellect (*ulul-albab*) (Al-Baqarah 2:269, Al-'Imran 3:7). In fact, the Quran addresses us as if we ought to remember. To those who doubt that they will be brought to life again after their death, Allah asks, "Does the human not remember that We created him from before when he wasn't a thing?" (Maryam 19:67). The word for remember and mention are the same, both from the root *dh-k-r*. It is in mention, repeated mentions, that the memory is roused to remember.

This is why the act of *dhikr*, remembrance of Allah, is so significant. "So, remember/mention Me, I will remember/mention you. And be thankful to Me and do not disbelieve" (Al-Baqarah 2:152). The act of remembrance is an indispensable cognitive capacity that the Quran consistently urges us to strengthen. The Quran itself was described to Prophet Muhammad ﷺ as *adh-dhikr al-hakim* or the wise mention, remembrance or reminder. Making the reading of it a habit is among the greatest ways to improve our cognitive capacity to recall. Remembering leads to acknowledging, heeding, and thanking Allah. It leads to a desire to fulfill our purpose.

Accompanying the majestic breath that holds the mystery of the human soul, and our testimony that Allah is our Lord, is a basic moral code. A code imprinted in every *nafs* or self that provides each one of us with an original state of goodness, innocence, or *fitrah*, so that we have the ability to rise above our basest instincts. "And the self (*nafs*) and He who proportioned it [her]. So, He inspired it as to what corrupts it and what makes it heedful. He has succeeded who purifies it, and he has failed who debases it" (Ash-Shams 91:7-10). This basic moral code that inspires every one of us as to what is good and what is evil, what is beneficial and what is harmful, propels us to live in ways that reflect the worship of Allah, whether we believe or disbelieve. It is only as such that we can, in all our diversity, share this earth and aspire to live in peace.

This moral code, transcendental handbook of wellbeing, guides humanity. It establishes the foundations of coherence, sense-making, orienting our minds towards unity, comprehensibility, reforming, and meaning. It allows us to prioritize and mobilize our resources, cope with stress and injustice, and successfully manage tension. Indeed, we were created in tension, we need it to survive – but too much of it can be unbalancing. "We have certainly created the human in tension. Does he think that that no one can overtake him? He says, 'I have spent my wealth frivolously.' Does he think that no one has seen him?" (Al-Balad 90:4-7). The greatest function of our moral code is to protect us against such transgressions.

The code then is not just a list of rules, that would hardly respect the complexity of our creation. Rather, it is an expansive guide that directs every being in a unique way as it combines with who they are and what they possess of strengths and weaknesses, of wealth and resources. It does not result in one path, but infinite paths that are charged by the same current, though the potential of each is the result of one's efforts. It is we who detail the course. No one can replicate the path of another. Even in our shared rituals which serve to unite, each one of us will have a unique imprint.

The difference between two good people, one who believes and the other a disbeliever, is that the believer seeks Allah's love, pleasure, and reward or avoidance of His dislike, displeasure, and punishment in his thoughts and deeds. He or she is animated by the central role of Allah in their life. The disbeliever respects as much as they can of this moral code for worldly gains or to avoid worldly consequences including his or her own feelings of guilt or satisfaction. They are animated by the central role of their *nafs* in their lives or self-interest. Their thoughts and behaviors are prone to change with changes in their internal and external environment. The moral code imprinted within them is subject to denial and suppression and in time forgetfulness, as they consistently adjust it to internal desires and external pressures. Most, however, can still thankfully identify and avoid fundamental evils. They may even live the good life as they envision it; indeed, it is Allah that grants it to them, but they hope little if at all for the real and eternal bliss of the life to come.

The challenge of *kufr*, disbelief, denial of purpose, in worldly terms remains undeniable despite this general appearance that all is well. A world that is filled with self-centred individuals cannot be good for the collective. The lack of understanding or genuine care for the welfare of others leads to ever increasing levels of corruption. The concepts of duty and responsibility are spurned, families are broken and redefined, communities are divided across superficial social, economic and political categories, and the rights of men, women, children and nature are violated as disbelievers experiment with the fundamentals of life. The earth continues to be polluted and disparaged as her truths, her beauty, her purpose, continue to be denied.

We can't genuinely fix any of this without belief in One Master, Owner, and a Day of Account. We cannot hope for a better future if so many of us deny the very moral code that is designed to afford us minimal levels of dignity and to the rest of creation protection from our greed. People can claim what they want to soothe their desires, to continue to live as they wish, but we cannot rise if our vision remains on a horizontal plane. We have within us the basics of a moral code to seek, know, and live our divinely stated purpose and to permit others to live theirs.

There is one more thing that Allah gave us that we may acknowledge and undertake our purpose, to worship Him alone – the splendid construction of our physique and faculties. The divine spark, personal testimony, and moral code would not be very effective if we did not have the physical and mental attributes with which to express ourselves. “Did we not make for him two eyes? And a tongue and two lips? And guided him to the two paths? But he did not tackle the obstacle. And how can you know what the obstacle is? It is the releasing of a neck [helping those in bondage], or feeding on a day of intense hunger, an orphan in proximity, or an indigent in misery” (Al-Balad 90:8-16). The physical and the mental go together. They reinforce our ability to fulfill our purpose. These *ayat* are telling us that we have no excuses. Are our hearts not capable of distinguishing the higher ground? Do we not see with our eyes those who need help? Are we not able to speak truth and justice with our tongues and lips? Can we not employ our bodies to help those whose bodies are confined, famished, or despondent?

On the Day of Judgement each *nafs* will know of a surety what it presented for itself and what it delayed (Al-Infitar 82:5). Those who disbelieved will be asked “Oh you, human, what has seduced you from your Generous Lord? Who created you, so [He] prepared you, so [He] adjusted you? In whatever image He willed He assembled you” (Al-Infitar 82:6-8). How is it that anyone can deny the *deen*, a life of purpose worshiping Allah, following His guidance? We have all been appointed guardians who know everything we do, who record it. A record that will be produced for or against us on the Day of Judgement.

All measures required for us to rise to our destiny were made inherent to our creation. “We have certainly created the human in the best form (*taqwim*) [reinforcements]” (At-Tin 95:4). But so too were the characteristics that tempt us toward our basest desires (At-Tin 95:5). The Quran tells us that we were created weak, ingrateful, arrogant, rejecting, despairing, disbelieving, unjust, argumentative, hasty, restrictive, stingy, unjust, and ignorant. But these are states that those who believe and do good – know their purpose and are willing to live it – are well equipped to overcome. Allah is our protector and helper.

For some people, this worldly life is shaped by a firm belief in Allah, who commands *tawhid* for the benefit of all. They are the truly humble, holding their Creator in the highest reverence. Their purpose is clear though there is a wide diversity in lesser convictions and practices. Through divinely ordained purpose, they avoid feeling and being lost or experiencing self-inflicted hardship (Taha 20:123). There is no fear on or for them, nor shall they grieve (Al-Baqarah 2:38). For other people, no such purpose is admitted. Instead, there is either a mundane search for meaning or a suppression of meaning resulting in loss, division, and instability. A life lived without accountability is detrimental to all creation. "Do you not see that to Allah prostrate whoever is in the skies and whoever is in the earth, and the sun, and the moon, and the stars, and the mountains, and the trees, and the animals (*dawab* – literally stomping creatures), and many people, and on many punishment is justified. And whoever Allah degrades, for him none can dignify. Indeed, Allah does what He wills" (Al-Hajj 22:18).

We are sentient beings, *bashar*, making different choices. Purpose shapes who we are and how we conceive of and relate to our Creator, ourselves, the world and everything in it. One purpose leads to unity, balance, justice, equity, and accountability through obedience to One Master. A deep consciousness of life – all life. The other leads to myopic thinking, a delusion of life and being alive, while merely living. A greed for the riches of this world and a general rejection of constraints on what one regards as freedom. Don't misunderstand, there is obedience – admitted or not – but it is to many conflicting masters. One gives us meaning, something to do with every breath with which we are blessed, there can be no despair. We come into being only to rise through Allah's guidance. The other is based on whims and desires, continually changing conceptions of wrong, of evil, a moral compass that deceptively destroys one's true purpose and that of others. "Say [Muhammad], 'Shall we inform you of the greatest losers in terms of their achievements? Those whose efforts were misguided in the life of the world, while they thought that they were building better. Those are the ones who disbelieved in the *ayat* of their Lord and His meeting, so their achievements were invalidated. So, We will not attribute to them any weight on the Day of Resurrection" (Al-Kahf 18:103-105).

In Islam, there is a hierarchy of beings in which the human being is responsible for his or her station or placement. We are not the most favoured of creation and indeed can be among the basest. By accepting and living out our purpose, we have the capacity to rise. Belief and good deeds are the two expressions of worship. Those who accept guidance, embark on a journey of purification, knowledge, and wisdom, will experience this life in a uniquely beautiful way only to find more beauty awaiting them in the life to come, with Allah's Mercy. We accept that only He knows the intricacies of His creation, their needs to flourish, the value of all things at all points in time, how everything fits harmoniously together, and the truth of matters. Only He knows what is revealed and what is hidden. Only He can guide us given how little all of us, even collectively, can ultimately ever know.

I like to imagine that when the brilliant stars rise to worship the One, the Eternal, the Light of the skies and the earth, in the colourless void of the night, we put on a spectacular show of lights for the inhabitants of heaven. The brilliant star rising, *at-tariq*, *an-najm al-thaqib*, as the Quran describes the most outstanding star in the night sky can be you and I. Waking every night, devoting ourselves to Him, to whom we will inevitably return. We cannot be absorbed by the darkness. Ours is a web of lights, surging across the earth and soaring to the heavens.

Ar-Rijal Qawwamun

Written as a letter to my son.

> Habibi Billal,
>
> *Assalamu alaykom wa rahmatullah wa barakatuh,*a greeting of peace, mercy and blessings from the Most High, and a greeting of love from your mama, a *nafs* whose happiness and wellbeing is forever bound by your happiness and wellbeing. You can never know the joy I felt when I found out that I was pregnant for the first time. I didn't know anything about you yet. But I immediately started preparing you for a life of faith, love, and mercy. On our slightly less than an hour's commute to work, I would sing you a self-composed song – *La illaha ila Allah, Muhammdun Rasool Allah* – and prayers on his family and companions. When I eventually found out that you were a boy, I prayed that Allah would bless you with a comforting face and some semblance of our beloved Prophet Muhammad ﷺ. He ﷺ, had a beautiful face, that radiated truth, trust, peace and compassion. Ya Allah, ya Rahman, how I've been blessed.

Ar-rijal qawwamun. You have a duty to uphold, reinforce and support those around you, whether male or female. More than your sisters, who hold no less a place of love, respect and elevation in my heart, you are commanded by Allah to go beyond with what you were favoured in strength, skills, aptitudes and wealth. Allah has granted you strength with the choice to be aggressive or constructive, daring with the choice to be reckless or protective, and virility with the choice to be unchaste or pure. He has blessed you with the ability to amass wealth well beyond your needs while further guaranteeing more wealth through your divinely ordained share of inheritance. Understand that these favours are not an indication of superiority but responsibility. Your masculine traits and divinely sanctioned share of wealth whether through striving or inheritance come with a tall order. I am not your equal. Nor is any woman. Not because we are lesser, but because Allah has granted to each what enables them to fulfill purpose, to worship Him in such a way that allows peace and harmony to be achieved in this life to the greatest extent possible. I was not granted the same favours that you were, but then again I was not burdened with the same duties and responsibilities.

Ar-rijal qawwamun – men are upstanding – not males. MEN. Men shoulder greater responsibility for the welfare, advancement, and protection of our Ummah. In worshipping Allah, a man can only make those choices that place the favours Allah has given him in His service. Strength, daring, and virility are all bound by Allah's guidance providing no justification for deviance. You are held to same standard as your female counterpart who doesn't share these traits. You are expected to manage your strength, measure your risks, and control your sexuality with no more leeway in terms of what is permissible than she is. In addition, you are commanded to share your wealth and other blessings with those around you, which is only voluntary in her case.

The degree or *darajah* that men are accorded in the Quran is based on the positive expression of this extra capacity and hence the fulfillment of the duties and acceptance of responsibilities necessarily associated with it. "… And for them [women] is accorded the same as what is owed by them according to what is customary, and to men (*rijal*) is conferred a degree above them and Allah is Dear, Wise" (Al-Baqarah 2:228). This degree is one of duty, responsibility and accountability to fulfill purpose, to carry the Trust. "And for each [individual] are degrees (*darajatun*) for what they did. So that He may fully recompense them for their works, and they will not be wronged" (Al-Ahqaf 46:19). For men and women are degrees in accordance with their actions. Know for a surety, dear Billal, that you are neither *qawwam*, nor in possession of any *darajah*, if you do not fulfill Allah's covenant with you as a *rajul* in this Ummah. Being male is a determination of birth, being a man is a choice, it is earned, it requires will.

I feel so much frustration when I look at the world that you grew up in and must continue to navigate and confront. So many complex, confused, and misguided messages. In the west as in the east, society is confusing young men about their roles, responsibilities, values, what they should stand for, and more importantly the need to defend masculinity against a torrent of destruction and disbelief. Selfish whims, base instincts, toxic feminism, and oppressive politics are supressing manhood, the sense of purpose that once defined what it is to be a man, husband, father. We live in times where males are captives of and in armies that defend falsehood, online and on the battlefield, where governments and businesses are teaming up to individualize society, disempowering all behind the thin veil of empowering some. The results are evident in the breakdown of family and deterioration of social bonds. It is not surprising that many men feel that they are losing direction. But you, and all young believing men, have an indispensable key to a life of purpose, meaning and engagement despite all this madness. You have Allah's guidance and the perfect example of its embodiment, Prophet Muhammad ﷺ.

Let us then start with Prophet Luqman's عليه السلام advice to his son. Indeed, Allah granted him wisdom so that his advice cannot be surpassed in its beauty, validity, and efficiency. It is only befitting that a prophet should start by advising his son not to associate anything with Allah. "…Indeed, *shirk* [associating anything with Allah] is a great injustice" (Luqman 31:13). Fully explaining the implications of this one bit of advice would fill volumes. Not associating anything with Allah is to live a life of *tawhid*. Oneness. Unicity. Submitting yourself completely and exclusively to Allah. He is your guide, your goal, your sustenance. *Shirk* is such a great injustice because it diverts people from truth to falsehood. Those who associate others with Allah, or disbelieve in Him altogether, think they know better than their Creator. They believe that what they know, even with their limited minds, is sufficient. As such, their decisions are often unjust.

"Oh my son, indeed if it [any deed] should be the weight of a mustard seed [hidden] within a cliff or the skies or in the earth, Allah will bring it forth. Indeed, Allah is Clement, Aware" (Luqman 31:16). This second piece of advice is an indirect warning to remain vigilant about everything you think and do. Nothing can be hidden from Allah, no matter how light, secured by layers of hardness, obscured by endless expanse, or buried in unimaginable depths. Allah knows of it and will bring it forth in due time. Even if something can be hidden from people until the Day of Judgment, it will eventually be revealed should Allah will. Do not belittle any act of kindness or harshness for every atom of good and evil is accounted for. Nothing is too small for Allah to reward and nothing, barring *shirk*, is too big for Allah to forgive. Never ever despair of His Mercy. Never.

"Oh my son, establish prayer (*salah*) and command what is good [in a good way] and prohibit was is reprehensible and be patient with what has afflicted you. Indeed, that is resolution [in one's] affairs" (Luqman 31:17). It is in this three-fold imperative that the first two lessons can be guarded. *Salah*, much more than the word prayer in English could ever express, is the foundation of your relationship with Allah for it shares its root with *silah* or connection. Five obligatory daily breaks from worldly concerns have been ordained for us to enter the court of the King, to set aside our struggles, to raise our spirit and stations. Alone or in congregation, joined by a community of believers from the past and present, this is where your humanity transforms and transcends the ephemeral. Perform your salah properly, with focus and intent, and you will be able to set things aright (Al-A'raf 7:170). They will shield you from what is indecent and reprehensible (Al-'Ankabut 29:45). To command what is good and beneficial, and prohibit what is wrong and harmful, you must first be able to distinguish. You must possess the knowledge and the heart that allows you to be a light for others. You must consistently seek purification and forgiveness from Allah. These habits will enable you to be patient with what afflicts you. How could you not be if you purify yourself, prepare mind and body to enter His court multiple times a day, to humble yourself, ask forgiveness and show gratitude.

"And do not give people your cheek [speak condescendingly] or walk in the land with exuberance. Indeed, Allah does not like any [and all] delusional, prideful [people]" (Luqman 31:18). Should you be capable of the threefold directive, which enables you to practice *tawhid* and remain vigilant of your thoughts and deeds, you mustn't think yourself above others, talking and behaving with arrogance. Would not your goodness then just be delusion and pride? If the previous lessons actually penetrate your being, you cannot be anything but humble. You cannot look to others except with empathy and a surety that you know nothing of their worth in the estimation of Allah. Not walking with exuberance is not a prescription to be unhappy; it is to recognize the source of your blessings, to be moderate, and to sensitize yourself to the condition of others.

"And tread incisively and lower your voice. Indeed, the most repellent of voices is the voice of a donkey" (Luqman 31:19). Allahu Akbar. What a final piece of advice! To tread incisively is to speak, walk and otherwise act with purpose, intelligence, and efficiency. Do not be windy, wordy, or wasteful. Set out on the straightest path and avoid distractions. Every step toward Allah is the destination. Prophet Muhammad ﷺ walked purposefully and efficiently. His stride demonstrated strength and energy as if he was wading through tall grass. He spoke clearly using common language and often repeated points that he wished to emphasize. He was calm and pleasant, a joy to hear for the listener. 'Aisha ؓ described his speech as *fasl* or decisive. To be able to do this is to know the boundaries, the limits, of one's communications so that the listener receives the correct message without being burdened with unnecessary information. His speech was quiet, never causing a disturbance to listeners or unnerving them. Nothing reveals a loss of nerve and temper more than a piercing, harsh voice. Loudness is distracting, annoying and repulsive. It does not deliver the message but rather obscures it in emotional pollution. In the words of Jalaluddin Rumi, "Raise your words, not voice. It is rain that grows flowers, not thunder."

Habibi Billal, it is clear from these ayat that manhood involves the mastery of the power of masculinity. Faith in Allah and guarding against *shirk* reminds you that your strength and everything good you achieve through it is a blessing from Him. *La hawla wala quwata ila billah* - there is no possibility or power except by Allah's permission or through His will. Everything you think and do is in a record with Him, so do not underestimate matters nor think for a moment that anything can be hidden from Him. Do not be arrogant when you have been advised as to what will benefit you and set you aright. "It is not for a believing man or a believing woman, when Allah and His Messenger have determined an affair that they have any choice in their affair. And whoever defies Allah and His Messenger, they have strayed in a manifest way" (Al-Ahzab 33:36). So, establish prayer, command what is right but practice it first, and forbid what is wrong but practice it first, and be patient with whatever should befall you. Be gentle and gradual in your dealings, in how you speak, and in how you act. Never belittle or look down upon others, for their condition may turn out to be a reflection of your shortcomings. This is nowhere more evident than in your relations with women.

As you are now a young man considering marriage, please pay close attention to what I will say next. Indeed, marriage and starting a family are sacred acts in Islam and are important dimensions of our purpose and accountability on earth. The journey you are about to embark on can be the greatest blessing, or sadly, the worst nightmare. The strength of your faith, your attitude, and especially understanding of purpose as you move forward will determine in large part whether you are content and happy or discontent and miserable

There are two serious misconceptions about manhood and masculinity that were brought about historically by cultures of the west and the east. The first is that a man is measured by his material wealth, and the second by his intellectual superiority. This does not mean that men are not financially responsible, nor that they are not required to become educated. It simply means that neither is a measure of their worth or purpose. The conflation of male value with wealth and power with control of the bank, had the unfortunate effect of female oppression. The easiest way that males could amass wealth was to unjustly take the share of women. While the simplest way to appear smarter, and maintain unjust advantage over wealth, was to prevent women from attaining literacy and exceling in intellectual pursuits. They were able to do this by misusing the masculine traits we covered earlier. The suppression and mistreatment of man's partner, mate, and friend, however, only had the effect of making her miserable, weakening family, and placing an undue burden on males themselves. The betrayal of their duties to Allah was a betrayal of peace and harmony on earth.

The discontent and gradual rebellion of women against injustice and a life of thankless servitude was only natural. She too had divine rights to a share of wealth and freedom to dispose of it as she wished. She too had an intellect that needed nourishing, that could make notable contributions for the betterment of her life and those around her. A man has no rights to what Allah has decreed for women, except as she voluntarily wishes to give. The opposite, however, is not true. While a man has a right to a portion of what he earns his portion must be shared with others and he is commanded to literally pay, financially or in kind, women for their contributions to his life and to the lives of those he is entrusted by Allah to provide for. "And do not wish for what Allah has favoured some of you above others. For men is a portion from what they earn and for women is a portion of what they earn. And ask Allah of His favours. Allah is of all things knowing" (An-Nisa' 4:32). As men were not respecting this divine directive, women sought economic independence in the labour market. Other men found it profitable to hire women because they could employ them for much lower wages than men and they could exploit them in other ways as well. From one form of servitude to another. Overtime, fortunately, women's economic leverage opened windows for education and a betterment of labour conditions – at least for some.

Today, girls and women excel in school and university, often surpassing boys and men. In this new world, many women are finding and deciding that they can do without men especially men who haven't figured out the 'how' of manhood and masculinity. This has always been the pivot defining a man's purpose in Islam. How to be a man, to fulfill your purpose and promise, demands intelligent observation of Allah's *ayat* and the life and times of Prophet Muhammad ﷺ as well as those of Allah's other chosen servants. So, let us recall together.

Service. Service for the sake of Allah. No other phrase better captures how Prophet Muhammad ﷺ, and other divinely guided men, fulfilled their earthly purpose. No matter who they were dealing with, weak or strong, rich or poor, ignorant or brilliant, human or nonhuman, the service of Allah through supporting His servants and protecting everything which glorifies His name was the 'how' of their existence. It was a young Muhammad ﷺ, barely two years older than you are now, who accepted an employment offer from a wealthy, brilliant, twice widowed businesswoman named Khadijah ؓ. Sent on a trade mission to Syria, the young Muhammad ﷺ would display unique business acumen, increasing Khadijah's ؓ profits, fortifying her connections, and furthering her reputation as a formidable tradeswoman in the region. So impressive was his performance, and previously established reputation of honesty, trust, kindness, and faith, that this woman of senior status in wealth, expertise, and even age, proposed marriage to Muhammad ﷺ, which as you know, he accepted. He was not the wealthier partner and had received compensation from her for his work. Nor was he the more experienced as she had already run a successful trading business, inherited from her parents, for many years prior to their encounter. None of these facts, however, diminished anything of his manliness. Their partnership would mark a new chapter in her and their joint prosperity.

Muhammad's ﷺ manhood was not constrained by material wealth or worldly experience. Rather, it was defined by the ways in which he made himself useful, the ways in which he supported and illuminated those around him, the ways in which he exhibited honesty, trust, generosity, and justice. Not only was there no need to diminish the wealth and power of women, but it would also have betrayed everything he stood for. *Ar-rijal qawammun* not through injustice, unwarranted superiority, and oppression but rather through giving of themselves and the favours and wealth that Allah has bestowed upon them whether abundant or limited. It is only fitting that when Prophet Muhammad ﷺ finally received his first revelation, rushing home shivering with fear, concerned about his mental state, that his noble wife Khadijah ؓ should assure him "Allah will never disgrace you. You unite uterine relations, you bear the burden of the weak, you help the poor and needy, you entertain the guest, and endure hardships in the path of truth." This is manhood, the power of masculinity leveraged for the achievement of all that is good. There is no mention of wealth, gold, silver, no mention of power, position, or tribal authority. Just beauty, kindness, justice, and generosity with nothing demanded or expected in return. Men are simply not allowed to diminish women – in any way.

This was not only taught by our beloved Prophet Muhammad ﷺ but is also part of Quranic truth. Whether dealing with a strong empowered woman or an orphan girl, a man is a prohibited from taking any of her wealth. And in fact, depending on his relationship to her is commanded to preserve and increase it on her behalf or according to her wishes. When Sulaiman ﵇ approached the Queen of Sheba it was to guide her and her people to Islam. He did not take over her dominion or subject her or her people in any way to his rule. Rather, he invited them to submit to Allah the One True Master. In doing so, he enriched them beyond measure. Perhaps nowhere in the Quran is this message of respect for a woman's wealth and agency driven more seriously than in the case of orphan girls.

"Indeed, those who consume the wealth of orphans unjustly are only consuming fire in their bellies and they will meet with a blaze [Hellfire]" (An-Nisa' 4:10). Men were commanded to safeguard the wealth of orphan girls under their guardianship until they came of age. Their wealth was not to be mixed, exchanged, consumed, or diminished by those in charge of their care (An-Nisa' 4:2). The possibility of injustice toward orphans led to a prohibition of their marriage to their guardians unless they gave them a suitable dowry commensurate with what others of similar beauty and wealth would have received (An-Nisa' 4:3). Nor was a man allowed to spend an orphan's wealth as she matured so that much of it would have dissipated before she assumed its management. In fact, if the guardian was wealthy, he was not to take any of the wealth for personal maintenance and if he was of limited means he could only take what was customary and reasonable. In the meantime, he was tasked with training and testing the girl until she reached marital age whereby her wealth was released to her if she exhibited the required intellectual capacity to protect her interests (An-Nisa' 4:6). Even in cases where a girl or young woman was mentally or physically infirm (*sufaha'*), her guardian was still commanded to provide for her needs and speak to her with kindness (An-Nisa' 4:5).

These Quranic commands were so counter intuitive, potentially outrageous, to the early Muslim community that they had to ask Prophet Muhammad ﷺ again: "They ask you [Muhammad] concerning women, say, 'Allah will inform you about them and what has been rehearsed to you in the Book about the orphaned women who you do not give what Allah as decreed for them and you desire to marry them. And the weak among children and that you establish equity for the orphans and what you do of good so Allah is of it Knowing" (An-Nisa' 4:127). Note the seriousness of Allah's response. He is showing the men that they are asking about something that has already been revealed, almost as if the command might change. Observe how Allah tells Prophet Muhammad ﷺ to say "Allah will inform you," even though the entirety of the Quran is Allah's Word. Here, in the clear presence of doubt on behalf of the men who asked, a reminder is in order. Allah is saying, out of mercy not necessity, I will repeat for you what you have already been made aware of. There is no change in Allah's *sunan* or ways. Consider how the *qiwammah* of men was being reoriented towards justice, equity, and generosity especially as it impacted one of the weakest segments in society. Allah, the Merciful, the Generous, the Kind, provides a direct command, repeated, to warn men about the protection and regard for women.

Reflect on the example of Musa ﷺ when he came across two women, sisters, who were struggling to water their flock. He asked about their situation, to which they replied, "...We do not water until the shepherds leave; and our father is an elderly man" (Al-Qasas 28:23). So, he stepped in and watered their flock after which he retired to a shaded area where he beseeched Allah for any good that He might bestow upon him (Al-Qasas 28:24). He did not ask anything of the sisters in return for his favour despite his dire need for relief. Instead, as any believer who does good is expected to do, he turned to Allah for help. His act of helping had no strings attached to it. It was purely a gesture of mercy, a way to uphold what was right, of practicing *qiwammah*. And it was not long before Allah responded to Musa's ﷺ supplication. One of the sisters came, approaching him with humility and reservation, to invite him back to meet their father. After a brief exchange between the two men, one of the sisters suggested to the father that he should recruit Musa ﷺ describing him as "... the strong and the trustworthy" (Al-Qasas 28:26). The father in his wisdom and perhaps sensing his daughter's unspoken wishes, decided to define this proposal with an even deeper bond – for Musa ﷺ to wed one of his daughters on condition that he agree to serve the father for eight years but if Musa ﷺ should complete ten years that would be of his choice (Al-Qasas 28:27). To this Musa ﷺ agreed, and the covenant between the two men was fulfilled. Again, you see the example of what defines manhood and the power of leveraging masculinity in Allah's service. Musa ﷺ had nothing material to offer but his goodness and abilities sufficed to earn him respect and position.

Even where Allah is clearly providing a woman with her material needs and she does not appear to require a man's support, he still has responsibilities. Think of Zakariah and his niece Maryam. Allah had accepted her consecration to Him by her mother and as such raised and provided for her without human intervention (Al-'Imran 3:35). Nevertheless, Zakariah was still tasked with her care, protection, and provision as encompassed in the Arabic word *kafalah*. "So, her Lord accepted her with a beautiful acceptance, and He propagated her a beautiful propagation. And Zakariah *kafalaha*. Every time he entered upon her in the manger, he found with her provision (*rizq*). He said, 'Oh Maryam, from where did this come for you?' She said, 'It is from Allah. Indeed, Allah provides for whom He wills without account'" (Al-'Imran 3:37). But this diminished nothing of Zakariah's responsibility toward his niece. Care for her was not only a duty but a privilege whereby both the caregiver and care receiver journey closer to Allah. This is the highest meaning of *qiwammah*, to provide for someone to the extent that they are freed to dedicate themselves to Allah. Maryam was indeed freed from all needs, *muhararah*, literally meaning 'freed from' but this changed nothing of the responsibilities, or *qiwammah* of the men around her.

Another example is to be found in the story of Ibrahim and Hajar when he left her and their son, a young Ismail, in an uncultivated valley by the Kaaba. You would be right to question what is the *qiwammah* in that? Leaving a mother in a deserted place with a toddler does not evoke pleasant thoughts. This, however, was not a normal situation. Ibrahim had been commanded by Allah to settle them there. He was deeply concerned. But through this event Allah showed that *qiwammah* does not mean control and micromanagement of women. It is also a reminder that any and all care and provisions given to women by men are ultimately due to Allah's blessings. It is Allah that provides. It is your choice, however, to be a vessel for that provision and hence to reap the rewards of fulfilling your duties.

Qiwammah entails trust and confidence in a woman's faith and capabilities. When Hajar found out that this was Allah's command, she dutifully submitted saying, "then He [Allah] will not neglect us." Both her and Prophet Ibrahim were placing the worship of Allah above worldly concerns. They both had a certainty of belief in *la hawla wa la quwatta ila billah* – there is no possibility or power except by Allah's permission or through His will. This did not preclude deep concern for his wife and son, as Prophet Ibrahim was a very gentle soul. It was only befitting of a father who had been granted two sons in old age that he should worry. "Our Lord," he said raising his hands towards the Kaaba as he walked away, "I have settled of my offspring in an uncultivated valley near Your sacred house. Our Lord, that they may establish prayer. So, make the hearts of some people incline toward them, and provide for them of fruits [and other produce] that they may be thankful" (Ibrahim 14:37). What a greater exercise of *qiwammah* than a heartfelt supplication to Allah to accept, dignify, and provide for one's loved ones. Whatever Allah grants to others through you is still from Him. Not giving is a loss to you. It is an injustice, an unlawful consumption of what was always intended for them.

It was not long before Prophet Ibrahim's ﷺ supplication was answered. The brief but intense trial that Hajar ؓ faced resulted in an abundance of water and eventual vegetation, as well as settlement by other people whose hearts did indeed incline toward mother and son. Through her desperate actions, running frantically between the hilltops of Safa and Marwa in search of provisions for her young son, beseeching Allah for succour, an Islamic ritual was born. Her footsteps have been memorialized in 'umrah and hajj for all Muslims to emulate and to reflect on the power of a sacred partnership between a man and woman in Islam. Purpose.

Because great men understood that women were their partners in life, with duties and responsibilities that shaped their responsiveness to Allah's call, they took seriously their role in supporting them. Support, as you can see from the examples above, was not limited to material provision. Education too was prioritized. In the same *ayah* informing men of their *qiwammah* is a comprehensive description of believing women, the women that warrant respect, care, and all kinds of sharing. Women who are aware of their purpose. "...So, the righteous [women] are devout, preservers of the unseen, as Allah has willed to be preserved..." (An-Nisa' 4:34). These women are not blindly obedient to men – they are obedient to Allah and respectful of men when their perspectives and wishes conform to Allah's guidance. The Queen of Sheeba submitted to Allah *with* Sulaiman ﷺ, she did not submit to Sulaiman ﷺ. She made-up her own mind. Hajar ؓ only conceded when she learned that her husband was carrying out Allah's will, not acting of his own desire. Women, like men, will be held to individual account and must be free to make their own decisions. This is why we saw women, who entered into Islam, migrate alone from Makkah to Madinah to join Prophet Muhammad ﷺ to avoid the persecution of their families including non-believing husbands.

Allah commands men to pay close attention to the intellectual development of girls and women with the goal of collectively serving Allah, not conflicting and competing with one another. After the Prophet ﷺ migrated to

Madinah escaping the persecution of the Makkans to establish his community, he was followed by many believers among whom were several women. Under the Treaty of Hudaibiyyah the believers, men and women, were to be sent back until Allah revealed the following *ayah*. "Oh you who believe, if there comes to you the believing women, emigrating, so test them. Allah is most knowing of their belief. So, if you ascertain that they are believers so do not return them to the disbelievers. They are no longer permissible for them, nor are they (the latter) permissible for them (the emigrant women). And give them (the disbelievers) what they spent and there is no offence on you if you marry them if you give them their dues (*ujurahun*) and do not hold to the marital ties with disbelieving women and ask what you have spent and they ask what they have spent. Such is Allah's judgment. He judges between you and Allah is knowing, wise" (Al-Mumtahinah 60:10). The Muslim men were commanded to support the believing women after ascertaining their faith. This means that these women would have received Islamic instruction while still in Makkah. They were not bound by disbelieving husbands. They had the right to seek, obtain, and live truth. The receiving community had the obligation to accept, protect, and free these women from any debt they may have owed their disbelieving (ex)husbands in Makkah – as entering into Islam voided their marriage bond. This secured their continued path of truth seeking and service of Allah.

In another clear demonstration of Allah's command to care for and develop women intellectually, we see the Quranic introduction of two female witnesses in commercial transactions. Commerce was, and potentially still is, a male dominated field. The Quran, similar to other social matters, took a gradual approach to female participation in commercial legal matters starting off by recommending a choice of two female witnesses in place of one male (Al-Baqarah 2:282). The primary female witness, however, was equivalent to her male counterpart since the second female was only intended to offer support and remind the first of any details should she have forgotten. It is so beautiful that Allah commanded the presence of two women to widen the circle of female experience. In fact, the primary female witness may not have needed the support of the second, but both would nevertheless benefit from participating. The objective of the command was not only to change the perception of women by including them as credible witnesses in a field they were not likely familiar with, but to train and mainstream them. The Prophet ﷺ was known to have called on one female witness and sometimes consulted with one woman over major affairs including his reception of the first revelation and the decision not to enter Makkah that resulted in the Treaty of Hudaibiyyah. Even in the Quran there are several other commands where sex was irrelevant in bearing witness. Do not misread the message of the Quran.

Read. "Oh wives of the Prophet, you are not like any other women. If you heed Allah, then do not be soft in your speech, lest he in whose heart is a disease should yearn, but speak with suitable words. And take your homes as a base and do not display yourselves as was the display in the times of ignorance. And establish prayer and give zakat and obey Allah and His Messenger. Allah intends only to remove impurity from you, family of the household [of the Prophet], and purify you [a distinctive] purification. And remember what is recited in your homes of the *ayat* of Allah and wisdom. Verily, Allah is ever kind, knowing" (Al-Ahzab 33:32-34). These *ayat* are intended specifically for the wives of Prophet Muhammad ﷺ. They are not like any other women and will be held to higher accountability. The command to stay close to home was meant to ensure that they could fulfill the duties of both learning the Quran and conveying it, as well as observing Prophet Muhammad ﷺ and conveying his teachings and mannerisms. Their homes were bases for learning that welcomed all kinds of guests. 'Aisha ؓ, Umm Salama ؓ, Maimuna ؓ and Hafsa ؓ would go on to narrate hadith and teach Quran proficiently. 'Aisha ؓ had her own narration of the script of the Quran and she was the second most frequent hadith conveyor. Their homes were very important bases for the acquisition and dissemination of knowledge for both men and women (both relatives and others) and there were few restrictions on who could frequent their homes for these express purposes. This is why they were commanded to strengthen their voices, speak and dress appropriately, and keep a barrier between themselves and their male guests. All to ensure that they could play active roles in propagating the message and supporting Prophet Muhammad ﷺ, their beloved husband and also Messenger of Allah.

Believing men know that educated and intellectually acute women are beneficial for themselves and everyone around them. You will find beautiful examples throughout our history of *rijal* supporting the development of outstanding women, starting with Prophet Muhammad ﷺ. They were not intimidated by a woman's intelligence, nor did they try to suppress her to appear authoritative. These men encouraged the education of women, and supported them in their quest to understand, preserve, and disseminate the Quran and serve the community. Many women relied on their husbands to learn hadith and then conveyed it to others. Men had the advantage of greater proximity to the Prophet ﷺ. They thus took care to share this knowledge and several women became notable repositories of Quran and hadith. So much so that their husbands and other men became their students. In time, it was customary to see men consult their wives on serious matters and juristic issues just as Prophet Muhammad ﷺ had done earlier. Women were, and continue to be, knowledge sources and transmitters. It is the duty of males and females to pursue knowledge in Islam. Neither should ever present an obstacle to the other in order to gain false advantage in this regard.

You are expected to carry this legacy forward. Encouraging the women in your life to grow, develop, and seek knowledge is your duty. Those who suppressed women in the past and those who continue to do so in the present wrong themselves, weaken their families, and burden our Ummah. Their actions certainly do not make them any smarter, just as diminishing a woman's wealth does not make them any richer. Such injustice just opens the door for all kinds of evils. Always champion the intellectual achievements of those around you. You'll be a better man for it.

Finally, my dear Billal, let me inform you of your name. Let us start with the last. You are Billal of *banu* Dhubyan, of the Ghatafan branch of Adnanites who trace their lineage to Ismail ﷺ whom as you know originates from the Hijaz. Prophet Muhammad ﷺ belonged to the tribe of Quaraysh of the Adnanites. What does this matter? We both know that it is righteousness, not ancestry, that determines one's closeness to Allah. Prophet Muhammad ﷺ said: "When Allah revealed the ayah, 'And warn your closest kin'[Ash-Shu'ara 26:214], the Prophet said, 'Oh people of Quraysh! Save yourselves, for I cannot save you from Allah's punishment; Oh Banu Abd Manaf! I cannot save you from Allah's punishment; Oh Abbas ibn Abdul-Muttalib! I cannot save you from Allah's punishment; Oh Safiyyah, aunt of the Messenger of Allah! I cannot save you from Allah's punishment; Oh Fatimah, daughter of Muhammad! Ask me anything you like of my wealth, but I cannot save you from Allah's punishment" (Sahih Muslim). That kind of intensely close proximity, let alone generations and centuries of separation, cannot avail a person anything should they betray Allah.

Your lineage, however, should not be so quickly dismissed. It may not carry favour, but it does carry responsibility. "And when Ibrahim was tried by his Lord through words [challenges, children, and commands] and he fulfilled them. He [Allah] said, 'Indeed, I will make you an *imam* [leader] for the people.' He [Ibrahim] said, 'And of my progeny?' [Allah] said,

'My covenant does not extend to the unjust" (Al-Baqarah 2:124). Prophet Ibrahim's ﷺ dedication and faith led him to become an *imam* for all people. This leadership role was not just limited to his time but extended to the generations of the righteous that would follow. Spiritual leadership and guidance are not automatically granted, they are reserved for the just servants of Allah. Possessing lineage, however, ought to at least make it that more shameful to swerve from Allah's guidance.

Now for *Billal*. Your honourable first name belonging most famously to Bilal ibn Rabah ﷺ, companion of Prophet Muhammad ﷺ and one of the most distinguished men in early Islamic history. Most Muslims know him for his courage, perseverance, and the honor of being the first *mu'adhin* (caller to prayer) in Islam. Indeed, Bilal ﷺ rose to a great station. Born into slavery in Makkah in the late 6th century, Bilal ﷺ and his enslaved mother Rabah, were of Ethiopian descent. Bilal ﷺ accepted Islam early in the Prophet's mission, which while making him of the earliest believers also subjected him to extreme torture by his master, Umayyah ibn Khalaf, a great opponent of Islam, who naturally wanted to force him to renounce the new faith. Despite the torture, Bilal ﷺ remained steadfast, repeatedly saying, "*Ahadun, Ahad*" affirming his belief in One True God.

When news of Bilal's ﷺ insistence and resilience in the face of torture reached Abu Bakr ﷺ, Prophet Muhammad's best friend, he was moved to negotiate his freedom with Umayyah. After some bargaining, Abu Bakr was able to purchase Bilal and free him from slavery. Bilal's beautiful and powerful voice made him the perfect choice to become the first *mu'adhin* in Islam, a role assigned to him by Prophet Muhammad ﷺ. He called the *adhan* for the first time in Madinah and continued to do so throughout the Prophet's life.

But Bilal's role extended far beyond the call to prayer. He became a close companion of Prophet Muhammad ﷺ and was entrusted with safeguarding the Prophet's treasure and distributing funds to the needy. He participated in major battles alongside the Prophet, including those of Badr, Uhud, and Khandaq. After the Prophet's passing, Bilal's grief was so profound that he could no longer bear to live in Madinah. With Abu Bakr's blessings, he moved to Syria where he continued to serve and spread the message of Islam. Your name was inspired by this legacy of faith, perseverance, and justice. By liberation from the shackles of men to the freedom found in the worship and service of the One and Only True Master. Bilal ﷺ was not only the first *mu'adhin*, but he also remains a symbol of the early Muslim community's stand against racism, classism, and social injustice. Bilal ﷺ is a testament to the transformative power of '*Ahadun,*

Ahad' – One and Only One – and the universal call to unity regardless of race, status, lineage, and other social barriers.

I pray that Allah guides your steps, protects your heart, and fills your life with peace and purpose. May you grow to be a source of pride and joy for your family, a light for your community, and a servant of Allah in all that you do. And most importantly, may you never lose sight of your purpose as a man, even in a world that sometimes tries to confuse or diminish it.

In Allah's love, light and mercy,
Mama

The Rituals of Purpose

> *Allah said: Whosoever shows hostility to someone devoted to Me, I shall be at war with him. My servant draws not near to Me with anything more loved by Me than the religious duties I have enjoined upon him, and My servant continues to draw near to Me with supererogatory works so that I shall love him. When I love him I am his hearing with which he hears, his seeing with which he sees, his hand with which he strikes and his foot with which he walks. Were he to ask [something] of Me, I would surely give it to him, and were he to ask Me for refuge, I would surely grant him it. I do not hesitate about anything as much as I hesitate about [seizing] the soul of My faithful servant: he hates death and I hate hurting him.*

Honestly, I don't know where I would be today had it not been for my acknowledgement and wholehearted acceptance of our Islamic rituals. Remembrance. Prayer. Fasting. Giving. Pilgrimage. These are the rituals of purpose, commissions of the first order, the acts that we perform when we sincerely admit that Allah created us to worship Him. These acts are meant to benefit us. They are purposeful but their undertaking should not be limited to that truth. We do not perform them only for the hope or expectation that they improve our lives and those of others but rather we believe that these are the enactments of our real and truthful purpose on earth. Trying to understand why we do *dhikr*, perform *salah*, practice *sawm*, give *zakat*, and undertake *hajj* is fine and indeed the Quran informs us of such matters directly, but we mustn't lose sight of the fact that these are *the rituals of our purpose*. We perform them because we worship Allah, not because we derive benefits from them even though we certainly do.

What would life be like if I didn't start my days in the wee hours of the morning with the remembrance of Allah? If I didn't glorify my Creator upon waking. *Alhamdulillah alazi ahyana ba'da ma amatana wa ilayhi an-nushur.* Praise be to Allah who revived us after our deaths and to Him is our return. This was Prophet Muhammad's first supplication upon waking from sleep. Who else can revive us from the lesser death that is sleep? "Allah deceases the selves (*anfus*) [people] at the time of their death and those that do not die in their sleep. So, He holds those upon whom He has decreed death and sends forward the others for a specified period. Indeed, in this are *ayat* for a folk who think" (Az-Zumar 39:42). Who has the power to send us forward to live in this life a little longer except Him? *Alhamdulillah* to the count of everything in the skies and the earth and everything in between and then some.

What would life be like if I could not prostrate myself before His Throne as He invites me to do at least five times a day? And then out of His infinite generosity leaves the gates of the Throne wide open so that I can approach it any time of the day or night for as long as I wish? Just beyond the floral print of my velvet mat is a world beyond this world, an expanse I cannot imagine but I know for a certainty exists as the indescribable feeling of magnetism draws my forehead to the ground. *Subhana Raby Al-A'la*, glory to my Lord Most High. How difficult it is to rise on some occasions as all my limbs submit to the extent that I can hardly distinguish them apart.

The rituals of purpose respond to our purest essence, they are the core of our humanity. Their performance only requires sincerity and purity of heart and body. We are lost without them. They are the foundations, the springs, the stimulants of our social obligations or second order commissions as well as all our discretionary acts or third order commissions in the hierarchy of worship. First, second, and third order commissions – tiers of priority – are all acts of worship. The rituals of purpose come first. Then the social duties of purpose including adequate care for all the relationships that shape a dignified life. And then the discretionary contributions of purpose that rely on our unique resources and capabilities in this life. Meaning will always be incomplete in the second and third orders if the first is neglected. With time social obligations diminish while discretionary acts all but disappear if we enter the twilight years. Only the rituals of purpose carry on with us until the last breath. They ground us, assure us of a life well lived, one that is meaningful to the last moment. There is no need for fear, loss, anxiety or a futile and desperate search for anything beyond. The Merciful Allah has relieved us from such a burden by giving us the basic formula for living our purpose. This is the Meaning of Life. Anything and everything beyond must yield both morally and materially to the rituals of purpose.

The rituals of purpose are diverse and versatile so that every moment of our lives can potentially be filled with some aspect when we are not otherwise engaged in worldly concerns. Aside from their obligatory minimal performance, we can increase practice in a show of love and reverence for Allah. I can give well beyond the two and half percent of my end-of-year accumulated wealth, as required by the *zakat*, to support people and beneficial projects. I can do so even when my situation seems tight just at the Ansar did with the

Muhajireen. They loved the emigrants and harboured no ill feelings toward them on account of what they were granted to ease their displacement, even giving them preference over themselves while some of the Ansar were in privation (Al-Hashr 59:9). I can increase my fasting beyond Ramadan to sharpen my will and improve my *taqwa*. Prophet Muhammad ﷺ used to fast out of Ramadan on Mondays and Thursdays as well as the 13, 14 and 15 days of the lunar month unless he was otherwise incapable due to travel or other circumstance. I can add prayers, or *nawafil*, during the night and day to draw closer to Allah and to remind myself of purpose.

There is not a moment that I cannot fill with remembrance or *dhikr* when my mind is not in use for something else. I can give praise, thanks, and glorify Allah while driving, washing the dishes, looking out at nature, lying in bed, sitting to rest, and so on. "Indeed, in the creation of the skies and the earth and the alternation of the night and the day are *ayat* for the possessors of intellect. Those who remember Allah standing and sitting and on their sides and who give thought to the creation of the skies and the earth [saying] 'Our Lord, You did not create this invalidly, Glory to You, so except us from the torment of the fire'" (Al-'Imran 3: 190-191). It is the simplest, yet greatest way – *wala dhikru Allahi akbar* to express our purpose (Al 'Ankabut 29:45). And it is the surest way to calm our hearts, to find unparalleled comfort. "Those who believe and whose hearts are reassured by the remembrance of Allah; for it is actually by Allah's remembrance that hearts are reassured" (Ar-Ra'd 13:28).

Bismillah, in the name of Allah, commences every lawful act we set our hearts upon. To pronounce the name of Allah demonstrates consciousness, intent. We recognize that what we are about to do in some way fulfills our purpose. It reaches Him and asks for His blessings, mercy and reward. Prophet Muhammad ﷺ said that "every action that does not start with *bismillah* is disconnected (*aqta'*)"(Musnad Ahmad). An act that is disconnected from Allah is incomplete, it unfolds only in the material world and has no life beyond this life. *Bismillah*, before we eat recalls the Source of all nourishment, acknowledges its Provider. *Bismillah* is an entreaty to receive only benefits from what we eat while seeking protection from any harms. It is an offering of gratitude for the sustenance and pleasures that wholesome food in all of its varieties gives us. *Bismillah* is a reminder to only put in our bodies what will fortify us and improve our health, helping us to fulfill other dimensions of our purpose.

Alhamdulillah, praise be to Allah, starts and finishes every act. *Alhamdulillah*, for what can we truly achieve without His help? It is only delusional to attribute success to oneself. Consider how many things have to be maintained, kept stable, within a range of normal, for you to be reading this book. Everything internal to you, your eyes, your understanding, your heartbeat, your breathing, your comfort level and so on. Then externally everything around you has to be guarded as well from the roof on top of your head if you are sitting indoors to the sky outside and everything in between. "Do you not see that Allah has facilitated (*sakhar*) for you what is in the earth, and the ships that run in the sea by His command, and He holds the sky so that it does not fall on the earth except by His permission. Indeed, Allah toward people is Compassionate, Merciful" (Al-Hajj 22:65). There are so many things that we either do not compass or take for granted. The simplest of tasks cannot be achieved without Allah's countless blessings. *Alhamdulillah*!

Our first calling to the rituals of purpose happens at birth, when we first come into this world. Prophet Muhammad ﷺ whispered the *adhan*, call to prayer, in the ear of his grandson al-Hassan ؓ just after Fatima ؓ had given birth to him. It is a profound beginning for any newborn to guide and ground an unknown future.

Allahu Akbar, Allahu Akbar, Allahu Akbar, Allahu Akbar

Allah is Greater. Allah is Greater. Allah is Greater. Allah is Greater. Greater dear little one than anything you will ever experience or encounter. He is Greater. Nothing can overcome Him. You are invincible in His love, light, and protection so do not think anything or anyone is greater. He is Greater than the greatest, bigger than the biggest, stronger than the strongest, and more expansive than the most expansive. You will always be safe with Him.

The first words you hear little one are not frivolous. They are not centred on anyone else in the room, not even on you, as exciting as your arrival into this world may be. They are a tribute to the Lord who made the moment, and all moments, possible. You were brought out of your mother's belly (An-Nahl 16:78). You were brought out; you did not come out of your own volition. You are given life through that mercy of being brought out, whether naturally or by medical intervention. You could not have come out on your own. You, and every human being, is dependent on Allah from the very start. "Indeed, We created the human from a strain of soil. Then We made him a droplet (*nutfah*) in a secure quarter. Then We made the droplet into a thing that clings (*'alaqah*). Then We made the thing that clings into [what appears as] a masticated thing (*mudghah*). Then We made the masticated thing into bones. Then We dressed the bones with meat. Then we raised him as a different creature. So, Blessed is Allah, the best of creators" (Al-Mu'minun 23:14). Prophet Muhammad ﷺ had further explained that the *nutfah* stage is around forty days, the *'alaqah* stage around the same, and the *mudghah* stage around the same, at which time Allah sends the Angel to blow into you *the Soul.* At about four months you have received the honour, partaking in *the Soul* that warranted the prostration of angels.

Ashhadu al-la-ilaha ila-Allah, Ashhadu al-la-ilaha ila-Allah

I bear witness that there is no god except Allah. I bear witness that there is no god except Allah. The *shahadah.* The foremost profession of Islam. You have One and only One Master little one. There are no gods except the One, True, Allah. It is only to Him that you owe allegiance. Every conflict, confusion, and challenge in your future can be resolved by recognizing this fact. You will not be torn, fragmented, and scattered by a world that seeks your subservience, your loyalties, to false gods. You will be strong, united, and decisive because you bear witness to the One, Sovereign, Master. No temptation, no matter how great can seduce you into worshiping anything other than Him, your Creator and Sustainer.

You have no refuge or escape from Allah, except to Allah. The world you have entered is as wide and sheltering as your purity will permit. If you choose to debase yourself, wrong others, and ignore truth and justice, it will appear small and insufficient. Honour the purpose of your creation. Declare the *shahadah* without reservations. It will witness for you when your journey is done, as your life is sure to pass even as we stand celebrating its first moments. Prophet Muhammad ﷺ said: "Indeed, Allah will distinguish a man from my Ummah before all of creation on the Day of Resurrection. Ninety-nine scrolls will be laid out for him, every scroll as far as the eye can see. Then He will say: 'Do you deny anything of this? Have the recording guardians wronged you?' He will say: 'No, my Lord.' He [Allah] will say: 'Do you have an excuse?' He will say: 'No, my Lord.' So, He [Allah] will say: 'Rather you [do] have a good deed with Us. There shall be no injustice against you today.' Then He [Allah] will bring out a certificate (*bitaqah*) within which is [inscribed] *Ashhadu al-la-ilaha ila-Allah wa Ashhadu anna Muhammadan 'abduhu wa Rasuluh.*' He [Allah] will say: 'Present your scales.' He [the man] will say: 'My Lord, what [good] is this certificate next to these scrolls?' So, He [Allah] said: 'You will not be wronged.' The scrolls will then be put on one side, and the certificate on the other side, so the scrolls will be cast off, as the certificate weighs down [the balance]. Nothing is weightier than the Name of Allah" (Sahih Muslim).

Ashhadu anna Muhammad ar-Rasulullah,
Ashhadu anna Muhammad ar-Rasulullah

I bear witness that Muhammad is the Messenger of Allah. I bear witness that Muhammad is the Messenger of Allah. This little one is the first man you must come to know. You will experience his manners in the gentleness of your mother and father. You will witness his teachings in your new home. You will hear his name, mentioned, praised and honoured, well before you can pronounce it. Muhammad, literally meaning the one worthy of praise, the seal of prophets, sent by Allah's Mercy only as a mercy to the worlds.

There is no more beautiful a life story than his, may Allah's peace, blessings and mercy be upon him. A life that will teach you about purity, the Quran, and wisdom. Through him you will learn how to love others, nature, and life, so that you may draw closer to the One who created all. Allah presents him as a favour to humankind. "Just as We have sent among you a messenger from yourselves reciting to you Our ayat and purifying you and teaching you the Book and the wisdom and teaching you that which you did not know. So, remember [mention] Me, I will remember [mention] you and be grateful to Me and do not disbelieve" (Al-Baqarah 2:151-152). If you truly come to know him ﷺ, he will become more beloved to you than anyone and anything.

He was the most generous and giving person. He once said, "If I had gold equal to Mount Uhud, I would be happy not to let three nights pass without having any of it left over, except for something set aside for a debt"(Sahih Bukhari). In other words, he ﷺ would give it all to help others. You were born to give but don't think of it as charity or sacrifice. To give, *infaq*, is to benefit yourself. It is an act of heedfulness and purification or *zakat*. To go beyond the minimal thresholds of *zakat* is *sadaqah* rooted in the concept of *sidq* or truth. To spend or give in Allah's way is to uphold truth. Allah tells us, "You will not attain goodness until you spend of what you love and whatever you spend of something, indeed, Allah is knowing of it" (Al-'Imran 3:92). Someday you may come across those who say, "… should we feed those whom if Allah willed, He would have fed?" (Ya Sin 36:47). These are the clearly lost, the truly wretched. They have no clue that any and all giving is commanded to purify them, to grant them blessings in this life and the next. Pay no attention to them. Allah provides blessings of all kinds to give you a chance to give so that He may purify you and reward you further. Do not look to minimize your contributions. Learn from your teacher, Prophet Muhammad ﷺ, who viewed himself only as a custodian of Allah's blessings. He always found something to give and when there truly was nothing he promised to help in the future.

Nothing will give you more joy, more reassurance, than to see our beloved Rasool in a night or day vision. He, ﷺ, said: "Whoever sees me in their sleep will see me in their wakefulness, and the *shaytan* cannot impersonate me" (Sahih Bukhari). May you, little one, experience this kind of beauty and be among his brethren as he named all those who would love him who had never met him. May you be a mercy to your parents, family, community and all living creatures. May the earth rejoice in your company and mourn your departure.

Hayya 'alas-salah, Hayya 'alas-salah

Come to prayer. Come to prayer. Hurry, come little one to the most reliable connection of your life. Your connection with Allah. Welcome to the community of believers who continuously congregate all over the world from dawn till dusk and some throughout the night seeking their Lord's forgiveness, approval, love, guidance, protection, mercy, and light. Come into the ranks of the humble, who seek to purify themselves. Come to a world where only goodness and heedfulness of Allah are the distinguishing features of such refined company. Here you will find no superficial division of colour, race, sex, profession, wealth or lineage. There is no more an equitable space than in the lines of those who truthfully respond to this call. Every boy, girl, man, woman, comes only as a servant of Allah. Hurry, this is your calling, the only race worth winning in this short life.

Salah is the ritual of purpose that distinguishes the believer from the disbeliever, or those who accept their purpose from those who deny or reject it. Prophet Muhammad ﷺ said, "between a man and disbelief and the association of others with Allah, is the abandonment of *salah*"(Sahih Muslim). Establishing *salah* is your acceptance of five daily momentary invites to converse with Allah, to demonstrate that you have received and understood His guidance. Spread throughout the day, each invite is a reminder of the Real, the Truth. These breaks from the world will soothe your soul and reframe your daily activities. They will help you put things in perspective no matter how great or trivial. Nothing should take priority over entry into Allah's presence even though He provides us with ample time to respond and allows exceptions and easements to encourage us to do our best to attend. "So, woe to those who pray, those who are inattentive to their prayer" (Al-Ma'un 107 4-5). Attendance is your genuine purpose on earth, and it is the foundation for all else that you do.

Know little one, that *salah* is an act of reciprocity. It fulfills a much greater purpose than can be acknowledged through a narrow focus on its performer. By not establishing *salah*, you withhold from others the benefits that should accrue to them through the offering of greetings of peace in addition to all the truths encompassed by its acknowledgements, appeals and intentions. Prophet Muhammad ﷺ taught us the *tashahud* or affirming the *shahadah* during *salah*, which includes the sending of greetings to Allah and the spreading of peace among his servants. And so we say:

> *Greetings to Allah and prayers and all things kind and good. Peace upon you, Oh Prophet and Allah's Mercy and Blessings. Peace on us and on Allah's righteous servants. I testify that there is no god except Allah, and I testify that Muhammad is His servant and Messenger. Allah, send prayers upon Muhammad and upon the family of Muhammad, as You sent prayers upon Ibrahim and the family of Ibrahim. And bless Muhammad and the family of Muhammad as You blessed Ibrahim and the family of Ibrahim, You are indeed Worthy of Praise, Glorious.*

These are words of mutual exchange, reciprocity, peace and love. The believer sends such greetings to others, wishing them well several times a day. You will do this in the direct and indirect presence of others. The *tahiyyat* or greetings reach Allah, His Messenger, and all righteous servants, including those you know and those you don't know, those who have lived before you, those who are living with you, and those who will live after you. And their *tahiyyat* will reach you.

Prophet Muhammad ﷺ made *salah* the gauge of integrity between people. He said, "the covenant between us and them is *salah*, so whoever abandons it has disbelieved (*kaffarah*)" (Sunan al-Tirmidhi). *Salah* is the treaty that binds all members of this Ummah to a common practice. You cannot genuinely respect this treaty and then go on to commit treachery, corruption, and injustice. It is only if you cannot – or refuse to – understand the depth and meaning of this ritual that you will go on to be unjust.

Hayya 'alal-falah, Hayya 'alal-falah

Come to success. Come to success. Let not the life of this world fool you little one. "He has surely succeeded who purifies himself and remembers the name of his Lord, so prays" (Al-A'la 87:14-15). Success will not be found in anything other than this gentle whisper, this call to *falah*. It encompasses the keys to contentment, stability, equity, justice and balance. Do not lose sight of this as the world packages success in academic achievements, a lucrative career, a fancy car, luxury travels, spacious dwellings, even a beautiful spouse and numerous children. These will be nice to have but they will not define real success. All of it is no more than blessings or burdens. Blessings should they support the calling to your Creator, easing your journey toward Him. Burdens should they temp and distract you, turning your life into a dull mundane existence that has all but extinguished the divine spark.

Allah tells us in surah *Al-Mu'minun*, the Believers, that we will surely succeed. We who earnestly experience humility and reverence when we pray, avoid vain talk, give the zakat, guard our chastity except with those with whom we share the marital bond, are vigilant of our trusts and promises, and who guard our prayers (23:1-9). The dual emphasis on our *salah* in the beginning and end of these *ayat* first highlights how we should experience them with humility and reverence and then on the importance of consistency, guarding their quality and timings.

When the time comes and you have reached the age of strength, fasting will help hone your skills for success. Fasting is the training of the human will. The acts of denying your body water, food, sex, and knee-jerk or intense emotional reactions will alert you to the potential mastery over yourself in other situations. That self-control, the ability to command yourself to yield to Allah as completely as possible is what makes fasting so unique.

> *Allah Almighty said: Every deed of the child of Adam is for him except fasting, it is for Me and will reward for it, and fasting is a prevention [from suspicious acts]. And when it is a day of fasting for one of you, let him not utter obscenities nor quarrel. So, if someone insults him or fights him, he is to say: I am a fasting person. And by the One in whose hand is the self of Muhammad, the bad breath of the fasting*

person is better to Allah than the fragrance of musk. The fasting person has two joys that make him happy: when he breaks his fast he is happy, and if he meets his Lord, he is happy because of his fast.

Every deed is for you except your fasting. That is for Allah. Fasting is singled out because it is the only ritual that teaches us something fundamental about ourselves and that is the clear distinction between our will and our other faculties. Your will is that faculty that allows you to make decisions when confronted with choice. Fasting distinguishes, insulates, elevates, your will demanding that it align itself with the guidance of its Creator. This is why fasting is commanded in many instances as a disciplinary measure in the process of repentance. Of all the rituals, it is the only one that acts as an expiation (*kafarah*) for sins and broken promises, and sacrifice (*fidyah*) for the incapacity to fulfill a ritual. Fasting will rebalance your inner peace, rid you of guilt, and remind you that Allah is the ever forgiving.

Fasting will enable you to dignify yourself over and over as your will exerts full control over anything that can control you. Fasting eliminates the noise, distractions, poisons, that obscure your inner voice and hence your ability to overcome and reject all kind of evils. This will make you stronger, less susceptible to worldly temptations and traps. No other ritual demonstrates our capacity to fulfill purpose more than fasting. Consider this your override switch even in the face of life's strongest seductions. Let it show you how strong you really are, how you can align your life choices with His guidance and in doing so to fulfill your servitude, refine your *taqwa*. Hayya, hurry, to success, and make everything that life gives you a means to goodness and heedfulness.

Allahu Akbar, Allahu Akbar

Allah is Greater. Allah is Greater. Again, little one a gentle reminder that Allah is Greater. Greater than anything you may hear, see, or feel in the journey ahead. Greater than any challenge that will inevitably be put in your way as you heed the calls to *salah* and *falah*. This is a repetition to secure your heart, calm your fears, and soothe the grief that is sure to come when you realize the depravity of some people, when you try and fail, and when you love and lose. This is a repetition to warn you never to lose hope, to keep the final prize always in sight. Even when all is good, when life offers the best there is on offer, and you are enchanted with its majesty, magnificence, beauty, and pleasures, still *Allahu Akbar*. He is far greater than the sum of everything He created. *Allahu Akbar* will be your refuge in times of ease and distress. There is no despair with a Lord that is Greater than all.

> *Oh child of Adam, so long as you call upon Me and ask of Me, I shall forgive you for what you have done, and I shall not mind. Oh child of Adam, were your sins to reach the clouds of the sky and were you then to ask forgiveness of Me, I would forgive you. Oh child of Adam, were you to come to Me with sins nearly as great as the earth and were you then to face Me, ascribing no partner to Me, I would bring you forgiveness nearly as great as it.*

Allahu Akbar. Never. Ever. Despair.
He is the Lord of Light, Love, and Mercy.

La ilaha ila-Allah

There is no god except Allah. Finally, little one, a restatement of the single most Truth of all existence. There is no god but Allah, something to which you and all people have already attested, this statement is not only Truth, it is a covenant, a promise, that you must spend your life doing your utmost to keep. To admit to One, and only One, God is to recognize the oneness of His universe. You, precious baby, are part of an incredible interconnected web of life both human and non-human that extends from the beginning of creation to the Final Hour. No matter how the world judges your destiny, whether you lead a simple or complex life, your words and actions will reverberate throughout time. So be kind, gentle and just. The promise of *la ilaha ila-Allah* cannot be honoured in any other way.

The rituals of purpose are a believer's surest way to the water. A man from the people of Najd once approached the Prophet ﷺ to ask about Islam. The Prophet responded: "Five prayers during the day and night." The man then asked, "Do I have to do anything else?" "No," replied the Prophet, "unless you do it voluntarily." Then the Prophet said, "And fasting Ramadan." So, the man again asked, "Do I have to do anything else?" "No," said the Prophet, "unless you do it voluntarily." Then the Prophet ﷺ mentioned the zakat, so the man asked, "Do I have to do anything else?" and again the Prophet ﷺ replied, "No, unless you do it voluntarily." The man then turned away and said, "By Allah, I will not do more than this, nor will I do less." Upon hearing this, the Prophet ﷺ said, "He will succeed if he is truthful" (Sahih Bukhari).

Indeed, there are many who are satisfied with performing the bare minimum while others can never be content as such. It's all good but I believe that anyone who performs the rituals of purpose with sincerity cannot help but hunger for greater closeness to Allah. Every ritual, performed with pure intentions and focus, is filled with blessings and mercy. Every ritual invites us to attain greater and greater proximity to the light, love, and security of the One. Our display of love and reverence is in turn met by love, mercy, and everything beautiful with which Allah grants His loved ones. Is there anything greater than Allah becoming the *hearing with which we hear, the seeing with which we see, the hand with which we strike and the foot with which we walk*? Perhaps you can think of something better, but I certainly cannot.

Citizens without Borders

Sheikh Muhammad Abdullah Draz, born in 1894, stood as a witness to a turbulent and painful era in the history of his people, and indeed that of humanity. Egypt, his homeland, was struggling under the oppressive rule of British colonization, which paved the way for Palestine's devastating occupation while two world wars left a considerable part of the world in material and psychological disorder. Yet, where such injustices may generate rage and justify aggression, Draz preferred to apply his knowledge and language skills to persuade international and local actors of the need for change. Firmly established in the rich heritage of Islamic scholarship and reared in the light of his father's example, he was confident in the Quran's guidance not only for believers but for all of humanity. Who other than Allah, the Proprietor, had the keys of the skies and the earth?

His acute sense of observation led him to believe that whether he was considering the behavior of the colonialists or his own countrymen who had been worn down or corrupted by decades of foreign domination, the challenge lay in people's perception and acceptance of moral duty. To Draz, the colonialist did not represent all his people, just as the treasonous Egyptian who sold out to the colonialist did not represent all Egyptians. Instead, there were people of *goodwill*, as he called them, on both sides who were willing to extend their hands to each other for the greater good of all. As Prophet Muhammad ﷺ taught: "The best of people are those that bring the most benefit to the rest of mankind" (Al-Tabarani). It is for these people who care about each other, who wish to live in peace, for whom Draz dedicated over a decade of his life to expound not only how they could but were intended to live by their Creator. His magnum opus, *La Morale du Coran*, was an offering to humanity of the universal principles that could guide all people to a just and peaceful existence. A treatise on duty, the second tier of human purpose, it is a work dedicated to citizens without borders or those who aspire to transcend the superficial lines drawn on a borderless earth to honour a shared humanity.

Draz believed that everyone of us kindled an innate light – a flame that illuminated their path and place in this life, which gave humanity some semblance of stability and predictability. This inner light, however, was not sufficient to understand Allah's *sunan* and hence to manage life's complexities. Only Allah, the All-Knowing, and the teachings of His messengers were the source of such knowledge. Prophet Muhammad ﷺ said: "The permissible and the prohibited have been made clear; but between the two are unclear cases. He who restrains himself when in doubt preserves his faith and honour" (Sahih Bukhari). Revelation was the necessary fuel for our inner light – the knowledge, the Truth, needed by people to live consistently dignified lives and to afford others the opportunity to do so as well.

From the Quran, Draz distilled the essence of human duty: the positive acts we are called to undertake and enjoin others to do the same and the negative actions we are commanded to avoid and likewise prohibit others. Duty, he taught, was the legacy of a life well lived. It emerged from inquiry and teaching, through moral effort and striving for the middle path. "And it is as such that We have made you a moderate [literally middle] ummah that you may be witnesses over the people and the Prophet be witness over you…" (Al-Baqarah 2:143). To be dutiful is to beautify oneself with sincerity, chastity and decency; to act with honesty, efficiency, and gentleness. It is to honour one's parents as the Quran says: "And your Lord has decreed that you not worship except Him, and do good by parents. Whether either of them reaches old age with you [in your lifetime], do not say to them *uffin* [expression of disrespect] and do not denigrate them but say to them a kindly speech" (Al-Isra' 17:23). It is to care for family and friends, and behave mercifully toward neighbors, the vulnerable, strangers, and all living creatures. Allah warns us in the Quran, "Do not give away the meanest of your earnings [things] that you yourself would not take except while cringing" (Al- Baqarah 2:267). Anything we would not give to Allah should not be given to others for He is ultimately the recipient of every good we do.

Duty was not a burden but rather an integral dimension of our purpose in this life. It gave individual and collective life meaning through the development of a just and empathetic society. "And We send down of the Quran that which is a healing and mercy for the believers, and it does not increase the unjust except in loss" (Al-Isra' 17:82). Duty encompassed everything from equitable treatment of spouses and supporting family to aiding those in need. It is reflected in kind words, truthful testimony, kept promises, and hospitality that rejects borders between self and other. "Oh you who believe, be upstanding for equity, witnesses for Allah, even if it be against yourselves or your parents and close relatives, whether one is rich or poor, for [your duty to] Allah has greater priority. So, do not follow whims that you may swerve and if you twist [the truth] or oppose [it], then indeed Allah is ever informed of what you do" (An-Nisa' 4:135). Duty was the way that every individual exercised their citizenship, adhering to Allah's guidance throughout His vast dominion by accepting, assimilating and uniquely reproducing it for the benefit of oneself and others. His Will becomes ours. The *fusion*, as Draz called it, of two wills.

The Quran and teachings of Prophet Muhammad ﷺ, Draz explained, also prohibited all actions that threatened human dignity and nature's balance. To commit suicide, lie, fornicate, boast, hoard wealth, be wasteful, to make illicit gains or benefit from anything immorally acquired, was to debase oneself while simultaneously corrupting the social and natural systems that sustain us. "And whoever accrues a bad deed, he only accrues it against his own self" (An-Nisa' 4:111). To abandon or mistreat the vulnerable, or to cause harm or ruin to the earth was to imitate the corrupt, to go astray and to walk in darkness. "Whoever is guided is only guided for his own self and whoever is misguided is only misguided to his detriment and no self will bear another's burden" (Al-Isra' 17:15). These errors, Draz reminded, betrayed our purpose and had repercussions well beyond our current place and time. Every permission and every prohibition are reminders of our purposefulness and the critical balance maintained when each of us honours their purpose for the unity of creation and the dignity of all life. "Then is the one who walks stooped over his face better guided than the one who walks steadily on a straight path?" (Al-Mulk 67:22). To neglect one's duties, in Draz's view, was to damage the noble balance in which we are created.

For Draz, the Quran's teachings were a comprehensive way of life that left no room for uncertainty concerning what we were placed on earth to achieve. It is only in the denial of divine guidance, the rejection of Allah's invitation to all that is good and wholesome, that the earth and our lives become corrupted. Draz focussed *La Morale du Coran* on the second tier of human purpose, duty. It is here that we have the opportunity to express the lessons gleaned from the performance of rituals. It is here that the light beam of remembrance, prayer, fasting, and giving becomes visible. The more we accept invitations to give, serve, uplift, be kind, the more we place items in the light path, giving it the splendour of a continuous beam. It is this beam that then illuminates the third tier of human purpose, which is the discretionary contribution that our unique presence on this earth offers. It is not duty but rather an expression of our creativity based on our aptitudes, interests, skills and even life opportunities but nonetheless dedicated to the service of Allah and His creation.

Islam tells us that duty, to feel obliged, is the key to a purposeful and dignified life. It is through the honoring of our responsibilities that we feel whole, needed, part of something bigger than ourselves. This is not based on blind acceptance of social pressure or from a temporary pursuit of passions but rather on a form of intelligence that can sense and read our inner code as well as it can read external guides. Literacy starts from within. The Quran points us to this code, it helps us to decipher it, reminds us of what is written, and presents us with infinite choices in living its meanings.

Duty presents us with both unity and diversity. In Quranic Truths, we all must carry out the same order, but we do so in dynamic ways taking account of individual and collective circumstances, capabilities, cultures, and the necessity of renewal. Duty provides structure and predictability while diversity tailors every act to time and place. Together, they reflect the majesty and greatness of divine design.

Duty also presents us with both authority and liberty. Allah is the author of the law, the logic that makes duty universally sensible and binding. Absolutely no human can change divine laws or ways including those related to human nature and social systems. If that was possible life would indeed be chaotic and there would be no basis for any kind of truthful knowledge. We are free, however, to accept and practice our duties to our benefit and that of others or to deny and reject them at our peril and that of our families, communities, and nature.

There is no doubt that duty can sometimes feel burdensome especially when we believe that our time can be better or more enjoyably spent doing other things. There are times when the simplest tasks feel unbearably heavy. This is when we have to remember that "Allah does not oblige any self except to the extent that He has given it" (At-Talaq 65:7). He also placed us within networks of relations that can help us fulfill our duties when we are feeling down, sluggish, tired, or unwell. We do likewise for those who come to our aide. Allah has given us the capacity and resources for what He asks of us. It is for us to determine how to apply ourselves in every situation.

Even as duty is commanded, it remains gentle, as Allah desires ease for us. There is no duty in Islam that leads to self-harm or exhaustion. "Allah desires ease for you, He does not desire difficulty for you" (Al-Baqarah 2:185). This must not be conflated with effort. Every duty requires effort, some of which will necessarily be out of our comfort zone. But when the events in our lives challenge us in ways that must be accommodated, Allah's *sunnah* provides for relief and adjustments. This does not change the essence of duty but rather its timing and possibly its intensity. We are equipped with the ability to determine when these facilitations may be needed to preserve ourselves.

In doing so, we are able to sustain what is asked of us and to proceed with calm, contentment, and balance.

I edited, simplified, and summarized Draz's monumental work, *La Morale du Coran*, a few years back to make it accessible for the ordinary reader. By removing much of the comparative literature that Draz had to include in his original work because it was a doctoral thesis, I hoped to honour his initial plan that the book only includes the moral laws of the Quran as supported by Prophetic teachings. My efforts sprung from a sincere desire to introduce Draz to a new audience. I was bewildered by the lack of knowledge that most Muslims had of this man and in particular this brilliant contribution to our lives. It was one thing to be Muslim, quite another to be a properly moral Muslim. Draz had made other contributions that perhaps are better known to the Muslim reader like his collaboration with his father Sheikh Abdallah Draz on Imam Al-Shatibi's seminal work, *Al-Muwafaqat* (The Congruences). Most will also be familiar with his unique and commendable exegesis of *Surah Al-Baqarah*, which he published under the title, *Al-Naba' Al-'Azeem* (The Great News). He was undoubtedly one of the most prolific Muslim scholars of the twentieth century and was worthy of his accolade as *master of the masters*, which was bestowed on him by colleagues and students alike.

During several Ramadans since, I have offered his work as part of special programming – trying to explain to participants how the moral world of the Quran functions. It is so important that believers know and understand their duties. That they appreciate the integral connection between duties and purpose and to anchor their lives accordingly. Very few realize that worship is not only in the form of rituals. Indeed, all acts that are animated and intentioned by belief are a form of worship. Intention transforms duty into an act of heedfulness or *taqwa*, and it is *taqwa* that saturates the mundane with a sacred hue. When we care for the orphan, tend to nature, lower the wing of mercy for the oppressed, captives, and needy, when we enjoin patience and truthfulness among those around us, we are not only tending to our humanity but also to revelation – for the source of both is the One.

It is incredible how so many people miss out on the beauty that a life of duty offers and disappointing how duty is complained about, neglected, or altogether avoided. The challenge is real. Personal desires and weakness of character often distract us from this path of duty, tempting us with illusions of freedom and momentary ease. But the believer is secure. Ultimate wellbeing is found in the embrace of responsibility and the acknowledgment of accountability. "So by your Lord, We will question them all about what they used to do" (Al-Hijr 15:92-93). Who can deny the messengers? "Most certainly We will question those to whom the Messengers were sent, and we will question the Messengers" (Al-A'raf 7:6). Prophet Muhammad ﷺ said that everyone will be questioned regarding, "in what occupation he spent his life, for what motive he acted, from what source he made his fortune and how he used it, and how he used his own body" (Jami' Al-Tirmidhi). It is in accepting and undertaking duty, as a bird trusts in the Mercy of the One who suspends it in the sky, that we learn to soar toward the Eternal. Duty is not a human construct, it is a divinely ordained dimension of human purpose that, as Draz taught, is crucial for our wellbeing in this life and the next.

There are those who journey in this life honouring what was required of them in terms of duty – a duty that possessed *sultan*, or authoritative truth, as commanded by Allah, their Lord, who knows every nuance of our advancement. They are patient and constant, capable of prioritizing their days, months, and years. Theirs is a covenant with Allah to guard and join what He commanded to be guarded and joined. Through duty, they honor their purpose while contributing to the fulfillment of the purpose of others.

Then there are those who reject all constraints, denying or else distorting their inner code, choosing instead to live in accordance with personal desires and the ever-volatile states of social systems that believe they have transcended the need for God. Allah is well aware of them. "Have you seen the one who takes as his god his own desire? Are you then to be a custodian over him?" (Al-Furqan 25:43). They have replaced the certainty and comprehensiveness of divine guidance with the limits and confusion of human impulse. Duty has become an unacceptable discourse. Instead, we are forced to reframe our conversations in terms of rights. But what rights are there if the responsibility for the duties that afford those rights are diluted or all together avoided among family members and nations alike? A world constructed on the basis of false independence and greed strives to erase any notions of shared or universal duty. It has shortchanged a good part of humanity while occupying individuals and groups with the futile search for a purpose that Allah has already made crystal clear.

Every member of the human race may indeed carry a light, but some have greatly dimmed or altogether extinguished its power. They have, in the expression of the Quran, purchased error for guidance. And "Their example is like the example of one who kindled a fire, so that when it illuminated what was around him, Allah fled with their light and left them in darknesses unable to see" (Al-Baqarah 2:17). The idea is that no one can illuminate the truths of Allah's universe for us if our inner light, the light that guides our understanding of what we see and experience, is burnt out. Although inner light is a personal phenomenon, it is the radiance of the collective that mostly influences our communal life. The second tier of our purpose in this life invites us to a humanity that rejects false borders, embracing family and community, rich and poor, friend and stranger without discrimination. It offers peace and stability wherever we find ourselves and whatever we are doing. It is a citizenship that transcends borders.

That is clearly not the citizenship that the modern nation-state has thrust upon us, one of false pride and nationalisms that thrive on superiority, racism, and military conflicts fueled by an insatiable appetite for the other's resources and world dominance. Shaped and disguised by major social institutions like the media, academia and the arts, it silences dissent through the twisted interpretation of constitutional rights. It urges members to cast off the chains of duty and tradition in exchange for freedom and individualism – an imminently preferable choice whether or not the state takes care of you. Such is the deception of modernity, post-modernity, and every other label that power invents to adorn its sins and cover up violations of the rights of others. Fragmented, unstable and unpredictable, the rhythm of life is irreparably disturbed by material and moral illusions, riding on the certainty of human greed and influenceable emotions. Not surprisingly, a significant dimension of human purpose is lost, and with it, the individual loses their footing. Searching for meaning, anxious, despairing and lost.

Like a trail splitting into two paths, one way leads to wholeness, the other to fragmentation. One way honors the sacred balance of rights and responsibilities, the other tips the scale in the service of those who perpetrate injustice though the self may be deceived. Indeed, the Quran tell us that there are people whose speech we may like in the life of this world, but they are nothing more than enemies. If they are to attain power or authority in the earth, they strive to corrupt her, exhausting fertile land (*harth*) and progeny (*nasl*) alike (Al-Baqarah 2:204-205). How can this compare to a universal citizenship that enjoins what is good and beneficial for all while rejecting and prohibiting what is unjust and harmful? To choose the path of duty is to find and experience peace and contentment while facilitating – or at least wishing – them for others.

The duties commanded throughout the Quran and exemplified by our beloved Prophet Muhammad ﷺ, are universal. They are an integral dimension of our purpose on earth. And while they are not dependent on the rituals of purpose, they certainly benefit from them as the rituals define who we are and not just what we do. I am Muslim. That is a notion of being. I acknowledge and perform commanded duties. That is a notion of becoming. These are not 'naturally' brought together. It is the believer that brings these notions together, as Draz explains, when we experience duty as an act of worship, infusing it with divine intentions of justice, wisdom, and goodness, seeking only His approval and acceptance. Allah's order – an order that transcends all superficial divisions and longed for by all creation in its unadulterated form – becomes our order.

The duties of purpose, unlike the rituals of purpose, are very rarely specified in terms of quality or quantity. They are in essence an orientation, a direction, to which the believer turns, each following a unique path given their potential, circumstances, and priorities at any given moment. This grants every person a significant role in how they fulfill their duties while at the same time facilitating respect for divine commands. While some may choose, or indeed be compelled, to undertake the bare minimum, others may choose to excel and go far beyond. The Quran establishes a baseline while encouraging people to greater and greater heights of good.

In his time, Draz and his contemporaries lived by their understanding of duty. They took to heart the teachings of their faith and example of Prophet Muhammad ﷺ who told us that Allah said: 'Oh my servants, I have made oppression unlawful upon Myself and unlawful for you. Do not oppress one another' (Sahih Muslim). The nationwide movement against British colonial rule with its blatant disregard for the rights of Egyptians, disruption of their culture, manipulation of their economy, and control of foreign policy for imperial gain demanded a suitable response. The actions that Draz and others resorted to in order to liberate their homeland made sense in their world. Today, however, those measures may seem inappropriate, insufficient or impossible given changes in local and global politics, technologies, and communications. Colonialism may be a thing of the past, but new forms of political domination, global economic inequities, and state-sponsored terror have gradually replaced it. A genocide is unfolding right before our eyes and the leaders of the world are letting it happen despite ongoing and intense protests by wide segments in every society.

The teachings of Draz are timeless based as they are on the Word of Allah. Today we are called to apply them in traditional as well as in new social structures and conditions. His emphasis on education, awareness, and persuasion as the most effective ways to deal with modern crises is as relevant as ever. We must, however, adjust their content and form in consideration of the specificities of our historical moment. And we must be able to critically examine the tools – communication technologies – that we think are at our disposal for this purpose. How do we interpret and translate Quranic guidance and the teachings of the Prophet Muhammad ﷺ to rectify contemporary manifestations of ageless challenges and what methods can we reasonably depend upon to do so?

I find myself returning to Draz's belief in the innate goodness of humanity, that inner purity which longs for justice, for dignity. It is not a belief in the ideal but the pragmatic – what other choice is there than to enjoin good and prohibit evil? To convince as many people of goodwill as we can that we owe ourselves and others, human and non-human, certain immutable rights as part of our very purpose on this earth. That we mustn't shirk our responsibilities. This is not only the most effective way of living through crises, it is the surest way to halt their progression and positively change the future.

Duty, after all, is an intimately human enterprise, born of reason and nourished by revelation. The Quran invites all of humanity to a dignified life and a noble end offering every believer who heeded Allah's guidance a path to the Hereafter. It is your choice to become a universal and eternal citizen, to live an integral dimension of your purpose. Responsibility is personal with each individual shouldering their own burdens. "For it [the self] is what it has earned; against it, what it has acquired" (Al-Baqarah 2:286). This much is clear, nobody bears the burden of another, and no parent can atone for their child, nor child for their parent (Luqman 31:33). Allah's justice is perfect, and He is Merciful yet swift in account. Every one of us will only answer for himself, for "verily, there is nothing for the human except what he strove for" (An-Najm 53:39).

Yet, the life of this world also exhibits collective responsibility and indeed the members of each community will be called to account at once. "And you will see [when the final Hour comes] every ummah kneeling. Every ummah invited to [observe] its record. 'Today you will be recompensed for what you used to do'" (Al-Jathiyah 45:28). The Quran warns us of the dangers that entire communities face when their members are complicit in injustices toward others, both human and non-human. It takes more than one individual or even a small group to create the economic systems that privilege the wealthy at the expense of the poor, or the strong against the weak, that pillage and destroy our natural world. This is the same for the development and maintenance of social structures that oppress people based on race, class, gender, or belief. When people normalize immoral behavior including sexual deviance, indiscretion, and exploitation they destroy the foundations of the single most important civilizational institution for the propagation of humanity – family. These are all communal acts. On top of all this and exacerbating each, is when Allah's guidance is completely ignored or distorted, when false claims are attributed to Him and His messengers, the entire community fabric becomes worn and vulnerable to disintegration.

Such choices, made consciously or passively, lead to a betrayal of the Trust that we covenanted to carry. The implications are suffered by all, as every living creature senses the imbalance and mourns the loss of beauty. The Quran's narratives and warnings serve as a reminder of our freedom to choose, to return to our original sense of dignity, and to live as servants of Allah and keepers of His earth.

Like the laden ship that by Allah's permission carries people across the seas and by His Will either delivers them safely or sinks, our collective choices can lead to rectification as surely as they can corrupt. Will we heed this warning? Will we, like Draz, accept our duties, own up to our responsibilities, and choose goodness, even as we feel overwhelmed by the forces of evil and injustice? The foundations of guidance and goodness are already within us. To fortify or destroy those foundations, is the question.

For Draz, duty bound people to the Creator, their own consciences, and communities. It gave every individual purpose. As it was an expression of the depth of the internalization of the essence of the rituals, it was also fortified by them – a symbiotic *yet extricable relationship*. Accepting duty, to feel obliged, is not an exclusively religious phenomenon. For the believer it is a matter of worship, for the non-believer worldly necessity. Duty is a universal *sunnah* irrespective of a person or community's belief. This is evident in the nature of duty; it extends well beyond the ritual acts. And its implications are obvious in the life of this world. When we do not follow the guidance of the Creator, the manual that provides us with the Truth of matters, there is nothing but suboptimal outcomes or worse destruction. The Quran justifies its commands, not merely basing them on hope or fear. Rather, it explains to me why I must live in a certain way so that others, all creation, can live too.

Draz's work, Allah willing, will remain a testament to the Quran's enduring relevance to address modern challenges and reinforce human dignity. His legacy endures as a reminder of our purpose in this life, of how we must be and what we must do to transcend all superficial boundaries, to become citizens without borders.

Al-Fakhoora: The Proud One

Brrrrriiiing, Brrrrriiiing, Brrrriiing. The sound of the school bell summoning children to an education, a way of life that centralizes knowledge and knowing in human affairs, instilling a respect for dialogue, persuasion, constructive criticism, and progress toward Truth. A Truth that can be shared with others, even as it is expressed and embellished by the diversities of our tongues, cultures, histories and future aspirations. For the children of Al-Fakhoora, The Proud One, a school in the Jabalya refugee camp in Gaza, this bell meant even more than this. It was the sound of some semblance of normalcy in a world that had all but stolen their childhood. *Brrrrriiiing, Brrrrriiiing, Brrrriiing*. Little boys and girls, eager to learn with beaming beautiful faces, line up to start their day. This was the foundation of a future of scholarship for some of them, enabling the pursuit of purposeful paths, producing the doctors, engineers, teachers, artists, poets, chefs, who could rebuild their homeland in a distant world where justice, peace and harmony prevailed.

Al-Fakhoora was no ordinary school. No school in Gaza is *ordinary*, a place of joy and peace, where students, teachers, administrators, and staff gather to build the foundations of a bright future. Here, schools double up as shelters for people seeking refuge from a continuous state of crisis. No place is safe. Al-Fakhoora was repeatedly targeted by Israeli military strikes while full of those beautiful beaming faces and others seeking refuge under the flag of the United Nations. Education, in particular, is intentionally targeted as Her Highness Sheikha Moza bint Nasser of Qatar, boldly asserted on numerous occasions. In her words, "…attacks on education rip away the vessel, destroying the lives of teachers and students and leaving nothing but emptiness. The future is annihilated. And there is no doubt that those who target education know what they are doing and do so with premeditation."[4]

It was Her Highness who paved the way that allowed me to develop a novel approach to policy studies, re-orienting my discretionary contribution in this life toward educational reform. I am so grateful to have had the opportunity to be part of one of her unique educational projects that birthed the idea of a *public policy in Islam*. Researching, designing, and then heading and teaching in the Master of Arts in Public Policy in Islam, the first of its kind in graduate

4 Her Highness' speech on the International Day to Protect Education from Attack, Doha 9 Sept. 2024. https://www.mozabintnasser.qa/en/media-center/speeches/her-highness-speech-international-day-protect-education-attack (accessed Jan. 12, 2025).

studies, transformed my career from a Canadian public servant to an academic and scholar. This experience reshaped the direction and distinctiveness of my discretionary contribution in this life, the third tier of human purpose.

Human purpose, as exemplified in the worship of Allah, is comprised of three interacting tiers that give everything we do in this life meaning. The first tier or that of the rituals is the very basic yet essential dimension of human life. To perform it well, even on its own, is to have lived a worthwhile life in recognition of Allah. Without this tier all else is lacking. It is the foundation of the true merit of your actions, giving everything a sacred hue. The second tier, that of your duties, is the dimension that ensures that we all have an opportunity to live dignified lives, to pursue purposeful paths with sufficient support from others, and to preserve or defend the world that we need to live in peace, harmony and justice. Finally, the third tier is that dimension of human purpose that is wholly discretionary, where we are encouraged to express our uniqueness, both as individuals and as groups. In this realm of personal creativity and initiative, we are invited to bring our special aptitudes, talents, resources, and interests to complete our worship of Allah. It is here that the homemaker, doctor, teacher, artist, poet, plumber, mechanic, cook, researcher, exert their creative effort to make constructive and productive contributions to their families, communities, and the world.

With this third tier, the trilogy of human purpose on this earth is completed. Everything we do has purpose and can be infused with intentionality to serve Him, assuming and retaining its sacred worth. "And strive for Allah with the striving rightly owed to Him. He has chosen you and has not placed on you any discomfiture in the *deen* [devoutly oriented way of life], the convention of your father Ibrahim. It is he who named you *Muslimeen* from before and herein so that the Messenger may be witness over you and you may be witness over the people. So, establish prayer and give *zakat* and hold strong to Allah. He is your protector. So, blessed is the Protector and blessed is the Vindicator" (Al-Hajj 22:78).

How can we strive in a way that is rightly owed to Allah? It is to go above and beyond, to challenge ourselves, to perfect what we set out to do in His cause and to use all the blessings that we have been granted to safeguard and beautify life. It is one thing to feed your neighbour, that is a duty, and another to open a soup kitchen that feeds the entire community, and yet another to design and execute a successful national or global strategy to eradicate hunger. Likewise, it is one thing to recycle and another to utilize your skills, knowledge and resources should you have them to develop innovative ways of reducing environmental damage. The third tier of human purpose responds to the Quranic exhortation to follow "the best that has been sent down to you from your Lord" (Az-Zumar 39:55) and to "race with each other in all that is beneficial" (Al-Ma'idah 5:48).

Through action we are led to our destiny. The Quran tells us that "whoever works righteousness (does good), of male or female, and they are believers, We will revive them a goodly life and We will reward them their dues in accordance with the best of what they used to do" (An-Nahl 16:97). It also states, "as for they who give and heed and affirm with beauty, so We will facilitate them toward ease" (Al-Layl 92:5-7). This ease comes from Allah's assistance as He supports, strengthens and blesses, those who assist others. The key is to move, get going, do something that reveals your commitment to Allah. "…Act, for Allah will see your actions" (At-Tawbah 9:105). "… How excellent is the reward for those who are doers" (Al-'Ankabut 29:58; Az-Zumar 39:74). We are encouraged to do our best in all circumstances. "So, give good news to My servants, those who listen to the word and follow the best of it, they are the ones whom Allah has guided, they are the people of intelligence" (Az-Zumar 39:17-18).

Like all tiers of human purpose, discretionary contributions must be based on voluntary choices. We must be capable of choosing what we wish to do with Allah's blessings on us when we have the opportunity, or good fortune, to do so. That means that we are capable of taking stock of our unique abilities and resources, strengths and weaknesses, as well as things like our social standing and influence, our position within social systems and organizations, and our links or relationships with others who may be called upon to play a role in what we wish to accomplish. It almost goes without saying that everything that we wish to do or are currently doing must be good, conforming to Allah's guidance both in its means and ends. Also, before and during embarkment on this third tier, we must be fulfilling both the first and second tiers of our purpose which should be firmly in place as they come in that order over our life course. Neither rituals nor duties can be compromised in the pursuit of discretionary contributions.

Fulfilling the demands of one tier cannot lead to unacceptable compromises in the others particularly as there are permissible flexibilities in each dimension depending on the specifics of any particular moment in our lives. Prophet Muhammad ﷺ illustrated this by reminding his companions: "… I wake and I sleep, I fast and I eat, and I marry. Whoever does not follow my example is not of me" (Sahih Bukhari). The fact that he ﷺ was also a governor, judge, warrior, and peace negotiator among other roles did not diminish anything of those other purposes. Believers accept, as Prophet Muhammad ﷺ said, that "Your Lord has a right over you, your body has one, your family another, and your guests have one – give each one their rights" (Sahih Bukhari). We choose what we wish to accomplish in the third tier, but it must not become the only or main preoccupation of our adult lives as it has become of late. The satisfaction of each tier contributes to a balance in life, both our lives and those of others around us.

Education is an obligation in Islam. It is both an individual duty (*fard 'ain*) and a communal obligation (*fard kifayah*). Every member of society, whether male or female, young or old, poor or rich, ordinary or gifted, is obliged to adopt a lifelong attitude toward learning – of *seeking Truth*. Social institutions whether situated within the formal system of education or outside it, are obliged to uphold this basic tenet so that we can advance and evolve while respecting the boundaries of Allah that make this possible. Prophet Muhammad ﷺ said: "Whoever takes a path in search of knowledge, Allah will cause him to walk in one of the paths of Paradise" (Sahih Muslim). Indeed, the Quran tells us that Allah raises by ranks those granted knowledge (Al-Mujadilah 58:11). Seeking knowledge is necessary for everyone to fulfill all three tiers of human purpose but for some it is also the central focus of their third tier. These are the individuals and groups who make the provision and production of knowledge and education their discretionary or special contribution in this world. And there is one name that has made an unparalleled contribution to higher education – Fatima Al-Fihri.

All of us, Muslim and non-Muslim alike, involved in higher education owe a debt of gratitude to Fatima Al-Fihri. It was she who founded the world's first and oldest university, named Al-Qarawiyyin, in 859 in Fez, Morrocco. Both Fatima and her sister Maryam were well educated by their father. He ensured that the girls had a strong Islamic upbringing and a solid knowledge of Quran, hadith and Islamic scholarship. Fatima was dedicated to the education of young people and used the great fortune that she inherited from her father and husband to advance this cause. Al-Qarawiyyin started off as a mosque that gradually transformed into a religious institute and university.

It was a centre for intellectual exchange, learning, debate, knowledge production, and dissemination.

Al-Qarawiyyin welcomed students from all over the world. Muslim and non-Muslim alike. It developed the formal degree system that professionalized the granting of credentials in different areas of scholarship. Its graduates, including teachers, doctors, mathematicians, chemists, astronomers, artists, and craftsmen had a great impact on the knowledge production and enlightenment of the time. These discoveries and extensions of knowledge became the foundations of European development and a leading contributor to its exit from the so-called dark ages.

Upon convocation, graduates of Al-Qarawiyyin University would wear gowns or *thobe* to imitate Muslim scholars, a symbol of proper training. The cap with the flat top symbolized the Quran, placed on the head to emphasise that it was the crown of all knowledge, the guiding light for Truth, Justice, Equity, Compassion and every other noble cause that education ought to be. The tassel, you guessed it, a bookmark that marked where a student had left off in his or her readings of the Quran. Almost every university around the world today, with minor differences, continues this tradition with most students, I dare say even professors, not knowing how it originated. According to UNESCO, Al-Qarawiyyin University is the oldest still operating university in the world.

When Sheikha Moza was a child, education for girls was still a novel idea in Qatar. Prior to 1949 education took place in traditional *kuttab*, a form of elementary school mostly limited to boys that focused on Arabic, Islamic studies and the Quran with other subjects included within this framework. It was not until 1956 that education for girls was officially formalized through the opening of a school for girls. Her Highness was born three years later and she would become one of the most celebrated champions for education and research at home and on the global stage.

A sociology graduate of Qatar University, Sheikha Moza recognized the value of education for her people early in her life. Her marriage to His Highness Sheikh Hamad Bin Khalifah Al-Thani in 1977 when he was still heir apparent cemented her future role in the governance of the country. When His Highness sought to establish Qatar Foundation in 1995 to support the development of his people, it was Sheikha Moza's leadership that would ultimately shape the direction and nature of that development. Taking the helm of a fantastic project in education, science, and research and based on her firm belief in the provision of quality education, she oversaw the establishment of Education City, a flagship project of Qatar Foundation. Her goal was to attract world class US universities to Doha. When I arrived in 2007, Education City with its 2500 acre campus on the outskirts of Doha, had already housed six branch campuses including Weil Cornell Medical College, Texas A&M engineering, Carnegie Mellon computer science and information systems, Georgetown University School of Foreign Service, Northwestern communications and journalism, and Virginia Commonwealth design. These would later be joined by HEC business school and University College London archaeology and conservation.

From 2003 to 2023, Sheikah Moza was UNESCO Special Envoy for Basic and Higher Education. She has used her growing global influence to promote education in Qatar and the wider Arab world. Prophet Muhammad ﷺ taught that "guiding someone to goodness garners the same reward as the one who performs it" (Sahih Muslim). A key aspect of her efforts on the global stage involves working to protect the right to education in conflict-hit areas of the world. In 2012 she launched Education Above All "to help provide education for hardest-to-reach out of school children affected by poverty, discrimination, distance, and conflict." Ten million marginalized children had accessed education by 2018 as part of the initiative's Educate a Child program.

Meanwhile, in a parallel universe, I too had taken an interest in education in crisis. But not quite the kind of crisis that Her Highness was concerned with. My graduate studies in public administration at the American University in Cairo during 1995/6 inadvertently unfurled the path of the rest of my life. Completing the MPA with straight As with the generous support the Nippon Foundation Scholarship for Young Leaders was certainly something to be proud of.

But I was crushed. Subjects were taught using outdated and imported ideas, content, theories, frameworks. Just master the content, write the papers, pass the exams. Learn to critique imported ideas using other imported ideas and methods. *Knowledge* was partialistic, fragmented, biased, and anthropocentric. There was no effort to consider let alone understand Truth and because of that understandings of reality were highly distorted. I knew that we could not talk about the public and its concerns without talking about the Designer, Creator, Regulator, of social order, of human dignity and duty, and of accountability. Imported curricula and strict censorship of course content meant that even in a predominantly Muslim society like that of Egypt, discussions of the sacred were unwelcome.

I returned to Canada in 1996 with the goal of completing doctoral studies in public policy and hopefully finding a route to incorporate my concerns. I was young. I was naïve. I really thought I could contribute to policy studies through my knowledge of Quranic guidance. My first term in the PhD was very challenging. Bringing faith, any faith let alone Islam, into class discussions to critique the works of others was completely rejected. The Quran has no value in secular academia. Not even as a book that may be accorded some level of curiosity if not respect. Apart from one professor, Phil Ryan, whom I later discovered shared similar interests from the Christian perspective, most would roll their eyes at what they considered unwarranted, unevidenced religious interventions by an academically immature student. It did not take many such incidents for me to stop. I learned to participate in class discussions, to critique the intellectual idols of the secular social sciences, in a way that would not offend secular sensibilities.

I learned neo-classical economics as the leading theoretical underpinning of public policy in the west and many global institutions like the World Bank, International Monetary Fund, World Trade Organization, and numerous others. Somehow its unrealistic and inapplicable assumptions did not seem to bother its proponents, somehow everyone was expected to suspend their disbelief at its outrageous claims and worse yet, destructive outcomes. Perfect information, no transaction costs, rational agents, market clearing, all concepts that have nothing to do with reality, were defining and shaping public policies around the world. To add salt to the wound, one had to accept that at the core of these models was a selfish and depraved human actor. The only demonstration of your or my preferences occurred through material exchanges and price signals in markets. There was no mercy, charity, justice, family, community or nation. There was no critique of human choices or objectives. Instead, the sum of the market behavior of all these selfish actors – somehow – resulted in collective welfare. Independence, consumerism, and free markets are the pillars of western secular public policy – at least in theory.

Something is terribly wrong. We are living in a world of family breakups, pandemics, genocide, environmental degradation, unjust wars, political oppression, poverty, racism, and greed. The market has not been a good gauge, equitable arbiter, or inclusive space. Indeed, as the Quran states: "Corruption has arisen on the land and the sea due to what the hands of people have earned; so that He may give them a taste of some of what they did, perchance to return" (Ar-Rum 30:41). Academia, I discovered, is an industry, a market like any other that is bound by the rules of wealth and power. It is an instrument for social manipulation and suppression, largely governed by a neoliberal ideology and a publication industry that rambles on and on so long as nothing it says or does ultimately disturbs the status quo. And then there are things that simply cannot be said. Things that much of the world now understands on account of Gaza.

I could never be convinced of a secular, godless, approach to public policy, and I agree with Phil Ryan, my former professor and now dear friend, that fruitful debates on religious matters offer society many positive outcomes – if not agreement on certain positions, at least understanding of each other's points of view. This opens channels for movement, the possibility that my actions and beliefs are shaped (not determined), as Ryan states, by my social interactions. There is a democratic imperative for dialogue between what he calls "sophisticated and thoughtful" minds.[5] That same imperative would deny any political leadership the imposition of religious beliefs that had not over the course of time and primarily in other social spheres made their way into – and consequently became acceptable to – the public conscience. This takes patience and time. But it is worth it.

To finish my doctoral studies, I needed to take a more pragmatic approach. So, with a massive grain of salt, I disguised my truths in the language of economics and innovation. I attempted to demonstrate how the new global intellectual property regime that would guarantee massive profits to the pharmaceutical industry was not beneficial for the developing world and would stifle innovation and access to much needed medicines. My book *The Illusive Trade-off* was largely based on this research. It was a shot in the dark as confirmed by the fiasco over the intellectual property of vaccines and therapeutics that occurred during the COVID19 pandemic and that had occurred previously during the HIV/AIDS pandemic in the late 1990s. Nothing had been learned. Perhaps something had. Once more we realized that wealth, power, and violence, secure their interests in international systems of governance that they largely establish ensuring the perpetuation of injustice. In this world of military might, profits, big business, and a populace convinced that it is the final arbiter of its own welfare through independence, consumerism,

5 For an interesting discussion see Phil Ryan (2014), *After the New Atheist Debate*, Toronto: University of Toronto Press.

and freedom – however delusional – public policy will always succumb to the dictates of the *market* with its mercenaries not too far in the shadows.

It would take Gaza to show global citizens just how impotent they were in the face of their own governments, how suppressed academics and students were in the face of their university administrations and funders, how corrupt the media was in face of political command and control. The insincerity of democracy became crystal clear to so many. "What we are witnessing in Gaza," lamented Her Highness Sheikha Moza, "has stripped away the world's imagined veil of civility unmasking its sheer brutality. We thought the world was civilized, but it was not so. This brutality extends beyond those who commit crimes and kill women and children. It includes all who have supported this depraved aggression with funds and weapons. It includes those who watch what is happening in Gaza; those who encourage it in private or in public; and those who choose to remain silent."[6] This is the challenge in a world where Truth is lost, denied, rejected.

So many of the so-called educated are not educated at all. They are indoctrinated. Nurtured on propaganda, basking in the temporary comfort of personal desires and social whim, willing to ignore, distort and conceal the truth for personal gain. Education has largely been divorced from knowledge as it loses its foundation of Truth. Except in cases of scientific necessity where we must agree as to what is real and truthful, almost all other disciplines have succumbed to the frivolity of human limits and desires. But when our shared foundations are lost, when one party denies the divine imprint in themselves and in the universe, and the truth codes of all creation are treated as unfalsifiable phenomena, it is not the challenge of scientific progress that we should worry about but the enablers of evil.

Education is about the acquisition of all kinds of knowledge. Knowledge that influences our beliefs, enhances our skills, improves our living conditions, perfects our morals, and corrects our values. Because of this knowledge, *'ilm* in Arabic, is intimately associated with Truth. To have *'ilm*, or to be a *'alim* or knower, is not to know just anything in any way, it is to know Truth through divinely sanctioned means and methods. Without this foundation of Truth, we only have information, material, that must be reconsidered in

6 Her Highness' speech on the International Day to Protect Education from Attack 9, Sept. 2024.

light of divine imperative – the Quran and Sunnah. At the beginning, the end, and core of our quest for knowledge is *La illaha ila Allah*, there is no god except Allah. It is this profound admission, this inescapable fact, that must guide education in all of its forms and for all of its purposes. To start, continue, and end with any other principle only leads to errors, oversight, and worse destruction.

As humans, we can only discover. We are not creators. Sure, we can discover then combine and recombine, we can even – to our own detriment – change the nature of things including that of our own selves, but we cannot make something – anything – out of nothing. We are not originators in the purest and deepest sense. How incisive are the *ayat* in which Allah reminds us of this. "We did not create the skies and the earth and what is in between them except with Truth and a specified duration and those who disbelieve concerning that about which they were warned [remain] opposing. Say, 'Have you considered what you invoke besides Allah? Show me what they have created of the earth, or do they have a share [in the creation] of the skies? Bring me a book from before this or any shred of knowledge (*'ilm)* if you are truthful'" (Al-Ahqaf 46:4). There is always a Truth foundation to any unit of knowledge. When that foundation is lost, whatever remains is noise, distraction, distortion, and lies.

To be clear, I am not saying that knowledge is homogenous, that there are no differences of opinion, infinite diversities in expression, or genuine yet contradictory routes on the same journey. But even in the presence of these conditions that are indeed necessary for human survival and pleasure, the Truth premise of all knowledge cannot be abandoned in exchange for our guesses and whims. Like everything in the universe, there are truthful, stable, unifying elements and structures that give order to and benefit our lives. These are adorned with the diversity of language, culture, levels of development and civility. Yet we must attempt to rediscover, beyond the nuances and details, the sacred: the difference between truth and falsehood, between what benefits and harms, and no less, between the rectifiers and the corrupters. Everything must be taken stock of in the framework of divine guidance, so that despite the complexity and difficulty, the sneers and opposition, we can honour the Trust, which is also the unity of all creation and the Oneness of the Creator. Our species can and must share fundamental truths in the hard and soft sciences, even as expressions remain different. It is the key to peaceful coexistence for all creation. Of all the fields of human endeavour, this is perhaps most critical for governance and policy where the quest for what is better and lasting – *khairun wa abqa*, as in the Quran – is at the very core of what we do.

My doctoral experience greatly altered my views on the integrity and possibilities of the academic enterprise. Consequently, I decided to join the public service of Canada instead of seeking an academic position. There seemed no escape from the requirement to separate religious-moral convictions from practice, to distinguish perception from social reality, to isolate problems and ignore complexity. Honouring the creed of my profession, despite all the grand posturing, was not *speaking truth to power*, but rather, loyal service to my political masters who were after all chosen by the people. Work in government led me to explore other policy areas beyond trade, innovation, access to medicines and intellectual property. But wherever I went the ignorance of divine guidance meant so much inefficiency, ineffectiveness, and contradiction across policy areas. Except for a deep personal attachment to my faith, to the Quran, and my love for Allah, I had largely abandoned any aspiration of integrating its teachings in policy. But the more I did this, the more unfulfilled and hollow I felt.

It was not until 2003, a few months after I had defended my doctoral thesis, that I received a very interesting request from a former professor of mine, Dr. Hatem El-Karanshawy, then dean of Public Administration, at the American University in Cairo. Among other ideas, Dr. Hatem, wanted me to work on designing and building a graduate program in public policy in Islam. He had known from previous communications that I was very disappointed in the master's program that I had completed at AUC and the challenge that the then Dean of the School of Business, Economics and Mass Communication, Dr. Farouk El-Hitami, had set for me when he responded to my complaints with a not-so-expected, 'well what would you suggest?' At the time I was waist deep in research, a full-time job, and a newborn. But now I was ready. Hope would spring once more!

We diligently set out to imagine what a graduate program of this nature would look like. What approach would we take, what courses would be required, what materials and faculty would be sourced, but most of all how could we convey the very idea of a *public policy in Islam*? There was no yardstick against which we could measure the potential efficacy of the program because there were no comparable programs worldwide. Just as the policy sciences had not considered Islamic studies as a potential source of knowledge, Islamic studies had not developed its own policy contributions. It was not long, however, before we had articulated our vision and mission. Our vision was to foster a progressive cadre of leaders, capable of and willing to govern in accordance with the noble values and ethics of Islam, promoting social and economic development and enhancing the quality of life of all citizens regardless of race or creed. Our mission was to develop the intellectual capacity and practical skills of leaders at all levels working or concerned with the public good. Through a combination of contemporary western scholarship and Islam's rich intellectual heritage, the Master of Arts in Public Policy in Islam was born – at least in theory. Even as we neared completion of the program, we still had no institutional host. That is, until Dr. Hatem – with the most generous blessings and grant of opportunity by Allah – presented the idea to Her Highness Sheikha Moza. The Master of Arts in Public Policy in Islam would be one of several programs establishing the first homegrown initiative of Education City – The Qatar Faculty of Islamic Studies (QFIS).

This resonated well with Her Highness who was seeking ways of balancing the impact of the foreign branch campuses that had set up shop in Education City. Firmly rooted in Her Highness's long standing pride of place, language, history, culture, and people, QFIS offered a suitable and unique opportunity. The Faculty was inaugurated in 2007, and would eventually be restructured and streamlined to form the foundations of Hamad Bin Khalifa University, which followed in 2010. This was not a simple decision, opening a program in public policy that focalized Islamic studies was both academically and politically courageous, but it was in keeping, with Her Highness's dedication to her faith, people, and mission.

In addition to supporting the establishment of QFIS, I headed and taught in the public policy program from 2007-2012. Those were indeed the glorious years. I could walk into a classroom and teach the relevance of the Quran – its lessons on purposefulness, connectivity, and holism – for making and critiquing public policy. It was a Muslim policy wonk's paradise. With the fantastic availability of financial resources, a renowned teaching cadre, talented officers handling finance, human resources, public relations, IT, and language instruction, our excitement was feverish. Remarkably, Her Highness, like her 9th Century noble predecessor Fatimah Al-Fihri who attended Al-Qarawiyyin, also joined the program, attended classes, completed assignments, and successfully received her MA in Public Policy in Islam – an achievement that she proudly displays on her official website. Her high profile gave a boost to the program's reputation, attracting the enrolment of other prominent state, academic, and business personalities.

When we started in September 2007 we had no building, only my-self as full-time faculty in the public policy program, and an entry cohort of 23 students. At the time of my departure, we had graduated two cohorts, attracted world-renowned faculty specialized in the objectives of the Shariah, Islamic ethics, and governance. Managing the program was perhaps one of the most profound learning experiences of my life. We had, no matter how imperfect, birthed a new discipline.

Upon returning home to Canada with my three young children, I poured my energy into articulating the theoretical and practical underpinnings of a public policy in Islam, a task that I was unable to fulfill while teaching and heading the department. This effort culminated in *Public Policy Beyond Traditional Jurisprudence: A Maqasid Approach* that has since been translated into several languages. At its core, I argued that we could understand public policy in Islam in the same way that we understood conventional policy as a course of action taken by a public authority to address a problem or take advantage of an opportunity. Unlike its secular counterpart, however, the qualification of *in Islam* meant that this course of action was guided by the *Shariah*. In particular, four principles appeared to define such courses of action in the Quran and teachings of Prophet Muhammad ﷺ: unicity (*tawhid*), purposefulness (*maqasid*), collective decision-making (*shura*) and rectification (*islah*). These four principles must be at the forefront of our minds when we are making or critiquing public policy. Each principle is associated with a cognitive capacity, including the ability to think holistically, purposefully, collectively, and positively. It is undoubted that such an approach to policy studies and policy making would have a profound impact on governance and leadership in our world today. Nothing saddened me more than when I learned of the closure of the program a few years later in favour of a conventional alternative to be a part of Hamad Bin Khalifa University. The need for a program of this nature could not be more dire.

Knowledge is the inheritance of humanity. Nobody has the right to withhold knowledge from others. Whether it is through measures that keep knowledge secretive, or those that restrict access for its seekers, it is all prohibited in Islam. Qatar's Al Fakhoora campaign, launched by local students in the wake of the 2009 military invasion of Gaza by Israel to express solidarity with their

Gazan counterparts and stress the basic right to education, held great hope for a better future. Fast forward to 2023, that confidence in a humane world had all but died. The world, including UNESCO, stood silent as a genocide unfolded. Yet, Her Highness vowed to keep the course. Her mission is clear. "Based on my deep conviction in rebuilding education, understanding that rebuilding education rebuilds hope for the future, I will continue in supporting the education sector in Gaza, through Education Above All Foundation, with the support and funding from the state of Qatar."[7]

In a poignant speech on September 9, 2024, on the International Day to Protect Education from Attack, Her Highness poured her heart out to the world: "After the veils have fallen, and we have lost our shared values, our principles, our very moral codes, what is left is Gaza: a litmus test against which all standards are measured." As believers, we accept Allah's decree that loss is a trial, a way to strengthen hearts, to distinguish true believers, and raise their ranks. "And We will certainly try you with something of fear and hunger and diminution of wealth and lives and productive endeavors and give good tidings to those who persevere" (Al-Baqarah 2:155). When all the tiers of human purpose – ritual, duty, discretionary contributions – are truly dedicated to the worship of Allah, perseverance in the face of loss becomes much easier to practice. Our resolve to build again and build better can only gain momentum. "And do not lose heart and do not grieve while you are the superior if you are [truly] believers" (Al-'Imran 3:139). Al-Fakhoora will always, Allah willing, remain the proud one.

7 United for Peace in Palestine Summit, 15 Nov. 2023.

Revival of the Fittest

Every Friday believers are called upon to read surah Al-Kahf (The Cave) to recall that as Muslims, it is not so much survival of the fittest that matters in this transient earthly life but revival of the fittest. "Oh you who believe, respond to Allah and to the Messenger when he invites you to what revives you" (Al-Anfal 8:24). Those who strive to fulfill their purpose – believe and do good – understand that all the blessings on this earth were provided to test people as to who is better in action, whose presence and contributions radiate the most light. To read surah Al-Kahf every Friday, taught Prophet Muhammad ﷺ, is to generate a light between you and the Kaaba, shine a light from you from one Friday to the next and for you from beneath your feet to the clouds of the sky that will also shine for you on the Day of Resurrection. It is also to have your sins forgiven between the two Fridays. For fifteen minutes or less of our time we are given a gleam of timeless examples of those who centralized Allah in their lives, providing maximum illumination of Truth and Reality.

Revival of the fittest is typified by purposefulness. "Say," as the Quran commands us, "Indeed, my prayer, my rites, and my living and my dying are for Allah, Lord of the worlds. No partner has He. And as such I have been commanded and I am foremost of the Muslimeen" (Al-An'am 6:162-163). To focalize Allah is to live in accordance with His exclusive worship, which involves acceptance and honouring of the purposeful paths of all creation and the nature of connection that allows all species to flourish, in cooperation not competition with each other. To believe in Allah is to know wholeheartedly that He is the provider, whether with abundance or within limits, for every creature is a share of suitable provision (Hud 11:12). Cooperating, supporting others, is a confirmation in this belief. When there is competition among the believers, it is to strive for Allah's Countenance, to abandon greed and all kinds of vice. Revival of the fittest is a path of return to balance both as it restores human dignity and protects nature's resilience.

The stories in Surah Al-Kahf present believers with four dramatic scenarios about how the deep resolve to exclusively worship Allah shaped the determination, perception, aspirations and life-course of their protagonists. First, we are presented with the example of those prevented from worshipping Allah because of a hostile environment. What are we to do in such circumstances? Are we to succumb to pressure and the temptation to go with the flow? Are we to pretend that we are something that we are not to appease those around us? Abandoning our purpose to worship Allah can only lead to ruin in this life and the next. The second example is all too common: dealing with those who see no need to admit purpose, to worship Allah. The abundance of wealth and children, with all the worldly advantages that these bring, delude some people into believing that they have no need for Allah, and should the afterlife even exist they contend that they will be rewarded there as well. How does this attitude impact their path and the purposeful paths of those around them? The third example relates to all of us as we sometimes struggle to accept the purpose of others. What happens when we cannot understand the wisdom of their actions, making hasty judgements of the events that we witness? The fourth and final example, presents the reality of those who know their purpose and are gifted with the means to actualize it. Perhaps we can see ourselves in every narrative, some more intensely than others. To routinely read this surah is to be reminded that having purpose – making our way to the water – can sometime be a struggle.

Every narrative is a quest for revival, a determination to fulfill purpose, to remain on the straight path, *as-sirat al-mustaqeem*, for light can only ever travel in a straight line.

The Cave: When you are prevented from fulfilling your purpose

Lending its name to the title of the surah, the cave is both a figurative and literal expression. Figuratively, it is not as is commonly understood to capitulate, but rather to seek refuge, to take asylum in a place and time of safe distance from harm. Caves figure prominently in human history as places of shelter and safety. Prophet Muhammad ﷺ meditated in a cave before and after receiving his mission, it is where he and his best friend Abu Bakr ؓ sought safety from the pursuit of enemies on their way to Madinah, and where he ﷺ took refuge on his way back to Makkah from Ta'if until being afforded protection by a local chieftain. Caves are a divine sanctuary, a sacred feature of the landscapes of rocky regions that have served people and other creatures throughout the centuries.

For us, a cave is anywhere we can distance ourselves from the pressures and distractions of life, where we can find peace and quiet. Most of us do not need to resort to caves as a matter of life and death, but unfortunately there are many people in our world who do. Many who are persecuted simply for saying our Lord is One, our Lord is Allah, His Law is our law. To resort to this divine sanctuary is not to surrender. It is to retreat for a determined time, so that you can reflect, regroup, replenish, and recalibrate yourself to strengthen your worship of Allah without compromise. This is an ultimate act of obedience; not to submit to the will of the oppressor but to find a way, even if it means sacrificing what you love, to stay the course.

In this wonderous story, literally about a cave, a group of youth, and their dog, we are invited to witness the determination to remain committed to Allah and the support that Allah extends when such efforts are genuine. These youth were firm in their belief that only Allah was Lord of the skies and the earth, that no one except Him was worthy of worship, and that there was no exchange for His words. But they were living in treacherous times among a people who had taken to the worship of multiple gods, violently pursuing those who opposed. Desiring to remain steadfast, the youth were compelled to retreat to a cave, calling on Allah to grant them mercy and straighten their affairs.

Confident in Allah's compassion, the youth placed all their trust in Him. So, Allah shielded their ears, guarded, and sustained them allowing them to sleep for many, many, years. There, they rested peacefully as the slow motion of individual histories conspired at the social level to reform their people. In the refuge of the cave, Allah turned them from right to left, while their dog stretched his forelegs at its entrance. The sun, on the command of her Lord, inclined away from them when she rose but lent them her warmth as she set. You would think them awake if you saw them, you would react with fear and flight. Those whom Allah guides are guided, while those who are lost have no one as a compassionate guide.

When the youth woke, they had not known how long they had slumbered, some said a day or part of a day. Others said that only Allah knew. To discover exactly how long they had been away, the youth sent one member into town with some currency they still had to fetch food. Fearing to be recognized and persecuted once more, the nominee remained vigilant. To his surprise the times had changed! A new social consciousness had emerged, and the people were gleeful at this discovery. Rather than stone them or compel them to renounce their faith, the youth became an *ayah*, a symbol of determination and resistance. Some townsfolk suggested that a monument be built for them, but the opinion that eventually prevailed was that a masjid should be built on the site of their refuge.

How impossible would it have been for the youth to envision such an outcome; that the coming of their tomorrow would become a sacred legend for believers and non-believers alike to reflect upon until the end of time. "And never say of anything, 'I will certainly do that tomorrow except [if you add] as Allah wills. And remember your Lord if you forget and say, 'Perhaps my Lord will guide me to what is closer to correct conduct'" (Al-Kahf 18:23-24). *Insha'Allah*, Allah willing. We say it not because something may not happen, or because we may ourselves be incapable or even perish, but because Allah may indeed have something better for us in store. *Insha'Allah*, because He is the Merciful, the Knowing, the Loving, the Generous.

The story of the cave, the youth and their dog came to be known so that people – then and now – may know that Allah's promise is true, and that the Hour is coming. Eventually, people would dispute the number of youth and the years of slumber. But neither of these details matter, the facts are that these youth along with their dog actually existed and they slept for a very, very, long time. The Quran hints that it was several centuries but reiterates that only Allah and a few others know the truth and that argument over such details is futile. Only those who wish to distract from the real moral of the story get hung up on such trifling issues.

For everyone else, it is amazing how we can see in this one narrative, the significance of man, the conventions, *sunan*, of social rectification, and the near timeless rhythm of the earth as they are weaved together in such an efficient way to help us understand the promise – if not immediate impact – of our singular purpose. We are called upon to understand how the threads of human life interact with those of time and space to produce a tapestry that ultimately reveals the unchanging Word of Allah. For this we must be patient, following Allah's guidance with unwavering conviction, for while each life is one among an infinite number of vibrations, our collective frequency will one day become a tsunami. Even in the grimmest of times there is Allah's Light and Mercy, a Light that endures and strengthens the hearts of believers, a Light that vindicates and reveals the Truth in due course.

Survival of the fittest – the idea that individuals and groups *naturally* compete so that only the strongest or most capable succeed and thrive – is an ancient phenomenon. This was and continues to be the reality of those who deny their true purpose, preferring to live in accordance with their desires or what society deems acceptable, causing distortions and destruction at the individual, group and social levels. Survival *is* actually selfish living at the expense of others and fitness is nothing more than the readiness and ability to unleash whatever it takes to dominate and reap the greatest possible advantage in this earthly life. Only our species is capable of such a travesty given the freedom to choose. Whoever wishes to believe may believe and whoever wishes to disbelieve may disbelieve and it spells out the consequences for both (Al-Kahf 18:29).

Survival of the fittest is more than a socio-political theory disingenuously claimed to have been discredited and abandoned. It remains alive and well in our modern world forming the foundations of colonialism, racism, and the dehumanization of certain groups leading to unjust wars, famine, slavery and genocide. However unpalatable to the compassionate members of the human race, this reality offers a lens through which we can understand the worldview and practice of those who deny purpose. The Quran is clear about these people, offering a truthful and timeless picture of the reality – not ephemeral perception – of their worldly success. Born of their disbelief and greed, survival of the fittest is the principle that saturates their chests, tainting their hearts through a centralization of the self instead of the sacred.

This is not to absolve the believer from survivalist tendencies, denying both Truth and Reality, but there is a big difference between those who recognize and struggle against evil inclinations, and those who accept it as *fait accompli*. The Quran clearly distinguishes between people in this regard. "Or do those who inflict harm think that We will make them like those who believe and work righteousness [good], equal in their life and their death? Wrongfully is that which they judge" (Al-Jathiyah 5:21). "Or shall We render those who believe and work righteousness like the corrupters in the earth? Or shall We render the heedful as the rebellious?" (Saad 38:28). "Shall We render the Muslimeen [those who submit] like the criminals? What is with you? How do you judge?" (Al-Qalam 68:35-36).

To reject purpose is to deny Allah's *ayat*, to lie with flagrancy, a most depraved act of disbelief (An-Nahl 16:105). Such immorality leads to further wickedness. A stained heart is neither sensitive to the truth nor intellectually astute (Al-Mutaffifin 83:14). It commands its possessor to follow his or her whims and can barely distinguish its voice from that of the devil. Perhaps the devil has done his work when we can no longer make this distinction. "And I will mislead them, and I will arouse in them [false] desires," promised Shaytan, "and I will command them so that they maim the ears of cattle, and I will command them so that they change the creation of Allah.' And whoever takes the Shaytan as a chief instead of Allah has indeed lost a clear loss" (An-Nisa' 4:119).

Believers seek revival, not merely survival at the expense of all else. To return to their Lord over and over again in this life and with hope for a share of the Hereafter. Just as the youth of the cave had done in keeping each other's company, the Quran suggests the extension of one's patience by associating with those who call upon Allah morning and evening seeking His Countenance. We are commanded not to let our gaze extend beyond these humble servants of Allah, desiring the luxuries of the life of this world. We are commanded not obey any whose heart is distracted from the remembrance of Allah and who follows their desires while their affair is fragmented.

Two Men and a Garden: When you believe that you no longer need to fulfill your purpose

In the second major narrative we are introduced to two men. One of whom has been given abundant wealth and beauty in the form of two fertile and picturesque gardens with a flowing stream in between in addition to manpower and progeny. Deceived by the apparent extensiveness of his dominion, he taunts his companion, "'I am greater than you in wealth and dearer in progeny.' And he entered his garden while he was unjust to himself saying, 'I do not think this will perish, ever. And I do not think that the Hour will happen and even if I should be returned to my Lord, I will certainly find better than this restituted'" (Al-Kahf 18:34-35). The arrogance of some people who are granted the luxuries of this world. How they misread the ayat of Allah who is the source of all blessings.

His companion, however, was well aware of Allah's favours and trials. "'Have you disbelieved in He who created you from earthen then from a fluid droplet then fashioned you as a man?" he retorted, "But as for me, He is Allah, my Lord, and I do not associate with my Lord anyone. And why when you entered your garden did you not say, what Allah has willed has occurred, there is no power except by Allah, when you saw me less than you in wealth and children? It may be that my Lord will give me better than your garden and will send upon it a calamity from the sky so it becomes slippery terrain, or its waters become submerged so than you cannot command it'" (Al-Kahf 18:37-40). Sure enough, the first man's produce was surrounded with ruin, leaving him bewildered and disappointed with all that he had invested in it. "'Had I only not associated anyone with my Lord,'" he lamented regretfully. There was no one to help or console him except for Allah, he could not even console himself. Allah is the authority, the best to reward and to determine.

Even as the idea of survival of the fittest is shunned in public discourse, it remains the basis of the beliefs and behaviors of those who believe in their indisputable superiority. "And they said, 'We are more in wealth and children, and we are not punishable" (Saba' 34:35). The perception of wealth, strength, intelligence and adaptability as self-generated is nothing but illusion. Every blessing is a gift from Allah and if He were to retrieve anything of His grants we would have no recourse. "Indeed, for those who disbelieve neither their wealth nor their children will avail them anything against Allah. And these are the fuel for the Fire" (Al-'Imran 3:10). Their success is not what drives human progress, nor does it justify their domination. "And do not admire their wealth and children. Verily, Allah only wills to torment them with such in the world and that their selves [persons] should weary [or depart] while they are disbelievers" (At-Tawbah 9:85).

You may think that harsh, but the suffering and elimination of weaker individuals and groups – human and non-human – is a direct result of the conditions that the lifestyles of these people perpetuate and even expedite. It is only begrudgingly and with miserliness that they tolerate social programs, charity, or any effort to aid others in this natural and for some, divine, process of selection. "And when it is said to them spend out of what Allah has provided for you, those who disbelieve say to those who believe, 'should we feed those whom if Allah had willed He would have fed?' You are not but in clear loss'" (Ya Sin 18:47). Do not feel sorry for them, rather, be a more keen observer. Nothing prevents them from believing when guidance is manifest or from asking for forgiveness from their Lord, but the sins of their predecessors catch up with them, wrapping them in the comfort of familiarity and advantage so that they cannot or do not wish to change. The disbelievers take the devil, a creature that refused to prostrate before man, an open enemy, who neither witnessed the creation of the skies and the earth nor his own creation, as an ally instead of Allah. Not surprisingly, Shaytan becomes a partner in their wealth and children (Al-Isra' 17:64).

Fact is, we are not free to do with our resources what we please. There is a wide scope for what we can do, but there are also constraints (Hud 11:87). It is an expectation of believers that they strive with purposefulness should they have the resources and capacity. "Those who believe and emigrate and struggle in Allah's way with their wealth and their persons are greater in degree to Allah and it is they who are the winners" (At-Tawbah 9:20). Only the disabled or genuinely weak are excused from certain forms of struggle in the way of Allah (An-Nisa' 4:95). Believers are not permitted to fake weakness or make dishonest excuses for themselves. Those who do so ally with evil and choose to conform to reprehensible social norms and unethical behaviors.

"Indeed, those whom the angels decease while wronging themselves saying 'In what [condition] were you in?' They will say, 'We were oppressed in the land.' [The angels will] say, 'Was not Allah's earth extensive [enough] that you may migrate within her?' So, for them, their refuge is Hell, and horrible is it for a destination. Except those [who are truly] oppressed of men and women and children who have no means to retaliate or find a way out" (An-Nisa' 4:97-98). For them there was no *kahf*. It is for Allah to forgive them and also to judge those who did not extend them support and protection. "And what is the matter with you, not fighting in the way of Allah while the oppressed of men and women and children are saying, 'Our Lord get us out from this town whose people are unjust and appoint for us from Yourself a guardian and grant us from Yourself a victor" (An-Nisa' 4:75). Those who believe fight for Allah, for justice, compassion, peace, co-existence, while those who disbelieve fight for the devil. I cannot help but think of the genocide in Palestine. The countless innocent lives lost, the cries for help, and the dishonest feebleness that so many around them have claimed either implicitly or explicitly. It is a fear of men and want of the riches of this world that prevents their interventions. They would do a good deal better to remember that the enjoyment of this world is little in comparison with the riches and felicity of the Hereafter (An-Nisa' 4:77).

Surah Al-Kahf suggests that we observe plants to understand the reality of life on this earth. They receive sustenance, water from the sky, sent down by their Caretaker. They grow, bloom, carry out their purpose, but then at a determined time they expire, turning into dry matter scattered by the winds. Another *sunnah*, an *ayat*. Are we with all our wealth and children really any different? Life is short, and it is fragile. And though we may enjoy our wealth and children, as they are, in the words of the Quran "adornments of the life of this world", it also reminds us that what remains of good deeds is better to Allah and more worthy for shaping our aspirations (Al-Kahf 18:46). "Oh you who believe, let not your wealth and children distract you from remembrance of Allah. And whoever does that then they are the losers" (Al-Munafiqun 63:9). "And know that your wealth and children are a trial and that with Allah is a great reward" (Al-Anfal 8:28). Ultimately, wealth and children may extend one's reach in this life, but they are not indicators of heedfulness or righteousness (Al-Isra' 17:6). These, in and of themselves, do not bring us nearer to Allah, that is only possible through belief and good works (Saba' 34:37).

Al-Khidr ﷺ and Musa ﷺ: When you assume you know how others should fulfill their purpose

The third narrative that we encounter, invites us on a journey with Prophet Musa ﷺ and an unnamed servant of Allah who had been granted mercy and knowledge. The story draws our attention to a common challenge in our understanding and practice of purpose, the dedicated worship of Allah, in all that we do. Simply put, it is the idea that our understanding and application of faith is optimal or is the correct way. Acceptance of the beliefs and actions of others is normally confined within a self or socially determined range, with which we have come to be familiar. Anything outside that range elicits a gut reaction that either approves or disapproves of what we observe.

We form hasty judgments, aware neither of the details of the past that merged into that moment, nor of the future that it will necessarily shape. We forget that Allah has a plan. And He is the best of planners. We forget that Allah has his soldiers, servants – human and non-human – tasked with carrying out His command. In our limited capacities with our worldly biases, even the best of us cannot compass how Allah governs His affair. With Prophet Musa ﷺ as the lead in this narrative, this point is clear. If he ﷺ, with all his divine favors, could not help but be impatient with what he had not received of knowledge then what of you and I, the common believers? We may not always agree with the purposeful path of others, but before we jump hastily into judgment we must pause and take stock of our own ignorance.

Parachuting into the unfolding of the story, we find ourselves traveling on a journey of knowledge with Prophet Musa ﷺ and his young servant. The junction of the two seas where they would catch up with a whale, an *ayah* from Allah, marked their intended destination. Prophet Musa ﷺ, however, forgot the whale and continued on so that the whale made its way to the open waters. Knowing exactly where they veered, the two men retraced their steps to find one of Allah's servants, Al-Khidr, a special man with a uniquely sacred mandate.

Eager to learn from this chosen servant, Prophet Musa ﷺ asked the man if he could follow him that he may learn what the man had been taught of correct guidance, *rushd*. Interestingly, the man responded that it was unlikely that Musa ﷺ would be patient with him and how could he be patient with what he had not been previously made aware of. But Prophet Musa ﷺ was insistent and assured him that *insha'Allah* he would be patient and not disobey any orders. Accepting the promise, the man instructed Prophet Musa ﷺ

not to ask about anything until he was informed of it.

What an incredible exchange between two godly men, each confident in their purpose and its modes of pursuit. We may not have been told much about Allah's servant, but we do know a bit about Prophet Musa ﷷ from other Quranic narratives. This is the man who with his brother confronts Pharaoh, who overwhelms the magicians, the one who liberates the Children of Israel. This is one of Allah's strongest messengers. Yet here, in this exchange, he expresses an unsurpassed humility in his quest for knowledge, the sacred truths of His Lord. He accepts being told that he will not be patient, and that he must not ask of matters before he is spoken to, he must follow and obey. In this alone are countless lessons.

In each of the situations that follow, Allah's servant undertakes a mission where Prophet Musa ﷷ just cannot hold back his perspective. In the first event, the men embark on a ship only for Allah's servant to damage it. In his astonishment, Prophet Musa ﷷ commented that its people would drown. What a serious thing this was! So, Allah's servant reminded him of what he had said, patience is difficult when you are not aware of the Truth of matters. Prophet Musa ﷷ acknowledged his mistake, asking for pardon and another chance.

In the narrative's second event, the servant of Allah comes across a boy which he kills. Expectedly, this triggered Prophet Musa's deepest instinct, accusing the man of killing an innocent soul, how deplorable! Again, the servant of Allah reminded Prophet Musa ﷷ of what he had said, patience is difficult with what one has not been informed. Again, the Prophet asked for pardon and added that there would not be any blame if the servant of Allah ended their companionship should this happen again. And so, the journey continued.

In the third and final event, the men reached a village whose inhabitants refused to feed or host them but the servant of Allah nevertheless took to fixing a wall for them so it would not collapse. Feeling that this was a generous act given how the villagers had treated them, Prophet Musa ﷷ expressed that he could have taken a wage. This was the parting between the two men but first the servant of Allah was to inform Prophet Musa ﷷ of the interpretation of the events for which he had little patience.

As for the ship, it belonged to poor seamen and was damaged to prevent a tyrannical king from possessing it forcibly. The boy who was killed would have exhausted his believing parents with his transgressions and disbelief. The servant of Allah only intended that Allah should exchange him for a better child, more pure and merciful. Finally, the wall was mended to protect a treasure that was hidden beneath it until its rightful owners, two orphan boys whose father was righteous, could reclaim it. Nothing, he told Prophet Musa ﵇, was done of his own accord.

Not one of us would be able to hold back their reactions to such dramatic events undertaken by a servant of Allah, let alone by anyone else. To get hung up on the miraculous details of the narrative is like endlessly arguing over how many youths there were in the cave or how long they remained. The point, rather, is to appreciate that no matter who you are, and none of us are remotely similar to Prophet Musa ﵇, you will lack the needed patience to accept let alone deal with that which you have no knowledge. To avoid passing hasty judgments on people and events potentially impeding purposeful paths or casting unwarranted doubt and disapprovals it is best to keep silent. "And do not follow that of which you have no knowledge. Indeed, the hearing, the sight, and the heart-mind – all of those – will be for such questioned" (Al-Isra' 17:36).

Our believing brothers and sisters may manifest their purpose in any number of ways. Sure, there is a shared foundation in our rituals and duties but beyond that Allah has gifted every one of us with a different combination of blessings. It is a sacred duty to make the discretionary contributions that we are uniquely capable of. I may not understand your choices or agree with your path, but as a believing member of this community, as a servant of Allah, I must have the humility, the expanse of chest, to dignify you, to honour your potential worth in the sight of Allah and admit my potential insignificance. The apparent urgency, significance, and righteousness of any one path in no way diminishes the value of other paths that remain obscure, veiled by the mercies of Allah to achieve what He wills.

Dhul Qarnayn ﵇: When you know your purpose and have the means to fulfill it

The last narrative in the surah brings us to the other extreme on the spectrum of purpose. We started with the youth of the cave, whose situation became so dire that they had to retreat in order to avoid being killed or coerced into renouncing their faith. Now we come to the story of Dhul Qarnayn - the one with two horns - who not only had a clear awareness of his purpose but was also given the means to achieve his mission wherever he went. While no ordinary person has this kind of power, much like the servant of Allah in the previous narrative, many are sufficiently blessed to be able to fulfill their discretionary purpose including what may not be strictly required but that they deem a part of their duty in return for Allah's gifts. These are the two glaring lessons of this story: to know what must be done and to do it, not for material gain or celebrity, but simply because Allah has put you, blessed you, in a position to do so.

Dhul Qarnayn was a man of great ability. Allah had established him in the earth by granting him a grasp of the causality of everything, enabling him to pursue causes. To know the causes is to understand how an object, event, process, or state leads to a certain effect, partially or wholly. By Allah's command, Dhul Qarnayn had a mastery of how things happened and as such he knew exactly what he could do to make them happen. He knew how things led to or followed from other things in the context of societies and the cosmos.

Traveling westward with the setting sun, Dhul Qarnayn came across a people whose corruptive behaviors had polluted a nearby spring, so much so that its waters had become muddy. With the choice granted to him by Allah to either punish or reform them, Dhul Qarnayn took the middle path. Punishing those who were unjust, while kindly dealing with and rewarding those who believed and did good. Then he went on to pursue another cause.

Coming to the rising of the sun, he found a people who had not developed any protection or shelter from its heat. More accurately, Allah had not provided a shield for them. But He had compassed Dhul Qarnayn with the needed expertise and again he was positioned to come to their aid, though the Quran does not tell us exactly how he does that. Then he went on to pursue another cause.

Eventually, Dhul Qarnayn reaches a pass between two cliffs, where he found a people who could barely understand any speech. Somehow, they managed to convey to him that *Ya'juj* and *Ma'juj*, great corrupters in the land, were wreaking havoc on their lives. Could he help them build a barricade between the two sides? While they offered Dhul Qarnayn a bounty for his efforts, he declined informing them that Allah's blessings were better. He then directed them on how to help him construct an impenetrable wall that would protect them as long as Allah willed.

Through this narrative we can see how purpose demands the exercise of justice, the application of knowledge, and the employment of material resources and physical strength. All these are blessing from a Merciful and Generous Lord, the ultimate enabler.

Allah is the ally of the believers easing their missions, facilitating and illuminating their path. "And as for those who strive hard for Us, We will guide them to Our Paths" (Al-'Ankabut 29:69). Surah Al-Kahf teaches the indispensable value of devotion to Allah. "And as for those who settle on piety, We increase them in piety and give them their reinforcement" (Muhammad 47:17). Its stories help us navigate the challenges of purpose by penetrating the heart-mind. The surah is intended to strengthen our determination, educate and humble us, while encouraging us to engage with the world, to seek to rectify all that needs something of the blessing that Allah has given us. "Surely as for those who believe and work righteousness their Lord will guide them by their faith" (Yunus 10:9).

We may seem small and insignificant in the grand scheme of life but what we believe and how we behave contribute to the broader trajectory of our communities and society, that then impacts the even broader and more long-term ways of the universe. That said, we are significant to ourselves even in the very short term. "Say, 'Shall we inform you of those who are the greatest losers concerning their deeds? Those whose efforts become lost in the life of this world while they thought they were doing [constructing] well" (Al-Kahf 18:103-104). Those who disbelieve in Allah's *ayat* and His meeting will have their works debased, remaining in the earthly realm since that is all that they cared for. Whoever hopes for Allah's meeting works righteousness and does not to associate anything with Him.

PART 3

Connectivity

Al-Fayood: The Overflowing

In my sleep, where the shackles of wakefulness, of the material world, are broken, I occasionally enter the realm of Truth and Beauty. Dreams, visions as some might call them, have influenced my relationship with Allah since childhood. And though we must be cautious about dream-telling, what we see in our sleep is sometimes intended by Allah to warn, guide or give us fortitude and hope. In the Battle of Badr, Allah diminished the size of the enemy army in Prophet Muhammad's ﷺ dream to give courage to the Muslims and eliminate potential disputes among them (Al-Anfal 8:43). Prophet Ibrahim عليه السلام saw himself sacrificing his son in a dream, a trial from Allah to test his mettle (As-Saffat 37:102). And then there is the multiplicity of dreams and their meanings in the story of Prophet Yusuf عليه السلام, from the first that foretold his journey, to those of his prison mates, to that of the king. What happens in our sleep can indeed be most profound, and so it has been with me on several occasions of which I will share one here.

There I was, sat reading from a book that I thought to be a vintage Quran with yellowed pages and dark print, the *ayat* arranged in the same rhythmic pattern as I was familiar with. But I hadn't read such words before, truthful as they appeared to be. My suspicions were confirmed when I read what was one of Allah's names: *Al-Fayood*, The Overflowing. I stopped. I stared at the page. I read and re-read. *Al-Fayood*? I couldn't go beyond it. I had never read or heard this name recited amid the ninety-nine beautiful names of Allah all too familiar to any believer. I awoke in puzzlement.

I thought about it, turned it over and over in my mind. Recalling the dream to my mother that morning, tears streaming down my cheeks, for the honour I knew that I had just received. The root of *fayood*, that which abounds or overflows, is *f-y-d*, meaning flood, overflow, abound. It is found in the Quran, describing the tears of the believers when they recognize the truth or when they are disappointed with being unable to strive in the way of Allah. "And when they hear what has been sent down to the Messenger, you see their eyes overflowing (*tafeed*) with tears because of what they know of the Truth, saying 'Our Lord we believe so record us among the witnesses,'" (Al-Ma'idah 5:83). Similarly, those who could not accompany Prophet Muhammad ﷺ in battle because there were no more mounts left turned back with eyes overflowing with tears (At-Tawbah 9:92). That day, my eyes overflowed with the tears of reverence and humility. Who was I to be given such a privilege? Sobbing.

Like everything we know, we learn about Allah through His names. "Allah, there is no deity except Him, to Him belong the beautiful names" (Taha 20:8). We are exhorted to call Him by them, for each name is a special comfort, a corresponding inner conditioning for the believer. "And to Allah belong the best names, so invoke Him by them…" (Al-A'raf 7:180). We choose the name or names that suit our invocation, that assure us of the exact powers required. When we seek forgiveness we call on the Forgiver, the Grantor of Forgiveness – *Al-Ghaffar, Al-Ghafoor*, for strength we call on the Strong, the Durable – *Al-Qawiyy, Al-Mateen*, for justice we call on the Judge, the Just – *Al-Hakim, Al-'Adl*, for mercy and love on the Merciful and Friendly – *Ar-Rahman, Al-Wadood*, and so on. They are all His names, His attributes. Whether we call on one name or all, it is the same. "Say, 'Invoke Allah or invoke the Merciful, whichever you invoke for Him are [all] the beautiful names…" (Al-Isra' 17:110).

His names are His Truth, all come together in the One, the Magnificence that He is. "He is Allah, other than whom there is no god. Knower of the unseen and the observed. He is the Merciful, the Giver of Mercy. He is Allah, other than whom there is no god. The King, the Holy, the Peace, the Secure, the Hegemonic, the Dear, the Compeller, the Supreme. Exalted is He above what they associate with Him. He is Allah, the Creator, the Brilliant, the Designer. For Him belong the beautiful names. Whatever is in the skies and the earth glorify Him. And He is the Dear, the Wise" (Al-Hashr 59:22-24). He is Allah. *Allah*.

Prophet Muhammad ﷺ taught that "Allah has ninety-nine names, one hundred less one; whoever takes stock of them enters Jannah" (Sahih Bukhari). These names are not listed as a complete set anywhere in the Quran or hadith. Instead, the version that has attained consensus today was compiled by Muslim scholars based on meticulous examination of those sources. It is of the majority opinion that these names are not the only possibilities as Prophet Muhammad ﷺ also stated: "Oh Allah you are my Lord, and I am your servant, son of Your (male) servant and son of your (female) servant, my forelock is in Your Hand, over me is your judgement, just for me is Your verdict: I ask You by every name that you named Yourself with, or sent down in Your Book, or You taught to any of Your creatures, or that You have kept in the knowledge of the Unseen that is with You, that You make the Quran the spring of my heart and the light of my chest, and the assuaging of my sorrow and the departing of my worry" (Musnad Ahmad). Might I have been one of those creatures. *Al-Fayood*, the One who Abounds, the Overflowing. Allah is the Overflowing in Light, Mercy, Provision, Forgiveness, Attentiveness and indeed He causes all kinds of things to overflow including the rivers, oceans, rains, and the tears of believers. Allah is *Al-Fayood*. How my eyes still well with tears as I contemplate the possibility.

What is it to *know* Allah, to take stock or preserve Allah's names as Prophet Muhammad ﷺ stated? It is to think deeply about each name, to study its mention in the Quran and Sunnah, to observe how it is expressed in everything around you, make connections, so that you can internalize its meanings and act accordingly. Stop and contemplate at every introduction to Allah in the Quran, for every name is a new invitation, a key to understanding why He places emphasis on certain attributes as opposed to others in a specific *ayah*. How does that impact meaning? How does it affect your understanding of His words? Can you extend your understanding to your own life and the world around you? Every believer must strive to know Him more than anything else in their life and then heed that knowledge as they journey onward. This is a very personal experience.

There is a limit to language and other forms of expression including the incredible perfection and beauty of nature that aim to teach us about Allah compared with how we ultimately come to *know* and apply His Truth. No two people who *know* Allah would describe their knowledge in the same way though the beauty and light that radiates from such individuals is testimony to the truth that their purified and refined selves have captured. They know that their ability to fulfill their purpose in all its dimensions is dependent on the depth of their knowledge of Allah, He for whose service they were born and wish to die.

Any believer's knowledge of Allah starts with this singular Truth: He is ONE. "Allah has not taken any son, nor has there ever been a god with Him. If it were such, then each god would have taken what it created, and some would have sought dominance over others. Glory to Allah regarding what they ascribe" (Al-Mu'minun 23:91). Allah is One and Only. No one shares in His dominion either by familial relation or divine competition. We can clearly see this in how the universe responds to Him, how it is regulated in an orderly way, and simply makes sense as He gradually allows us to unravel its logic. To know Him, therefore, is to practice both *inqiyad,* or submission to Allah's guidance and *ikhlas*, which is to do so exclusively.

Our connection to Allah is that of absolute dependence. A dependence that is not reciprocal. We depend on Him while He in no way depends on us. "I do not want from them provision, nor do I want them to feed Me. Indeed, it is Allah who is the Provider, Possessor of the Strength, the Durable" (Adh-Dhariyyat 51:57-58). He is not in need of anyone or anything. "And your Lord is the Self-Sufficient imbued with mercy, if He wills, He could eliminate you and succeed after you whatever He wills as He propagated you from the progeny of other people" (Al-An'am 6:133). This is not to be taken harshly or as a threat, it is intended to underscore that what we do, we do to and for ourselves.

Everything we do to nurture this special connection is reflected back on us. In other words, when we excel in cultivating our relationship with Allah, we benefit ourselves, and when we fall short, we harm no one but ourselves. Prophet Muhammad ﷺ taught us that "Allah, Exalted is He, has decreed: 'Oh children of Adam, if you will commit yourselves and worship Me, then I will enrich your hearts and deliver you from poverty. But if you refuse, I will fill your hearts with concern, and allow you to stagnate in the poverty of your own selves'" (Musnad Ahmad). It is in our commitment to Allah that we uplift our hearts, honour each other, and guard other creatures. When our commitment to Allah wanes so does the beauty and balance of our world. Only He knows how we should behave to preserve life's delicate balance. Only He can rectify our deeds even as we try our best.

How often have I heard people say, 'I love Allah' and then go on to live in accordance with their whims. Some people justify not praying, and even rationalize sinning, with the pretence that it is okay because they love Allah! By binding our love for Allah with our followership of Prophet Muhammad ﷺ, the Quran clearly rejects this reasoning. "If you love Allah, then follow me, Allah will love you and forgive your sins. And Allah is Grantor of Forgiveness, Giver of Mercy" (Al-'Imran 3:31). To love Allah, just as it is when you love anyone special you must be willing to communicate with them in an appropriate way, respect their likes and dislikes, maintain their trust, keep their confidence, preserve their wealth, defend their territory. However, when it is Allah that you love, unlike any worldly affair, all of these demands are intended to benefit you not Allah. No one understood this better than Prophet Muhammad ﷺ. Neglecting his teachings but then claiming to love Allah is simply delusional. Love is never based on ignorance or self-soothing bias; it must be grounded in belief and good works, the likes and dislikes of who we claim to love.

There is so much that we can learn about Allah from His likes and dislikes as elaborated in the Quran and Sunnah. Prophet Muhammad ﷺ taught that "Allah is Beautiful, and He loves beauty, and He loves the magnanimity of affairs and hates pettiness" (Sahih Muslim). This is a call to rise above, to nurture a resilient personality that not only does good but that can pardon, forgive and avoid vanities. Those who can be abundant, spending in good times and in hard times, controlling even suppressing their anger, and pardoning people for all sorts of shortcomings (Al-'Imran 3:134). He loves those who are neither disheartened nor weakened when struggling in His way (Al-'Imran 3:146). Those who remain equitable irrespective of their feelings towards those with whom they are dealing (Al-Ma'idah 5:42). Allah loves those who put their trust in Him (Al-'Imran 3:159) basing their decisions on His guidance with complete confidence in His decree regardless of the forces that may oppose them (Al-'Imran 3:173). They are ready and willing to fight in His way (As-Saff 61:4) defending everything that is fair, just and truthful. All the while purifying themselves in heart and body (At-Tawbah 9:108) and giving gratitude (Az-Zumar 39:7). There is so much more that Allah loves but that is for you to discover.

Understandably, Allah does not like anything evil or unjust. This includes the mistreatment of parents, usurpation of the rights of relatives, the poor, the needy, travelers, and orphans. He does not like spendthrifts and wasters, meanness in actions or words, murder, fornication and all kinds of sexual impropriety, cheating in business, pursuit of what we know nothing of, hubris and arrogance, and the association of any partners with Him. All of these actions are hateful in the sight of Allah (Al-Isra' 17:38). He does not like corruptors, liars, hypocrites, aggressors, betrayers, ingrates, boasters, misers, and sinners. Nor does He like those who reject faith, who break their promises, abuse others, desecrate nature, and spread immorality, including those who ally themselves with any of the individuals or groups who behave as such.

Our connection to Allah is unfailingly reflected in the quality of our beings, which is not separate from our treatment of others, both human and non-human. The strength of our connection is a function of how hard we try to align ourselves with everything good, everything He loves, and distance ourselves from everything evil, everything He hates. Our efforts to come closer to Allah involve sincere and tireless performance of all the tiers of our purpose: rituals, duties and discretionary contributions. Every narrative involving Allah's righteous servants in the Quran is a revelation in this regard, helping us to understand how to be in this world so that we can *be* with Him in the next. This is by far the highest honour. Ever.

Two of those narratives concern two outstanding women whose connections with Allah are beautifully reflected in their sublime knowledge of His failsafe responsiveness to those who wholeheartedly turn to Him. Neither woman is addressed by her name in the Quran, not as a diminution of their status or the magnitude of the events they experienced but in keeping with the Quran's method of allowing generalizations to others. The two incidents could involve any member of our community. Of course, not any member would have handled these situations as these two special women did, but the guidance of Allah and the rulings that He decreed on their account are universally applicable. For those who are seeking a closer connection to Allah, examining each woman's approach is invaluable.

One of those two women is a mother of the believers, 'Aisha bint Abu Bakr ﷺ. She relates to us how during an expedition she was accidently left behind after she had gone searching for a necklace. No one noticed that she was not in her carriage as it was covered, that is, until the army reached the next stop. Finding the camp had departed she sat down to rest, hoping that someone would come back to get her. Soon it was night and she fell asleep. The next morning, she was spotted by one of the emigrants, Safwan ibn Mu'attal, an honourable young man, who had been tasked with checking if anything had been accidently forgotten. He offered her his camel while he led on foot. Their arrival together, however, gave occasion to the rumor mongers to circulate a scandal.

The word *ifk* – intentional fabrication of falsehood, lies, or slander – occurs three times in the Quran. Two of those mentions are here, in the story of 'Aisha ﷺ in Surah An-Nur. "Indeed, those who came with the slander (*ifk*) are a group among you. Do not think it bad for you; rather it is good for you. For every person among them is what he has earned of the sin, and he who took upon himself the greater portion from among them – for him is a great torment" (An-Nur 24:11). These people thought this to be a trifling affair, but it was very serious in Allah's estimation. "When you spread it by your tongues and you said with your mouths what you have no knowledge of, and you consider it trivial, and it is with Allah great" (An-Nur 24:15). Evil is spread through people's tongues and what their mouths articulate, enticing others to hear it and sullying the senses of everyone involved. It spreads when people speak of something of which they have no knowledge, when they assume the worst of others, and do not extend the courtesy and discretion they would want extended to themselves. Matters are only made worse by a dismissive attitude regarding the dislikes of Allah.

This slander was a serious injustice, not because 'Aisha ؓ was the wife of the Prophet ﷺ, a mothers of the believers, which is not mentioned in the Quranic narrative, but because there was no evidence. "Why did they not come with four witnesses regarding the matter. So, if they had not brought four witnesses so they are with Allah liars" (An-Nur 24:13). This was an innocent person whose life was literally being destroyed by her own people. A pure and loyal wife having to withstand being told by her husband in front of her family, "If you did it, ask Allah to forgive you, and if you didn't do it say it." How incredibly hurtful is that? 'Aisha ؓ answered by saying, "Indeed, it has settled in your hearts. If I said I am innocent, and Allah knows I am innocent you would not believe me. And if I say that I did it and I didn't do it, you will believe me. And I am not going to say a word other than what the father of Yusuf said," at which point she turned her back to them saying "So beautiful patience, and Allah is the One resorted to for help regarding what you describe."

Like Yacoub, the father of Yusuf, a name she could not recall in her grief, 'Aisha ؓ resigned herself to a beautiful patience – *sabrun jameel*. This was her family; these were her people. "Why, when you heard it, did not the believing men and the believing women assume good of their own selves, and say 'this is a clear lie (*ifk*)'" (An-Nur 24:12). *Their own selves*, of each other. The *Ummah* is one body, it is *intra*dependent. "And why did you not when you heard it say 'It is not for us to speak of this. Glory to you. This is a great defamation.' Allah cautions you that you may never return to this. Ever. If you are believers" (An-Nur 24:16-17). Despite the seriousness of the crime, Allah offered the perpetrators room for repentance and potential for forgiveness. "And Allah makes clear for you the *ayat* and Allah is Knowing, Wise" (An-Nur 24:18).

Casual talk about people's honour and their personal affairs is prohibited for believers. People that engage in such sins must be corrected before their indiscretions lead to wider social ills. "Indeed, those who love to see immorality spread among those who believe have a painful torment in this life and the Hereafter. And Allah knows and you know not" (An-Nur 24:19). Whether it is through slander or any other method, the spread or normalization of immorality including all forms of sexual impropriety are strongly proscribed in Islam.

Breaking the barrier of shame, the human state of modesty or *hayaa'* that compels us to avoid all kinds of sins, is a great loss to individuals and communities.

'Aisha ﷺ could barely believe what eventually transpired. Traditional accounts put her suffering at around a month before the *ayat* confirming her innocence and reprimanding her accusers were revealed. "By Allah," she admitted, "I never thought I am worthy in the sight of Allah, that He will send the Quran to be recited to the end of time confirming my innocence." She could see the Quran being revealed to Prophet Muhammad ﷺ because his demeanour changed, and he smiled saying "your innocence came from the heavens." Everyone rejoiced. Her gratitude to Allah was immeasurable.

"Those who abuse (*yarmuna*) chaste, unassuming (*ghafilat*), believing women, are damned in the world and Hereafter and for them is a great punishment" (An-Nur 24:23). *Yarmuna* - is to literally 'commit an excess against' which encompasses more than speech to include all kinds of transgressions against the *ghafilat*, the innocent, unassuming who are just going about their own business. In vindicating 'Aisha ﷺ Allah's response served to reform her society and every society thereafter. Allah could have simply revealed an *ayat* confirming her innocence, but instead in His infinite wisdom and mercy, He taught us just how serious sexual impropriety is in all of its forms. Here in Surah An-Nur – The Light – we make the necessary links between our purity, chastity, and connection to Allah. Through her suffering and turning to Allah, her patience and invocations, the community was corrected until, as she rightly noted, the end of times. "And had it not been for Allah's favour on you and His Mercy! And Allah is Compassionate, Giver of Mercy" (An-Nur 24:20).

Our other exemplar is a woman by the name of Khaula bint Thalaba. She too had suffered a great injustice. Like 'Aisha ﷺ Khaula's knowledge of Allah, His justice and grant of dignity to His servants, saw her through a major crisis and resulted in the rectification of the broader community. Khaula, may she be honoured by Allah, was married to Aus ibn al-Samit, whom she reportedly loved and from whom she had several children. Upon losing his temper, as most inevitably do at some point in a marital relationship, Aus would pronounce *zihar* – a custom in pre-Islamic times where a husband would disparage his wife by stating that she meant *no more to him than his mother's back*. Through these words a man signified that he no longer had marital responsibilities including intimacy with his wife resulting in emotional and physical hurt while also damaging the family.

Khaula's indignation with her husband's insolence inspired her to take the matter to Allah and His Messenger. Her keen inner sense and virtuous nature knew instinctively that such words must be unacceptable to the Lord of justice and mercy. Disrespect to both wife and mother, and an affront to the sacred marital relationship, must be impermissible. A man is simply not at liberty to abuse or deprive his wife and family of the duties he owes them. She had emotional, physical and material rights that he was obliged to satisfy. No fit of rage could justify otherwise. So, Khaula vowed not to allow Aus to touch her until the matter was settled by Allah and His Messenger. *Al-Mujadilah* – the one who argues – is the title of the surah as it describes her persistence in approaching Prophet Muhammad ﷺ to find a solution for this odious marital behavior. The Prophet ﷺ, however, would repeatedly turn Khaula away with no satisfactory answer as he had not received any revelation concerning the matter. But she would return to argue and reargue her case.

In due course, as with Allah's *sunan*, Allah would reveal that the practise of *zihar* was not only false, but it was also harsh and sinful with no place within the boundaries of the marital relationship. "Allah has heard the speech of she who argues with you concerning her husband and her complaints to Allah and Allah hears your exchanges. Indeed, Allah is Hearer, Seer. Those who impose *zihar* on their women, they are not their mothers. Indeed, their mothers are they who gave birth to them. And indeed, they say this contemptible speech and falsehood. And indeed, Allah is the Grantor Pardon, Forgiveness" (Al-Mujadilah 58:1-2). The reprimand did not stop there. Reoffending would have been all too easy. From henceforth those who committed this sin were subject to expiation.

"And those who impose *zihar* on their women then retract what they said, must free a neck [someone in bondage/slavery] before they touch each other. As such, you are admonished. And Allah is with what you do aware. So he who cannot find [someone to free], then fasting two months consecutively before they touch each other. So, he who cannot withstand [fasting] then feed sixty needy people. It is as such that you may believe in Allah and his Messenger, and these are the boundaries of Allah, and for the disbelievers is a painful torment" (Al-Mujadilah 58:3-4). Men could no longer behave with impunity. Now there was restitution and retribution – a penalty that contributed both to personal reform and to rebalancing life that the injustice of *zihar* represented. As I reflect on Allah's response, I realize how the enormity of the expiation demonstrated the gravity of the offence. Two consecutive months of fasting. Not one like Ramadan but two whole months without a break or the feeding of sixty people. That is what it would take to rebalance the marital relationship, to reform the man's behavior, and to fix the harms that may not be so obvious to family and community. This is Justice. This is Allah. Ever mindful of His servants, vindicating those who turn to Him when they are wronged.

Connecting with Allah is the most beautiful and reassuring dimension of this life. You can connect with Him any time and anywhere. *Alhamdlillah*, He is pervasive. Wherever you look, whether toward the east or the west He is there. He is the Expansive, *Al-Waasi'*, the Knowing, *Al-'Alim*. "And for Allah is the east and the west. So, wherever you turn there is the Face of Allah. Indeed, Allah is Expansive, Knowing" (Al-Baqarah 2:115). East and west are inseparable, they meet, overlap. Whatever is to the east or to the west depends on where you are positioned. The Kaaba is to the east when I am in Ottawa, and the west when I am in Kuala Lumpur.

It is not the direction to which we turn that matters. It is our heedfulness of Allah, our deep respect for His guidance, and our mercy toward His creation. "It is not virtue (*birr*) that you turn your faces toward the east or the west but virtue is [found in] those who believe in Allah and the Last Day and the angels and the Book and the prophets; and giving wealth for His love to the relatives and the orphans and the needy and the wayfarer and those who ask and those in bondage (*fi al-riqab*); and establishing prayer and giving zakat and those who fulfill promises if they promise; and the patient in tragedy and harm and during hardship. These are the ones who are truthful, and these are the ones who are heedful" (Al-Baqarah 2:177). *Birr* is not a mechanical exercise but a conditioning of the heart. Humility. Sincerity. Mercy. Connection. It is an affirmation of loyalty, servitude.

Those who worship Allah, who believe in Him, know that He is close. "And if my servants ask you about me, verily, I am close. Answering the appeal of the appellant if they appeal to Me. That they may answer to Me and believe in Me that they may be guided" (Al-Baqarah 2:186). What a beautiful affirmation of Allah's presence in our hearts and in our lives. *Truly, I am close.* Allah hears, sees, and knows what we reveal and conceal. He does not *need* us to ask. But asking, appealing, pleading, invoking, all these acts, condition our hearts reminding us of the nature of our dependency and our vital need for Him.

We must understand that to answer to a call or appeal does not necessarily mean to fulfill it, let alone fulfill it with any immediacy. It means *to respond to it.* The response may not come in the form we expect or even desire. When it comes from Allah, however, it is the response that best meets our needs and takes account of all the variables that we do not even know have to be accounted for. Sincerity in our *du'aa*, invocations, includes resignation to Allah's decree, the wisdom of which in many cases we will only fully understand in the next life. Whether we bear with patience like 'Aisha ﵂ or we commit to action and persistently argue our case like Khaula ﵂ we must remain steadfast and confident that Allah does respond.

Trusting the process requires us to answer to Him and to believe in Him - *fal yastajibu li, wal yu'minu bi.* This is not a chronological ordering that means we ask Allah first, then He responds, then we believe. He is always responding, and we are always answering and believing. It is an indivisible occurrence. There is a certainty that the believer experiences when invoking His names, asking for help, seeking His guidance. He will respond, He is responding.

It is impossible to strive to connect with Allah through all the dimensions of our worship and not fall in love. For me, it is impossible. He is the source of all good and beauty, the entirety of humanity could not produce anywhere near the perfection that He has provided for us. Look at the world, the skies, mountains, oceans; look at your food, the colours, tastes, varieties; look at the animals and insects; look at the seasons; look at your own self! His universe is breathtaking. It is people who spoil the good, commit injustice, and corrupt on account of their limited awareness or disbelief. "Whatever befalls you of good is from Allah, and whatever befalls you of harm is from yourself. And We have sent you [Muhammad] to the people as a messenger, and Allah is sufficient as Witness" (An-Nisa' 4:79). It is crazy to me how so many people blame Allah for the havoc that they are wreaking on themselves and others.

Let's be clear, to love Him does not preclude fearing him. "And as for he who fears the station of His Lord, and forbids the self from desire [whim], then indeed the Jannah will be his refuge" (An-Nazi'at 79: 40-41). There is a threshold where the boundaries of love and fear are blurred. I am what I am, and I do what I do because I love Allah, but I also fear displeasing Him because I am aware of His Power, at least to the extent that He has permitted me to appreciate. I do not want any part of His torment but the fear of disappointing Him is what stirs my heart. Prophet Muhammad ﷺ told us that there are "three whose eyes shall never see the Fire: one whose eyes were watchful in the way of Allah; one whose eyes were filled with tears in awe of Allah;

and one whose eyes were closed regarding that which Allah had prohibited them to look upon" (Al-Tabarani). May you and I and all our loved ones be among those three. *Ameen.*

In a sacred narration Allah says, "I am as My servant supposes Me to be, and I am with him if he remembers Me. So, if he mentions Me in himself, I mention him in Myself. And if he remembers Me in company, I remember him in a better company. And if he advances toward Me an inch, I advance toward him an arm's length. And if he advances toward Me and arm's length, I advance toward him a yard. And if he comes to Me walking, I come to Him running" (Sahih Bukhari). This is Allah, my Lord of Abundance, of Overflowing generosity, mercy, care, provision, wisdom and every other attribute that He approves for Himself.

Inspiration of the Nafs

Love envelops the believer. There is this deep certainty that the highest calling of the *nafs* – the self – is to love for the sake of Allah including the love of one's own self, desiring for its success in this life and the next. I find a great lesson in the story of Thamud, an ancient Arabian tribe, that denied the essence of the *nafs*, its possibility for transgression (Ash-Shams 91:11). Intoxicated by the abundance of blessings from Allah, with palatial and mountain dwellings and authority in the land, Thamud believed the *nafs* to be beyond sin, disbelieving in the One who created and equipped it. Though not obvious to them, the denial of the nature of the *nafs* is the most devastating of all acts for the welfare of a group and its individual members. It is the greatest indication of self-destruction, sooner or later.

Knowing and caring for myself for the sake of Allah has been a lifelong journey. In loving for the sake of Allah, our first admission is His presence. We love *who* we love because of their heedfulness, their firm belief in and service of Allah. Likewise, we love *what* we love because it is good and pure, because it eases or reinforces our heedfulness. We, you and I, are no less subject to this kind of love than those we bestow it upon. I must love myself for the sake of Allah, to love everything about myself that is pure and strives for His Countenance and to dislike everything about myself that inhibits my connection to Him. How else can I identify what needs improvement? No one is born with this kind of self-awareness; it is developed over many years of self-reflection and connection, through the experiences that reveal to us the strengths and weaknesses of our *nafs*. Without this ongoing effort, I would be like Thamud, captive to the transgressions of my *nafs* yet at the same time denying such a possibility.

Allah, Glory to Him, created the *nafs*, preparing and ordering her before making her mate and propagating from them both, many men and women. "And the *nafs* and He who ordered her (*sawaha*), inspiring her as to her rebelliousness (*fujuraha*) and her heedfulness (*taqwaha*). He has succeeded who purifies her. And he has failed who debases her" (Ash-Shams 91:6-10). Prophet Salih ﷺ was sent by Allah to Thamud to awaken their *nafs*, to urge them to purify it, reminding them of Allah's favours, exhorting them to worship Allah alone and obey His commands that they may succeed. To support His messenger's call, Allah provided him with an *ayah*, a sacred she-camel – *naqat Allah* – that emerged from a rock. This beautiful and unique creature was to be left unharmed, grazing freely in Allah's pasture and drinking from Thamud's water source on designated days. This was a test of obedience.

I can imagine how it must have been for Thamud given their denial of the possibility of sin, their delusion that through their power and wealth they were above the law. I can see how those who are given so much can lose themselves in arrogance and greed. I can see how even the slightest command to share with another of Allah's creation becomes too much, as Thamud denied Allah they also denied His Dominion, His Messenger and His allocation of resources among His servants. They wanted it all.

Despite witnessing the *ayah* of the she-camel, and receiving clear instructions concerning her safety, Thamud became consumed with resentment regarding her mere existence. She was an unwelcome agitation to the *nafs*, the collective self, embodying the people's conscience. She threatened their hegemony, what they perceived as the singular determination of their own destiny. To get rid of her would have no consequence except to increase them in power and wealth. Without a god, the *nafs* could not transgress. It was not long before they hamstrung and slaughtered Allah's she-camel in open rebellion calling on Prophet Salih ﷺ to bring on Allah's wrath. Within three days, three short days, Thamud were punished for their sins as they had been warned. A devastating earthquake and thunderous blast reduced them to lifeless corpses in their dwellings, *fasawaha* - the *nafs*, had been ordered once again.

The world in which we live is riddled with Thamud, hurting from the disorder and loathing of so many *anfus* (sg. *nafs*); the arrogance and greed is so rampant that my *nafs* and those of so many others – no matter how strong or loving – can only be a contribution to a future victory that will inevitably arrive. I know that so many are trying to live as I do, striving to know the *nafs*, diving into the Quran that I may recall her inspiration and strive for success.

The Merciful has given the *nafs* many designations, *asma'*, to teach us about her diverse nature and needs. I am of course of *bani* Adam, a child of the first *nafs* in human form – *insan* – given a code of conduct to ensure the preservation of my dignity and respect the purposeful paths of all creation. Allah, in His infinite justice, has provided all nations with messengers to convey His guidance, warn of His wrath, and assure of His mercy and forgiveness. "And for every ummah [nation/community] is a messenger. So when their messenger comes, judgement will be applied among them with equity, and they will not be wronged" (Yunus 10:47). Every group and its members are invited to follow the right path, to purify their collective *nafs* and individual *anfus*. And to Prophet Muhammad ﷺ it was said, "Indeed, We have sent you with the Truth as a bringer of good tidings and warner. And there was no ummah except to which was dedicated a warner" (Fatir 35:24). The provision of messengers in different times and places meant that there were many paths leading to the One, all of them illuminated by the same Light.

The Quran and its Messenger were a gift to all of humanity. Nevertheless, it was common then as it is now for some people to reject the Messenger ﷺ because he did not belong to *their group*. "And they said, 'Why was this Quran not sent down on a great man from [one of] the two towns?'" (Az-Zukhruf 43:31). The disbelievers were beside themselves as to why the Quran was not revealed to a man from among them, someone of greater power and influence – at least as they perceived it. "And we did not send into a town any warner except that its elite said, 'Indeed, we are disbelievers in that with which you have been sent.' And they said, 'We are more abundant in wealth and children, and we are not to be tormented'" (Saba' 34:34-35). This idea that one is not to be held to account, that one is beyond sinning, is the surest path to connecting to the lowest self. But the *nafs* knows instinctively when it receives Truth. It is only a matter of acceptance or rejection, to purify or debase.

Many philosophers, psychologists, scientists, theologians, and others have explored and theorized about the self. Thinkers of the Enlightenment, who perhaps thought that they were introducing something new when they rejected the concept of sin, the transgression of the *self*, were merely following in the footsteps of their disbelieving predecessors. Seeking to release people from divine authority, thinkers like Voltaire, Rousseau and Kant grounded moral behavior in human reason and ethics. Injustice no longer violated divine law and did not require repentance. People were capable of formulating their own moral judgements, freeing themselves of the guilt that accompanied divine sanction. Although I can agree with Kant that ethical behavior is a rational duty, this does not alter the idea of sin as a religious and indispensable Truth. The first is required for the harmonious coexistence of disbelievers with believers, the second as a source of knowledge, rectification, and elevation for believers. The concept of sin may have been misused by the church to control people's lives, but in Islam it is an authoritative truth necessary for the security, control, and connection with the self.

But what happens when sin, as Rousseau sought to demonstrate, is merely regarded as socially motivated behavior rather than innate evil? What happens when we abandon the Creator's manual of the self and all its rich remedies for our human ailments? This knowledge is foundational for the validity of academic disciplines that deal with human and social behavior. Even more broadly it is crucial for human welfare on an individual and collective basis. The Enlightenment's decoupling of sin and human nature had serious implications for the understanding and management of the self. Some thinkers separated the self from the body, denied it permanence, connected and disconnected it, elevated and debased it, factualized and fictionalized it. Some attempted to convince us that we could not understand the self at all, it is illusive and ever-changing. As a result, concepts of guilt, rectification, and responsibility have been greatly distorted in modern secular thought.

A most stark example can be found in the sinful, downright evil, behavior of soldiers in war, progressively explained away as trauma, mental illness, or some form of environmental response over which they had no or little control. The preparation of the self and the nature of the battle are not even footnotes in examining the aftermath of war. Bessel van der Kolk, author of the New York Times Best Seller *The Body Keeps Score*, goes even further to argue that the heinous acts which result in trauma-related symptoms are legitimate psychological responses to overwhelming events. He tells us how Tom, a Vietnam war veteran, who went on a rampage killing innocent villagers and raping a woman *suffered* moral injury as he was haunted by the memories of his crimes. Tom was considered a trauma survivor who was worthy of a non-judgemental space to process his thoughts and heal! Two-million, 2 000 000, Vietnamese civilians and soldiers lost their lives due to the American invasion on their country – a country they only sought to keep united. Tom's case demonstrates how the Enlightenment's emphasis on reason and understanding had become a travesty for crime and impunity.

Compare this case to that of Mohammad Ali Clay, one of the greatest boxers of all time, who refused to fight in that same war based on conscientious objection. Clay believed the war to be unjust noting that the Vietnamese people had never harmed his country. His belief in Allah and Islamic notions of mercy and justice led Clay to oppose the war and refuse to serve. Even as he was charged with draft evasion, banned from fighting, stripped of his fighting titles, and revocation of his passport he held his ground eventually winning a Supreme Court case against the United States for denying his conscientious objector status. Through a deep connection to self, Clay recognized who the real victim was and decided to take no part in harming himself or others. I can't help but think of Aaron Bushnell, an active member of the US Airforce, who set himself on fire outside the Israeli Embassy in Washington, D.C., while crying "Free Palestine!" Once he had recognized what Clay had understood close to sixty years ago, his heart broke. No Palestinian had ever harmed his country. I only wish he had taken Clay's path and spared his precious life.

The amount of corruption, confusion, contradiction, and pure speculation regarding the *nafs*, is part of the explosion of mental and physical illnesses worldwide, and our inability to deal with them effectively. The institution of the church that so greatly upset Enlightenment thinkers has been replaced by an insidious capitalism that maintains even greater power and control over the individual because it has convinced so many of the self's immunity to transgression. Fortunately, the self is not a human construct, and if we are to connect with its higher dimension, to turn to it in love and compassion, that we may achieve dignity and respect each other's paths, then we must turn to its Creator.

Muslim scholars have drawn on the Quran, hadith, and mystical legends to examine the *nafs* and present to believers some understanding of this central concept. For most the *nafs* is a non-physical entity that was inspired by Allah regarding its potential for wickedness and righteousness. Although not inherently evil, the *nafs* has tendencies to pursue passions and pleasures, committing injustices against itself, if it is not reigned in and purified.

From the Quran, the scholars gathered that the *nafs* could exhibit three states or alternatively pass through three progressive stages. *An-nafs al-amara* or the self that commands into temptations, choosing to ignore or override the instructions that it has received to be righteous and commit to rectification. Spoken by Prophet Yusuf ﷺ in the context of asserting his innocence, the Quranic *ayat* states: "And I do not absolve myself (*nafsy*). Indeed, the self commands to vice except as my Lord bestows mercy. Indeed, my Lord is Grantor of Forgiveness, Giver of Mercy" (Yusuf 12:53). In this state or stage the *nafs* has the potential to debase itself. It is only a potential because it has the capacity to recognize the wrong and desist from enacting it even as it feels the pull to give in. For the *nafs* to suggest the wrongdoing is not necessarily to do it. Prophet Muhammad ﷺ stated that "Allah, may He be glorified and exalted, will forgive my Ummah for whatever crosses their minds so long as they do not act upon it or speak of it" (Sahih Bukhari).

The temptation to give in, whether or not one actually does, or simply not to do one's best in all that is good, leads to self-blame in the case of *an-nafs al-lawwama* or the reproaching self. In this state or stage, the *nafs* recognizes its weaknesses, it does not try to extricate itself from the happenings of life, but rather admits what it has prioritized and what it has neglected. Allah swears by this state of *nafs* pointing to its Truth and inviting us to reflect on its importance (Al-Qiyamah 75:2). It is difficult not to reproach ourselves when we recognize how limited we are in our abilities and knowledge, an admission that leads to pleas for Allah's Mercy and Forgiveness. The *nafs* takes responsibility and realizes that it is only through Allah's benevolence that it will be saved on the Day of Account. For some, this state of the *nafs* precedes graduation to the assured self.

The assured self – *an-nafs al-mutma'inna* – is invited by Allah to return to Him contentedly and contented (*radiyyah, mardiyyah*), to enter among His servants and enter His paradise (Al-Fajr 89:27-30). This *nafs* complements its deep faith with hard work in order to accumulate all that it can of goodness, deeds that it would be proud to present to its Lord and Creator, evidence that it heeded His guidance. "What is it to do good?" Prophet Muhammad ﷺ was once asked. He ﷺ replied, "To do good is to obey Allah with the same presence of mind as if you were seeing Him; and if you do not see Him, surely He sees you" (Sahih Bukhari).

The assured self is a *nafs* that practices genuine trust in Allah, knowing that something good comes out of even the harshest challenges it may face in this life. Of this self, Prophet Muhammad ﷺ said, "Bewildering is the affair of a believer, for his affair is all good, and this applies to no one other than the believer. If happiness afflicts him, he is thankful, so it is good for him. And if harm afflicts him, he is patient, so it is good for him" (Sahih Muslim). This is a *nafs* defined by steadfastness, peace and calm, ready, without hesitation or fear, to accept its Lord's invitation to what is infinitely better than the life of this world.

When we think of the *nafs* in this way through heart-mind states and stages, it is natural that we focus on specific ways of purification, *tazkiyyah*. These might include asking for forgiveness (*istighfar*), remembrance (*dhikr*), self-accountability (*muhasaba*), heedfulness (*taqwa*), and struggling against the self's rebellious tendencies (*jihad an-nafs*). The *nafs* is clearly and rightfully established in relation to its Lord and Creator in a non-material way. But the Quran is much more comprehensive than this.

The *nafs* cannot be dissociated from the body, neither the individual's body nor the communal body. We are no less without our bodies on the other side as we are without them when we sleep. "On a Day when their tongues, and hands, and legs will bear witness against them as to what they used to do" (An-Nur 24:24). Body parts will bear witness in some cases without the aid of the tongue. "Today [Day of Account], We will place a seal on their mouths, and their hands will speak to Us, and their legs will bear witness with what they used to earn" (Ya Sin 36:65). What did those hands do? Where did those legs go? Did they concur with how they were employed or were they misused? "Until, when they come to it, their hearing and their sight and their skin will testify against them regarding what they used to do. And they will say to their skin, 'why did you witness against us?' They [their skins] will say, 'Allah made us verbal, as He verbalized everything else, and He created you the first time and to Him you are returned" (Fussilat 41:20-21). Every aspect of our creation from the very beginning has a latent ability to speak, to express itself, to witness. Every aspect, whether of body and faculties, uninhibited by the constraints of earthly life, will pour out its memories at Allah's command. The body does indeed keep score.

It keeps score as every breath – *nafas* – gifted to us by Allah is mediated by the quality of the messaging our *nafs*. There is no coincidence in their shared root *n-f-s*. Every *nafas* carries signals that reach every cell in our bodies having the potential to nourish, heal, and illuminate or just keep us alive. Every *nafas* transports thoughts, actions and memories to every cell in our bodies. It is not surprising that medications are ineffective in treating soldiers returning from war. Drugs cannot erase memories of body parts and faculties; at most they can offer a temporary numbing like alcohol. Van der Kolk is correct in suggesting that a whole person approach is required to deal with these experiences. He is not correct in asserting that these soldiers suffer from a disconnection from the self, rather they have experienced prolonged or intense connection to their wickedest self through shameful actions – sinning. And they have been cheated out of the real and most effective tool to heal, the one offered by their Creator. Self-compassion must be accompanied with repentance – *tawbah*. In fact, it is embodied in it.

There is an important function for guilt and blame, their intensity corresponding with the injustice that has been committed and the sensitivity of the self. *Tawbah* demands a confrontation of this internal dialogue; why we feel the way we do and what can be done to rectify the injustice that is giving rise to these feelings so that we can heal effectively, so that we can earn the right to heal. The *nafs*, out of its Creator's Mercy, is bolstered by its faculties and emotions. When we do good, we feel satisfied, comfortable, elevated. And when we do wrong, we feel guilty, constricted, lowly. We turn to repentance in an effort to rebalance and recalibrate our original sense of dignity. Our slipups cannot be remedied simply by feeling bad or worse by supressing those feelings. The *nafs* demands a remedy that will prevent recidivism.

A sound heart is able to distinguish between things for which one is ultimately at fault and those for which one is not. To abdicate responsibility or care only for oneself is not self-compassion. It is irresponsible. *Tawbah* requires three indispensable actions. To desist from the wrongdoing permanently, to fix any harms that our actions resulted in, and to participate in a better future. It is only in engaging the entirety of the self that not only the individual can heal but that the world in which they committed their injustice can do so as well. Self-restoration must also be an act of social rectification.

Understanding the comprehensiveness of the *nafs* and striving to purify it is the only way forward, even as I struggle to accept that some kinds of aggression deserve nothing short of Hell. I want to believe that all selves can be reformed, but my heart is sore, broken daily in a million pieces. Those who appear to have so clearly chosen to be the lowest possible version of themselves cannot by reason know Allah but reason is not the only faculty involved in the movement of the *nafs*. "And if they [the enemy] incline toward peace, so you too incline toward it, and place your trust in Allah, it is He Who is the Hearer, the Knower" (Al-Anfal 8:61). My only solace at this time is that an ordering of the *nafs* eventually comes, whether in three days as in the case of Thamud, or three centuries as in the case of the companions of the cave. That is the way of my Lord, that is His promise.

Amidst the backdrop of a genocide, and the violence that we are witnessing against the Palestinian people is a Quranic invitation to the occupier, the perpetrator, to return to the ways of their Lord. The possibility feels undeserved, unfair. It could be mistaken for the idea that what is happening is forgivable, forgettable. Can such arrogance and violence turn back and be honoured once again? Anger and grief are mediated by the weight of Allah's words, "Perhaps your Lord will have mercy on you. And if you return [to sin], We will return [to retribution]. And We have made Hell for the disbelievers a pallet (*haseerah*)" (Al-Isra' 17:8). It is through a Quranic command to the Children of Israel, *bani Isra'il*, that humanity is taught a most beautiful lesson: he who kills a *nafs* or corrupts in the earth is as if he killed all people and he who revives a *nafs* is as if he revived all people (Al-Ma'idah 5:32). This is His Word, and this is His World, and every fibre of my aching *nafs* must yield.

Everyone has the potential to nurture their better self, inspired to recognize the duality of the *nafs* – rebelliousness and heedfulness – as well as in its human form. “We have certainly created the human in the best disposition (*ahsan taqweem*). Then We returned him to the lowest of the low (*asfala safileen*). Except those who believe and work righteousness, for them is a reward incalculable” (At-Tin 95:4-7). Two extreme poles – the sacred, beautiful, devout and the profane, irreverent, ungodly. Every human has a diabolic companion who challenges his struggle for heedfulness. Prophet Muhammad ﷺ had warned of this: “Everyone is shadowed by a diabolic companion,” he said. “Even you?” someone asked. “Even me,” he replied, “but my Lord has helped me conquer him and he has submitted” (Sahih Muslim). All devoted believers are subject to this favour. “Surely, he [Satan] has no authority over those who believe and in their Lord place their trust” (An-Nahl 16:99). It is through our relationship with Allah that consciousness sharpens, moving us along a spectrum from mere wakefulness to fidelity or heart-vision – *ru'yat al-fuad* – the most compassionate and truthful power of a purified *nafs*. Our connection with Allah is a connection with our highest self.

It is important to understand that duality does not mean only two possibilities. But rather, a complex spectrum that tends towards one or the other. Each possibility is tempered by the unique characteristics of our personalities and resources adding even more layers of distinction from one person to the next. But humans do share many characteristics that are important to recognize if we are to address them effectively. The human – *insan* – tells us the Quran, was created weak (An-Nisa' 4:28). He turns to Allah in crisis but when it is resolved he moves on as if Allah's mercy never touched him (Yunus 10:12). Yet the removal of mercy leads the human to despair and ingratitude (Hud 11:9). “And the human supplicates for evil as he supplicates for good, and the human is ever hasty” (Al-Isra' 17:11). Haste is often accompanied with anxiety. “Indeed, the human was created anxious (*halu'a*). If misfortune touches him, he panics [breaks down]. And if good touches him he is restraining [holding back his generosity]” (Al-Ma'arij 70:19-21).

The Merciful does not leave us in this state. He presents a prescription, an elixir that offers His servants the keys to balance, to managing the *nafs*. Sure, everyone suffers anxiety…

Except those who pray
Those who are consistent with their prayers
And those in whose wealth is a known right

For the one who asks and the deprived
And those who truthfully affirm the Day of Deen
And those who are distressed by their Lord's punishment
Indeed, the punishment of their Lord is not secured
And those who preserve their privates
Except for [in the presence of] their spouses or whom they hold-by-oath, so they are not to blame
So, whoever seeks beyond that, so they are the transgressors
And those who regard their trusts and promises with vigilance
And those who are in their testimonies upright
And those who guard their prayers
These are in gardens honoured (Al-Ma'arij 70:22-35).

The remedy is a connection to the self, to the Creator of the self, and the creation of the Creator. It is comprehensive psychological, physical and social experience, not focused exclusively on the self but necessarily extending to the context that ensures the sustainability of its welfare. Prayer connects us to Allah in a consistent pattern, it reminds us of Reality, the Truth of matters. It regulates our daily activities and instills a sense of calm. A share in our wealth for those who need ensures the fulfillment of our and their purposeful paths. It mitigates our greed, reminds us of the true source of blessings, and promotes compassion. Belief in the Day of Judgement reminds us that we must continually strive to purify ourselves and never become complacent. We will be held accountable. Our sexuality must be guarded because it has such destructive potential for ourselves and others. It is confined to a lawful intimate space that necessitates marriage and encourages the formation of families. Our trusts and promises must be fulfilled as the paths of others depend upon them and our testimonies must be truthful for their potential to benefit or harm. These promote a sense of belonging and the need to invest in long term relationships. Finally, an emphasis on prayer once more because between genuine and regular communications with Allah that humble and remind, all efforts in the middle are eased and rectified.

The comprehensiveness of the *nafs*, its inclusivity of our entire being, further underscores the importance of everything that enters our bodies. Like the *nafas* that can bring the breath of consciousness to every cell in our bodies, proper nutrition can strengthen and heal. Allah thereby commands us to eat of what is permissible – *halal* – and wholesome, pure, delicious, obtained with mercy, justice and sustainability – *tayyib* – and to be grateful for

His favours (An-Nahl 16:114). "Oh you who believe, eat from the wholesome things (*tayyibat*) which We have provided for you and be thankful to Allah if it is indeed Him that you worship" (Al-Baqarah 2:172). Even the messengers received a special warning as to what they should eat to preserve the quality and strength of their *anfus*. "Oh messengers, eat from what is wholesome (*tayyibat*) and work righteousness. Indeed, I am knowing of what you do" (Al-Mu'minun 23:51). Whether messengers or ordinary folk, like you and I, eating healthy is indispensable for the maintenance of our *nafs* and its efforts to achieve balance.

Consuming what is prohibited, what is not beneficial for our bodies, opens the door for the *shaytan*. "Oh people, consume from whatever is on the earth, permissible (*halal*) and wholesome (*tayyib*), and do not follow the footsteps of the *Shaytan*. Indeed, he is to you a clear enemy" (Al-Baqarah 2:168). What we put in our bodies can make us sick, heavy, and lazy, affecting the clarity of our thoughts and the proficiency of our actions. The *ayat* on consumption do not refer only to foods but to everything that can be consumed by our bodies. Believers are warned against wasteful consumption of wealth, unjustly consuming the wealth of others and in particular orphans, inequitably and exclusively consuming inheritance, and consuming *riba* (all kinds of interest on money and goods). One must also be vigilant not to consume false ideas and corruptive forms of entertainment thereby staining their hearing, vision and hearts. All of these things facilitate the devil's mission to divert our attention from Allah or abandon faith altogether. There is an inseparable link between what we consume, and our ability fulfill our purpose to worship Allah with gratitude and humility.

It is hard to believe that I have been here for over half a century, plenty of time to understand and discipline my *nafs*. This is a decade more than the age when one is supposed to have reached their greatest capability, *ashudahu*, as the Quran names it. Forty years, the age when Prophet Muhammad ﷺ received the revelation, a span long enough for the *nafs* to have settled and matured. "And We have advised the human to be best toward his parents. His mother carried him by decree and delivered him by decree; and his detachment [from her complete care] is thirty months. Until he reaches his greatest capability, and reaches forty years, he says: 'My Lord enable me to thank for Your blessings with which You have blessed me and my parents and that I may do good that You accept and rectify my progeny for me. Indeed,

I have repented to You and indeed, I am of the Muslims" (Al-Ahqaf 46:15). In another *ayah*, we see the same invocation but rather than ending with an appeal for one's children, it ends with "and enter me by Your Mercy among Your righteous servants" (An-Naml 27:19).

To me, the refinement and elevation of the *nafs* is a journey of connecting. Connecting to Allah, to myself, to others and to nature. Sensitizing myself to Allah's inspiration concerning what can elevate and debase me has allowed me to navigate many of life's challenges with compassion and calm. The higher ground is always a choice, though perhaps not the easier one. But it is harder to think and behave in such a way that would compromise the wellbeing and security of my *nafs*. Me. The me that loves all of Allah's creation, that would rather hurt than hurt others, that wishes nothing but happiness for everyone, that sees the struggles of others to just be in this world and prays for the ability to give and heal. This *nafs* is worth my efforts and your *nafs* is worth yours. The *nafs* that Allah has so generously gifted me and the one He has likewise gifted you.

How beautiful it is to have a welcoming attitude to the finest inspiration of the *nafs*. To choose with little or no hesitation everything that increases us in heedfulness. Loving Allah is to love oneself for His sake. Belief and doing good are the tonic for the *nafs*, nourishing and elevating, helping us to keep up with Allah's order so that we commit the least possible injustice. Connecting with our higher selves pushes us to be better, to monitor our actions and purify our intentions. We are constantly seeking to be wiser, kinder, humbler, finer. *An-nafs al-mutma'ina*, may Allah grant us this invaluable state. But like I said, this is a journey. It may start with a complaisant attitude where one finds themself more often than not connecting with their rebellious nature due to the pressures or temptations of life. *An-nafs al-amara* requires greater discipline. It needs to respond more fully to its sense of shame, reminding itself that Allah is ever-present. From there, the self may graduate to a more favourable attitude, where it connects with greater consistency and joy to its higher calling but still not to the full exclusion of the lower. *An-nafs al-lawama*, by which Allah swears, constantly questioning its actions reflects the majority of us.

The task assigned to us all is to purify the *nafs*, for each to learn about their unique self so that we can exercise *taqwa*, to succeed in this life and the next. To exercise *taqwa* means to be heedful of Allah as if we see Him, and if we cannot then to be certain that He sees us. To become heedful is to know that every *nafs* is part of the grand unity that Allah intended us to be. We are all part of something bigger, the *Nafs*, to which we can all trace our origin. Every *nafas*, contributes to a shift of our *Ummah*, hopefully for the better. In *taqwa*, equity and justice are non-negotiables. It is as such that we will be a mercy and fulfill our responsibilities.

To have *taqwa* is to know that any act no matter how small generates a ripple in time that shapes the earnings of our *Ummah*. When *sadaqah* is translated as charity it loses its core meaning which is truth from the root *s-d-q*, an affirmation of truth to be precise – the truth of mercy, kindness, empathy, gratitude, and above all, exclusive submission to Allah's guidance.

Some of the companions of Prophet Muhammad ﷺ once complained that wealthy people would have more rewards because they did everything that the less well-off did and also had the advantage of giving from their wealth. Prophet Muhammad ﷺ responded by saying, "Has not Allah made things for you to give as *sadaqah*? Truly every *tasbeehah* [saying *subhan*-Allah] is a *sadaqah*, and every *takbeerah* [saying Allahu Akbar] is a *sadaqah*, and every *tahmeedah* [saying *Alhamdullillah*] is a *sadaqah*, and every *tahleelah* [saying *la ilaha ila* Allah] is a *sadaqah*. And commanding the good is a *sadaqah*, and forbidding an evil is a *sadaqah*, and in the [permissible] intimacy of each one of you [with his wife] there is a *sadaqah*" (Sahih Muslim). On another occasion he ﷺ mentioned that "Your smile to your brother is a *sadaqah*" (Musnad Ahmad). Every lawful act with a foundation of truth, and performed with pure intentions is a *sadaqah*. Life, by Allah's command, must respond to the simplest acts of goodness that we dispense.

Willing or not, we are all servants of Allah whether rebellious or heedful. Those who choose not to admit this out of negligence or defiance, cannot step out of His order. Their actions are still bound by His Word, the design of His universe, and the Truth of their *nafs*. "Indeed, those you invoke besides Allah, are servants like you. So, invoke them that they may respond to you, if you are truthful" (Al-A'raf 7:194). All are servants within Allah's grand scheme, if not supporting, purifying, and elevating themselves, then through their misgivings allowing those who do believe the opportunity to struggle against them in order to carry the Trust. Through their rebellion, they invite the believers to greater heedfulness, to reach the heights of Allah's inspiration. They provide the opportunity to pardon, enjoin the good, and seek refuge in Allah from the *shaytan* (Al-A'raf 7:199-200). Everybody is willy nilly a servant irrespective of what dimension of their *nafs* they strive to express in this life.

Our bodies return to the earth only to be resurrected, each *nafs* reunited with its earthly form. "And he," tells us the Quran about the human, "makes an example of Us while forgetting his creation, saying 'who will revive the bones when they are ash?' Say, 'He who first initiated them will revive them and He is with all creation Knowing" (Ya Sin 36:78-79). We will be brought back but not in the same form. The appearance of each *nafs* will reflect its earnings and state in the life of this world. Was it heedful or was it rebellious?

"The first group to enter Paradise," taught Prophet Muhammad ﷺ, "will be shining like the moon, and those who follow them will be like the most brilliant star in the sky" (Sahih Bukhari). The believers, those who had *taqwa*, will be beautiful, healthy and eternally young. Those who disbelieved, who were nasty, will be deformed and darkened, disfigured by all the evils they committed during their lifetimes. Of these, Prophet Muhammad said, "The people of Hell will be made to look like blackened, charred coal" (Sahih Muslim). The *nafs* merely transforms, undergoes a kind of metamorphosis, changing in form in accordance with the realms that Allah decrees it to enter.

Whatever we hope to transform into after the taste of death, must have been nourished in heart and body in this life. Not unlike a caterpillar that is shrouded in a silky cocoon or molts into a chrysalis, hidden for a determined time under leaves or buried in the ground as it digests itself, then emerges as a butterfly. Some are destined to fly low, close to the ground, while others soar thousands of feet into the sky. We too will be resurrected after having been absorbed by the earth. Each displaying all the beauty or ugliness that he or she necessarily was in their earthly phase, soaring or plummeting in accordance with their station with Allah.

He Called me Assam

I miss my dad. I've missed him every day since he passed into Allah's mercy in 2019. Perhaps I started missing him before that when physical frailty and some form of dementia had already begun delivering him to the other side. It was a long journey. Three years to be exact. Long for a man who had been full of life, full of movement, full of joy. Long for me, as I struggled to deal with how life had to continue apace while my dad lay in hospital then a nursing institution. I refuse to call it a *home*. Eventually, the hope of leaving, getting better, turned into a quiet anger based on a mistaken belief that we had abandoned him. We refused to take him home – at least that is how he saw it. And then there came the contented resignation to the truth that this miserable situation actually was – the inevitable attendance of death, asking him to prepare for departure. Three years of purification, and *insha'Allah* the rising in station. Even now as I write these words, I am choked with sadness and wish to burst in tears. But no, I will hold back. I want to tell you about his life and how so many of Allah's *ayat* shaped his story, my story, and the infinite stories of those whose lives he touched.

Born Ibrahim-Fahmy Mohammed Abdelgafar in the Egyptian countryside of the Nile Delta in 1941 to a family of limited means, Dad was from the very beginning destined to be a hard worker. He was the sixth of nine surviving siblings of my grandparents who, not too long after his birth, relocated the entire family to Cairo. There he attended school and aspired to become a physician. My grandfather's sudden death when Dad was only 17 dashed all such dreams. He started to work in the well-digging industry in the Sudan to support his mother, brothers, and sisters. Although his grades met the cut-off for medical school, he transferred to arts so that he could attend university part-time allowing him to continue to work. He graduated with an honour's degree in History from 'Ain Shams University. Despite the hardships, he would speak fondly of these years and his love for Sudanese people for the rest of his life. These were also the years that he romanced and married my mom, Afaf Eid, who was studying sociology and psychology at the same university. They graduated together in 1970. She would remain the love of his life until his passing.

In 1972 my sister Shrouk whose name means sunrise was born, and I, unexpectedly, laugh out loud, followed in 1973 shortly before yet another war with Israel over land that it had illegally occupied in 1967. It would later return the Sinai Peninsula to Egypt, but this story is not quite about that. The war, however, unnerved my parents with their two infant daughters. My father began to explore possibilities for a better life overseas and Canada soon became the most plausible alternative as one of his cousins who had emigrated earlier sent him an invitation and proposed sponsorship. Although my mother was hesitant at first, Dad never looked back. He wanted to give us the best life, something he could not envision in a country embroiled in conflict. Indeed, Allah's earth is vast. I was seven months old.

Later in life, I would learn that Dad had for some time wanted boys. Not because he preferred them but because he believed that he could treat boys differently. One particular wish, had he had a boy, was to send him to Al-Azhar to become *hafiz* – to learn and recite the Quran by heart – like his blind brother, Sheikh Ahmed. But Dad knew, like any believer, that "To Allah belongs the dominion of the skies and the earth, He creates what He wills, granting to whom He wills females and granting to whom He wills the males. Or He pairs them males and females and makes who He wills sterile. Indeed, He is Knowing, Capable" (Ash-Shura 42:49-50). Girls were a blessing, but they were different.

Girls could not be sent off. They had to be guarded, protected like pearls. They were beautiful, glamorous creatures. Capable of everything boys could do but requiring more care and protection along the way. A mission that Dad was more than happy to undertake. Prophet Muhammad ﷺ said, "Whoever has three daughters, and cares for them, is merciful to them, and clothes them, then Paradise is certainly for him." And in another narration, it is said that the people asked what about two? He said, "Even two," leading some to think that had they asked about one, he would have said even one (Sunan Abi Dawood and Musnad Ahmad). Many years later when I finally had two daughters after four male grandchildren, Dad was over the moon.

In Ottawa Dad found work as a waiter at the Holiday Inn. It was not his dream job, but he had responsibilities and an insatiable desire to make this new life work for his young family. The hours were long, the shifts unpredictable, the language a challenge, but he was used to hard work and the tips were good. He had also come from a family of extreme hospitality and generosity. Hosting people came natural to him. He enjoyed it. That is not uncommon for folk of limited means in Egypt. They share. My grandmother was an incredible cook, and she expressed her love by shoving roast duck and rice in your mouth with her fingers. Dad was not much different though he settled for overloading your plate.

He and my mother soon bought their first home. It was a small townhouse that they furnished and decorated so beautifully. It was the heart of their happiness, their achievements in this new place, but most of all it was safety for their daughters. I remember mom – who set aside her career for our care – sitting us on the floor by the kitchen heater during Ottawa's cold and long winter nights to teach us how to recite the shorter *suwar* of the Quran. I was three and my sister was four years old at the time. We often giggled at the sounds and at our mistakes as she made us repeat after her. She was patient, persisting night after night, despite sometimes having to move on to other activities – like sewing homemade dolls or baking bread – because we just could not get our laughter under control. And though we did not understand a single word, we eventually could recite *al-Fatihah*, likely the very first *surah* that every child learns. Then came the *mu'awwidhat*, the three short *suwar* at the end of the Quran – *Al-Ikhlas*, *Al-Falaq* and *An-Nas* – that are recited to invoke Allah's protection. Once committed to memory, they were recited every night before bed, after a bath and a warm cup of milk. It was mostly thanks to my mom that both of us learned to speak Arabic fluently.

Home was where my Dad's love for beauty, fine food, the good life finally began to blossom. With his family happily settled, he could focus on work, on providing for us and his family back in Egypt. We were proud to be Canadian, an identity that would forever hold memories of Egypt, sometimes with joy and sometimes with grief.

It was a conscientious decision on the part of my parents to choose integration with Canadian society over isolation in a small immigrant community. Our house was always open to everyone, every culture, every faith. Prophet Muhammad ﷺ taught us that "the neighbour that is the best to Allah is the one that is best to his neighbour" (Sahih Bukhari). Twice a year in April and August on the birthdays of my sister and I, Dad would light up the house, decorate the entire ground-level, stock up on food, drinks, and all kinds of goodies and then literally invite the entire street. Egyptian, Irish, Italian, Chinese, Portuguese, Jamaican, Czech and Canadian (those who are not sure from where their ancestors came but are certainly not native), poured into our home for a few hours of joy. Allah created us in all our diversity to know each other (Al-Hujuraat 49:13).

From his work in hospitality, Dad knew a local mariachi band, three Mexican friends, that he invited to perform live in Spanish in our living room. These were evenings eagerly anticipated in the neighbourhood. One where immigrant identity did not matter. Here families could relax, contented with the restoration of their dignity that was reflected in the brotherly treatment of each other, forgetting for a few hours the struggle of first-generation immigrants. "Allah does not prohibit you from those who do not fight you in your *deen* and do not evict you from your homes, that you extend goodness (*tabaruhum*) and act equitably toward them. Indeed, Allah loves the equitable" (Al-Mumtahinah 60:8). My parents chose to connect with all people, to show the beauty of their culture and faith through food, hospitality, and gifts. Prophet Muhammad ﷺ taught *tahadu tahabu* meaning exchange gifts so that the love between you may increase (Sahih Bukhari). They dignified and treated all their guests with generosity. They became the hosts in a place that was hosting them. This gave them a sense of belonging, but it also rooted them in the traditions of their distant home. It was a most enchanting childhood.

Family is a big deal in Islam and Arab culture. It is not a social unit to be manipulated according to social trends, human whims, or sexual preferences but a sacred institution mandated by Allah for the propagation, protection, and purposefulness of humanity. "And it is He who has created from water a sentient being (*bashar*), then connected him through lineage (*nasab*) and marriage (*sehr*). And ever is your Lord capable" (Al-Furqan 25:54). Strong and cohesive families are symbols of honour, loyalty, and strength. In his magnum opus the *Muqqadimah*, Ibn Khaldun, a renowned Arab social scientist of the Middle Ages, observed that the growth and success of civilizations is indisputably associated with the strength of family and tribal bonds. Strong families are an important contributor to social stability and progress. When family connections weaken and fragment, societies breakdown becoming vulnerable to all kinds of internal and external threats.

Both the Quran and Sunnah emphasize the importance of treating parents, spouses, children, near and far relatives with dignity, generosity, mercy, and beauty. We do not choose these connections; we are born into them and must bear our responsibility. "Worship Allah and do not associate anything with Him, and do good unto parents, and to relatives, and orphans, and the needy, and the near neighbour and the neighbour further away, and the wayfarer, and those possessed by oath. Indeed, Allah does not love those who are vain, proud" (An-Nisa' 4:36). Our treatment of immediate and distant family establishes the bar for the quality of broader social connections. It is the heart of any successful community.

The treatment of parents and in particular that of mothers is singled out and prioritized. "Say, 'Come, I will recite to you what your Lord forbade you. That you do not associate anything with Him, and toward parents to do good...'" (Al-An'am 6:151). The respectful treatment and lifelong attention to parents is a non-negotiable for believers. "And we advised the human regarding his parents. His mother carried him, discomfort upon discomfort and his weaning in two years. Show thanks to Me and your parents. To Me is the finality" (Luqman 31:14). When asked about who is most worthy of our kindness, Prophet Muhammad ﷺ said, "Your mother, then your mother, then your mother, then your father, then your nearest, then nearest" (Sahih Bukhari).

My grandmother's passing was very difficult for Dad. I remember him just going up to his room, closing the door, and sobbing. I was around five years old. It was the first and only time I heard my father cry, it was excruciating. I can still hear it so many years later. He rarely teared in front of anyone, and when he did, it was silent. Only his mother drew such pain. He must have wished that she could have visited us in Canada, to see her son in his new life. But almost every other close family member eventually paid us a visit. Aunts, uncles, cousins and my maternal grandparents who unlike the others made that Atlantic flight many times.

Our home was always welcoming, somehow always big enough. Dad would set aside his small metallic green Dodge Colt in favour of a large car or van for the summer, something that could accommodate the guests. It was cheaper to buy and resell than to rent. He would plan a trip to the major tourist attractions. All trips included visits to the Thousand Islands, Niagara Falls, Marine Land, African Lion Safari, and Wonderland to the west and then Montreal to the east. Sometimes he even took them south to New York. From one motel to the next, my parents presented their vision of the best that Canada had to offer. But no one took the bait. It was summer. They knew that Canada was no place for sun-loving Egyptians in the winter.

In alternate years, we visited Egypt. Dad rarely accompanied us because of work. This was my mother's mission. Every second year she would fill five of the six pieces of luggage that we were entitled to with gifts, the remaining bag contained everything the three of us would need for our six-week vacation. She would often plan a longer than usual transit to introduce my sister and I to a new city – Brussels, Rome, Barcelona. I digress. Our travels to Egypt were a connection with family, places, culture, language, and history. They were a sharing of the bounties of our new home, and it brought so much joy to everyone. "And give the relative his right, and the needy and the wayfarer, and do not waste flagrantly" (Al-Isra' 17:26). The next day of our arrival was the day of gifts distribution, from clothing to Fruit Loops cereal, to plastic bags (not yet understood as a threat to our planet), bringing hugs, laughter and gratitude. Mom also brought money. Money that she had saved and that Dad had sent for the less well-to-do members of the family, friends, and strangers often still living in the countryside. He also sent money to maintain his mother's grave and pay for an annual Quran recitation in the village where she was buried.

When we returned home, Dad would greet us at the airport in Montreal with intense hugs and kisses, occasionally biting our cheeks. My sister and I could never wait to get into the car where he had two snack bags prepared for each of us with our favourite junk food on the backseat. It made the two hour drive home so much fun after a gruelling flight. It was the best welcome home.

While we were away, Dad used his spare time, which was not much given how much he worked and now studied, to redecorate their bedroom. Every other year he would bring the latest design ideas to that one room in the house. Paint, floral or textile wallpaper, paneling, crown molding, gold accents, and bed coverings to match. Then there was my mom's gift that was always placed on the edge of the bed.

There is no more a beautiful bond than that of marriage, bringing together a man and woman in a sacred union that connects families while potentially producing offspring. "And of His ayat is that He created for you mates from yourselves (*anfusikum*) that you may dwell with them and placed between you friendship and mercy. Indeed, in this are *ayat* for a people that think" (Ar-Rum 30:21). Marriage is a sacred space where two people assume responsibility for each other's well-being. This process of finding, pursuing, persuading, and settling with a mate is an *ayah*, an inexplicable blessing from Allah. Human power cannot institute this kind of friendship, love and mercy between two people let alone between their families. No matter how hard we try we simply do not have that ability. Only Allah can place genuine love between people.

We pray for a suitable partner in life, and when we find them, we pray that they remain suitable and that Allah increases us in love, respect, generosity, and all the beautiful things that marriage is intended by Allah to be. This is a place where our hearts and bodies find refuge, nourishment, and healing. "And those who say: 'Our Lord, grant us from our spouses and progeny those who will be a comfort to our eyes and make us leaders for the heedful'" (Al-Furqan 25:74). The coupling of good family and leadership is not haphazard. Peaceful settlement and contentment on the home front is the foundation for successful public endeavours. Indeed, the Prophet ﷺ said, "Whoever Allah provides with a righteous wife [spouse], Allah has assisted him in half of his religion. Let him be heedful of Allah regarding the second half" (Al-Tabarani; Al-Bayhaqi).

The contractual arrangement of marriage in the Quran does not diminish anything of its essence as an organic, living relationship. "Your women are tilth (*harth*) for you, so approach your tilth as you wish and present for yourselves [something to them] and heed Allah and know that you will meet Him and give glad tidings to the believers" (Al-Baqarah 2:223). This likening of a wife to land is a call to understand the character of the earth with its diverse and integrative reality. To live with each other in kindness (An-Nisa' 4:19). Those who take offense from such an allusion do not understand its complexity or majesty. To be likened to the earth is not an insult. It is an honour, inviting the addressee to seek knowledge and assume responsibility. Each must play a role essential to the other's flourishing. The *harth* demands care if it is to yield flowers and fruit, if it is to embrace its guests, absorb the warmth of the sun and dance with the wind. It needs exchange, communication, watering, fertilizing, weeding, harvesting, rotating and rest. These practices demand patience, commitment, generosity and intimacy. It should come as no surprise that being happily married is associated with better mental and physical health.

Well before Dad passed and even before his illness, I dreamt that I was standing beside him in an open space, our arms engaged, as he was waiting to wed a *hur'iyn* – those beautiful creatures promised to the believers in the Hereafter. There in the distance she stood, gorgeous, dressed in white with massive greenish eyes and light coffee-coloured long tresses, alongside her was her brother who was some masculine version of her. But Dad did not advance towards them. He sensed something else, something I was too preoccupied with their vision to notice. Then he turned. A bit further away and in the other direction, in the white open space, we could see my mother coming toward him. He let go of my arm and started to walk toward her with the gait of an excited teenager. She was his love and clearly no *hur'iyn* could compete.

My relationship with both my parents was close though each had a different zest. Dad's pride and joy was education, lots of education. He valued intelligence, perhaps just as much as he valued beauty; to him, they may have been one and the same. At the age of four, He started calling me the philosopher and made sure that I had female role models in my life whose minimal achievement was a doctorate. Of course, I had no idea what that was at the time, but I could see the respect he proffered and his beaming face when he dealt with everything intelligent. It affected me deeply.

I excelled in academics in no small measure to his constant efforts and expectations. Both my sister and I were furnished with all the latest technologies. From gadgets that improved maths and spelling, to our first personal computer in 1987. He even humoured us with a remote-control robot, an eccentricity at the time. Knowing my love of writing and poetry, he once came home with two big boxes of English literature books that he had picked-up from one of his retiring colleagues – Dad was now a teacher of hospitality at a local college. This was my introduction to Sir Thomas More, Walt Whitman, Robert Frost, John Keats, Rudyard Kipling, William Blake, and Elisabeth Barrett Browning whose words will forever ring true. Dad, "I love thee with the breath, smiles, tears, of all my life; and if God choose, I shall but love thee better after death."

A small glitch in this otherwise untainted educational process occurred in my last year of high school when he and my mother decided to ship my sister and I off to Egypt. Their concern over our quickly transforming cultural ideals overrode all my pleas to continue my studies in Canada. I wanted to go to med school, and I had entry scholarships for undergraduate studies. But he would hear none of it. The matter was settled. It was the American University in Cairo, or nothing. My respect for my parents and their wishes precluded any wild decisions despite my deep resentment for what I believed to be a grave mistake. "And Allah has decreed that you worship none but Him and to parents that you do good. Whether one or both attain old age during your life do not say to them *uffin* [an expression of impatience and discontent] and do not disparage them and address them with dignified speech" (Al-Isra' 17:23). So off I went where I studied business, minored in economics, and mastered in public administration. My mother accompanied us but once we were settled, she would go back and forth.

Dad came to visit a couple of times and in between we exchanged letters. There was no internet back then. Six, seven, eight pages long, he wrote to me at least once a month as every letter took about three weeks to arrive and I wrote back. Every letter started with "*Bismillah Ar-Rahman Ar-Rahim* Dear Assam," and concluded with "watch your prayers, take care of your *deen*, and don't forget your glamour, Love, Dad." He called me Assam. It was one of my many nicknames, a sign of love and closeness in Egyptian culture. One actually hardly hears their birth name except in formal settings. I was Assam, Suma, Bisbis, Simsim, and Assooma. But only Dad called me Assam, something I realised a couple of years after he passed when I read an Assam Tea label in a grocery store and felt a sharp, painful void. I had not heard that name in a long time. Assam. He took her with him.

Emphasis in the Quran and hadith on the station of mothers must not in any way be misunderstood as a diminution of fatherhood and the bond between father and child. The Quran is replete with examples of fathers that loved their children and who were loved back. Perhaps the most outstanding example is that of Prophet Yacoub ﷺ and his son Prophet Yusuf ﷺ. In his profound grief over the temporary loss of his son, Prophet Yacoub lost his vision. "And he turned away from them and said, 'Oh, my regrets over Yusuf,' and his eyes became white from grief, as he was a suppressor [of anger, emotions]" (Yusuf 12:84). His sadness was so prolonged and intense that his other sons who were responsible for Yusuf's disappearance thought he may become fatally ill or die. Many years later when Prophet Yacoub sensed that Prophet Yusuf was well and alive, we get to witness his emotional reaction. "And when the caravan had departed [from Egypt], their father said, 'Indeed, I sense the smell of Yusuf though you might think me senile" (Yusuf 12:94). It was the smell of his beloved son and soon he would regain his vision and set his sights once more on his lost treasure.

The details of Prophet Muhammad's ﷺ life are also outstanding in this regard. He was an exemplary father full of kindness and love for his children and grandchildren. He used to hug and kiss them, showing affection in private and public. When he was asked about this by a man who claimed to have never kissed his now mature son, the Prophet ﷺ replied, "What can I do if Allah has withheld the mercy from your heart?" The Prophet ﷺ was fair and generous to all children and advised believers to do likewise, "Heed Allah, and be just among your children" (Sahih Muslim).

Prophet Muhammad ﷺ was playful with his children and grandchildren, carrying them on his shoulders and back. He would let them play around and on him when he prayed and wait for them to get off his back to rise. Boys, girls, he loved and showed affection to them all.

Perhaps it was his relationship with his daughter Fatimah that was the most outstanding. He ﷺ informed believers that "Fatima is a part of me. What harms her, harms me" (Sahih Bukhari). He was known to stand to greet her when she entered the room, kiss her forehead, and make space for her to sit beside him. Theirs was an intense love between father and daughter. When Prophet Muhammad ﷺ neared the end of his life and fell ill, Fatima's heart became very heavy, visiting him often to care for him and cool her eyes. On one of their final visits Fatima was overcome with grief and tears. Her father gently called her to his side and informed her that she would be the first of his family to join him in the afterlife. "Oh Fatima, do not cry, for your father will not leave you. Rather, you will be the first of my family to follow me." To this news, Fatimah smiled. They were soon to be reunited.

When I completed my doctoral studies in 2003, he was there at my defence beaming with pride. This was his moment. That young woman, not yet 30, and soon to be mother of two, was his baby. His philosopher. To this day, I'm not sure to what extent the determination to finish was based on my drive or his. My sister would also go on to earn a double masters after her undergrad studies.

Dad was older now. A grandfather to four boys and two girls. He attended every birth he could. He loved his grandchildren, and they adored him back. They brought back the birthdays, the balloons, the joy that had since my maturity turned into a dozen roses every August. Prophet Muhammad ﷺ said, "The best among you, the worthiest and most noble, are those who are the best, the kindest, and most considerate to their family" (Sunan Al-Tirmidhi). And Dad certainly was.

Without the preoccupation of teaching and running the college restaurant – for which he entered the Ontario Restaurant Hall of Fame - Dad turned more fully to the service of his local Muslim community. Hajji Ibrahim, as he was called, was given the keys to a nearby masjid – keys to a House of Allah – where he would open for *fajr* and perform the call to prayer. There were many early winter mornings when I would sneak down to clean off his car from the snow and turn it on to heat. I could not bear him doing that, even more so because his health was changing. "And lower for them the wing of humility from among [the many wings of] Mercy and say: My Lord have mercy on them as they raised me from infancy" (Al-Isra' 17:24). Dad was loved by the masjid community as he was by his friends, former colleagues and students. On several occasions after his passing, we would discover from the memories that others shared just how much and what he was he doing when he was not at home.

On one such occasion we were told of an incident by a young Chechen refugee family that he had met at the masjid and with whom he had developed a friendship so much so, that they too gave him the keys to their home. One day upon returning home from picking up her children, the young woman found Dad cleaning her kitchen after he had stocked their fridge with some groceries that he had brought. Finding the kitchen sink full of dishes, he could not just leave. He knew just how difficult this new place was no matter what they had left behind. They had two young infants and hardly knew any English. An all too familiar narrative. Life had come full circle. "And they feed [nutritious] food out of love for Him, to the needy, orphan and captive. Indeed, we feed you for the countenance of Allah. We do not want from you reward or thanks" (Al-Insan 76:8-9). This was his secret life, a life about which he never spoke.

The aftermath of an infection during a quadruple bypass when he was about seventy years old finally took hold of his health five years later. Very quickly Dad became physically weak, and his mental capacities diminished as well, though he never forgot anything of real importance. Till the end, he knew who he was and who we were as well as all of his friends. Most important, he knew his Lord, His Messenger and the Quran.

He hated the nursing institution to which he was forcibly committed. I had tried my best to support my mother when she would call me at two and three in the morning telling me that Dad had fallen and she needed help getting him back in bed. I would rush over, and we would struggle to get him off the ground. He eventually fell down a whole flight of stairs, denting the wall with his head. That day he was whisked to hospital by ambulance, never to return home again. He spent three years between hospitals and nursing care before the end was finally in sight. An end that he welcomed. "The days pass, the weeks pass, the months pass," he once told me, "and I'm still here." Four patients had died in his shared room during his stay.

When asked by his palliative care nurse where he wanted to die, he did not respond. So, she prodded, "Ibrahim, do you want to die here?" To which he said, "Nooo." Then she asked, "Do you want to die in hospital?" Again, he affirmed the negative. My heart was crushed by this exchange, it seemed so cold. "Ok, Ibrahim, where do you want to die?" He then looked at me, and in the most heart wrenching, gentle, and broken voice said, "Home." I was devastated, that was not possible given his state.

I visited Dad often in those final days. He was completely silent at this stage and his appetite only admitted small sips of water. He was pale and his facial features were accentuated likely due to dehydration. But he was still beautiful. We all knew the end was near. I held his hand, kissed his face, wet his lips with a moist cloth. Then I gently whispered, *La illaha ila Allah, Muhammadan Rasool Allah*, in his ear. Under normal circumstances you are supposed to say the first part, *La illaha ila Allah*, to which the other responds, *Muhammadun Rasool Allah*, thus completing the *shahada*. In this case I had to say both as he just stared out of the window to the left. I was not sure he heard me. On the way out that day, I stopped by the nursing station and told them that they were to call me when he passed, not my mother or my sister. I did not think they could handle it as well.

I drove home that day with the most horrible feeling in my gut. Everything in my body was sore and the lump in my throat so huge I could barely swallow. That night, in my dream, the exact same scene that had unfolded earlier in the day recurred. There I was whispering the *shahada* in Dad's ear, but this time he responded. He said his part as he had always said it throughout his life. Dad never just said *Muhammadun Rasool Allah*, but rather *Sayyiduna wa Nabiyuna Muhammadun Rasool Allah* – our Master and Prophet Muhammad Messenger of Allah. He had heard me; he had corrected me. Prophet Muhammad ﷺ was most dear to him, something He had never failed to express. "The prophet is more worthy of the believers than their own selves and his wives are their mothers. And uterine ties are more worthy of one another in Allah's Book from among the believers and emigrants. Nevertheless, you must do good towards those you guard. This is outlined in the Book" (Al-Ahzab 33:6). May Dad's affirmation forever echo throughout the heavens, amplified by the chorus of angels.

On Saturday morning shortly before 8am, I received the call. I picked up. "It's Dad, right?" The voice said, "I'm sorry." His funeral procession was long, winding through the streets of a city that he had loved so dearly and that loved him back. Burial arrangements were swift as is customary in Islam. His body was moved to his beloved masjid for a brief overnight stay. He had eventually made it *home*, the Home of Allah that he had tended to with such joy and sincerity. The last arms to embrace his body, to place him in the earth on that peaceful Autum day, were those of my nephew, Amr, whom he had named and been the first to embrace twenty-four years earlier to the day. September 7, 2019. *Ina lillahi wa ina ilayhi raji'oon* – To Allah we belong and to Him we are all returning.

Al-Mithaq Al-Ghaleez: The Deep Covenant

Quranic Truth and Prophetic teachings present divorce – *talaq* – as the closing of a book, a concluding act that recognizes the sacred ink that filled the pages of a marriage with friendship and mercy. It is the divergence of paths of two partners who once journeyed together, dwelled within each other, not with bitterness and greed but with reverence for the deep covenant – *al-mithaq al-ghaleez* – that they exchanged with each other. Revelation does not present divorce as an occasion to lay blame, to hurt, and damage each other. Rather, it is a divinely guided act of release, a beautiful release, to maintain connection between believers, honouring the Trust not to sever what Allah has commanded to be joined. Those who are not joined in marriage, are still joined through kinship. Divorce changes nothing of the *ayat* that remind believers that they are of each other, *ba'dukum min ba'd.* The marital bond merely transforms back to the mutual guardianship that is characteristic of believers.

The Quran is cognizant of the fact that many couples break-up and make-up. Because there is no fornication in Islam, those splits and reunions are set within the boundaries of a marital relationship with all of its rights and responsibilities. Break-ups take one of two forms of *talaq* – revocable and irrevocable. "Divorce (*at-talaq*) is twice, then either holding on (*imsak*) with goodness or releasing (*tasreeh*) with beauty..." (Al-Baqarah 2:229). *Talaq* is revocable only twice, which means that the couple can choose to make-up within a specified period or *'iddah* based on their original marital agreement. A third break-up is considered irrevocable meaning that after the *'idah* the couple must part.

Talaq is a verbalized intention to end the marital relationship. It commences a waiting or cooling period that encompasses three menstrual cycles if a woman is regularly menstruating, or three months if she is not regular or is no longer menstruating. If she is pregnant then the *'idah* is extended to the duration of pregnancy and birth. "And for those who are despairing of their messes of your women, and you are unsure then their period is three months and for those who have no messes. And for those who are pregnant their time is until delivery. And whoever heeds Allah, He makes ease out of his affair" (At-Talaq 65:4). Patience, kindness and generosity are demanded of both partners during this time.

During the *'idah* a woman is to maintain exclusivity, *tarabus*, of herself and all marital rights and responsibilities with the exception of intimacy are to be maintained by both partners. "Divorcees (women) are to maintain exclusivity (*tarabus*) of themselves for three periods and it is not permissible for them to keep secret what Allah has created in their wombs if they believe in Allah and the Last Day. And, in such [circumstances], their husbands are more correct to return to them if they [both] wish reconciliation. And for women are rights just as there are duties on them in accordance with what is good (*ma'ruf*) and for men is a degree (*darajah*) on them. And Allah is Endearing, Wise" (Al-Baqarah 2:228). That added degree is that of duty upon the husband, and potentially father of an unborn child, to support the wife during this difficult period irrespective of how he feels or the ultimate outcome of the process.

The wife, short of rebellious or lewd behavior, has the right to stay in the marital home, to be housed as the husband is housed. During this time her life must proceed as normal, and she is not be restricted or harmed in any way. "House them where you are housed from your means and do not harm them so as to restrict them and if they are pregnant then provide for them until they deliver. So, if they nurse for you then give them the recompense and confer among yourselves with kindness. And if you find yourself in difficulties let another nurse for him" (At-Talaq 65:6). The father is responsible for the financial care of the mother while she is nursing their child. And if for some reason she cannot nurse, then he is responsible for compensating another woman to nurse the child. This removes the economic burden from the mother while she cares for their baby irrespective of whether they stay with each other or part.

The Quran is clear that it is not demanded from men what is beyond their capacity. A husband can only spend of what he has but spend he must. "So that he of means spends in accordance with his means, and he whose provision is limited must spend of what Allah has provided him. Allah does not task a *nafs* except to the extent of what He has given it. Allah will provide ease after difficulty" (At-Talaq 65:7). Allah is knowing of the difficulty that these accommodations and financial demands place on men, not to mention the emotional control that they must exercise in dealing kindly with someone with which they wish to part or who wishes to part with them. But the promise of rewards for heedfulness are great, as are the punishments in the case of rejection of Allah's guidance.

There is no *'idah* if consummation of the marriage has not taken place. "Oh you who believe, if you marry the believing women then divorce them before touching them, you are not due from them a waiting period (*'idah*) that you count. So, pleasurably provide [gift them] and release them a beautiful release" (Al-Ahzab 33:49). In cases where a couple has tied the knot to get to know each other lawfully, in the light of Allah, but have not consummated their relationship there is no waiting period and no financial obligations on the man except for the provision of a good-will parting gift according to the man's measure of wealth (Al-Baqarah 2:236). If a duty or dowry has already been agreed upon, then the woman is entitled to half unless she willfully remits any amount. "And if a man divorces a woman before consummation but after a 'duty' has been set then half of that duty is to be fulfilled, unless the woman pardons or whoever is tasked with overseeing the fulfillment of the marital contract. To pardon is closer to heedfulness and not to neglect the favour among the parties involved" (Al-Baqarah 2:237). The act of pardoning the man is an appeal to the woman to act with generosity as well. She is entitled to half the duty, but since the marriage was not consummated, she is encouraged to forgive part or all of this sum. It is, however, a pardon because she is not obliged to do so. Such is the gravity of a marital promise in Islam, which becomes even more serious if the couple has taken the deep dive.

A consummated union is one where the parties have laid everything bare before each other, not just in the raw physical sense but more so in heart. This is an act of trust before it is one of pleasure, for to give and receive pleasure our guard must be let down. The ability to see and sense each other is only possible if the instinct to cover is overcome. That willingness to expose, to express vulnerability, requires inner negotiations, a process of self-persuasion that everything is going to be okay. There is no dearer gift than the giving of self, to allow another to move in, to make space as they gradually settle with the belongings of their heart and body. Allah knows that this process is more intense for women and so when it ends men are commanded to be patient, generous and beautiful in their treatment.

Heedful men owe their divorcees provisions based on what is customary (Al-Baqarah 2:241). They cannot take back any of the gifts that they had given their wives, let alone to extract wealth from them that was never theirs. "...And it is not lawful for you to take anything of what you have given them except if it is feared that Allah's limits will not be upheld. So, if you fear that Allah's limits will not be upheld then there is no offense on them regarding what she sacrifices. These are Allah's limits, so, do not violate them. And whoever violates Allah's limits are the ones who are unjust" (Al-Baqarah 2:229). A limited flexibility is introduced to this command based on a woman's volition to give back something of those gifts to avoid enmity, to keep within the limits of Allah that demand the maintenance of kinship between them. This is a permission for her to give back and him to receive what would otherwise be unlawful for him to demand or to reacquire especially in cases where she is the party wishing to end the marriage.

The prohibition of a man taking anything he had once given to his wife is driven with even greater severity in the case of him deciding to marry another woman. Allah acknowledges the hurt that always results from such changes of heart. "But if you do decide to take one wife in place of another, you may not take any of what you had given (to her) even if it was a veritable treasure. Would take it through slander and clear sin? And how would you take any of it and you have become so intimate with each other, and they have taken a deep covenant (*mithaq ghaleez*) from you?" (An-Nisa' 4:20-21). The expectations of a woman's magnanimity, her capacity to pardon, are strongly mitigated when the husband is leaving her for another woman. The tone now changes with the husband, and he is not permitted to even entertain taking anything back no matter how much he had given. It is here that the expression *mithaq ghaleez* is warranted as a reminder to him of the depth and complexity of what was once shared and correspondingly the depth of the hurt and challenge of healing.

Such a *mithaq* is only mentioned in two other instances in the Quran. "And when We took from the prophets their covenant (*mithaq*) and from you [Muhammad], and from Noah, and Ibrahim, and Musa, and Issa son of Maryam, and we took from them a deep covenant (*mithaq ghaleez*)" (Al-Ahzab 33:7). The five named prophets are distinguished from the rest by a much deeper covenant because of the complexity, challenges, and dangers of their missions. The second mention is in the context of the extraction of *mithaq ghaleez* from the Children of Israel to not transgress in the Sabbath (An-Nisa' 4:154). Think about these *ayat*, then consider that this is the same expression that Allah uses to explain to men the nature of the promise they made to their wives. You will not only understand the depth of the marital bond but also realize the understanding, mercy and compassion that Allah has for His female servants.

On one occasion when Umar Ibn Al-Khattab ﵁, the second caliph, had just completed a sermon where he asked the men, "Why do you go to excess in women's dowries even though during the lifetime of the Prophet the companions used to pay 400 dirhams or less in dowry? If the increase in the dowries was a sign of piety or honour in the sight of Allah, you would have not surpassed the companions in this regard. So, let me not hear that any man paid a woman, a dowry of more than 400 dirhams." As he descended the pulpit, a woman who had attended the sermon challenged his order. "Oh Commander of the Believers! Do you forbid the people to pay more than 400 dirhams as women's dowries?" He answered, "Yes." To which she replied, "Did you not hear what Allah said in the Quran about dowries?" He asked, "Which verse do you mean?" to which she responded, "Did you not hear Allah saying, 'If you have given one of the women a *qintar* (great amount) in gifts then do not take back from it anything. Would you take it in slander and clear sin?" To this, Umar ﷺ conceded, "Oh Allah I ask You for pardon. Everybody is more knowledgeable than Umar… The woman is right while the man has erred."

With the duration of *'idah* reached and the question of generosity settled, it is now time to part or reconsider and reconcile. "So, if their time is reached either hold onto them in kindness or part with them in kindness and call to witness two people endued with justice from among you and uphold the testimony for Allah. This is how he who believes in Allah and the Last Day is counselled and he who heeds Allah, he will make for him away out" (At-Talaq 65:2). Either way, two people must be present to witness how the couple wishes to proceed. They must witness with fairness and equity whether both partners wish to resume their marital relationship. This protects against any unilateral decision the husband might wish to make including a coerced return to his wife. *Both must agree to reconcile no matter who initiated the break-up*. The option to reconcile, however, is only open after the first two break-ups.

Allah has prevented the possibility of reconciliation immediately after the third *talaq* while demanding the maintenance of all the duties and rights of *'idah*. The relative ease of making-up during the process that follows the first two pronouncements of *talaq*, is now replaced with the command that the wife must marry another man (Al-Baqarah 2:230). If for some reason that marriage should dissolve, then there is no offense on the former parties should they wish to return to each other (Al-Baqarah 2:230). This intense injunction is intended to re-establish the solemnity of the marital bond that is clearly being taken for granted. It sanctions the couple for hasty behavior, instability, and causing each other, particularly the wife, grief. Neither party is permitted to be so ill tempered, impatient, or immature, so as to utilize divorce in such an impulsive way. I once knew a couple who had divorced nine times because she threatened to kill herself every time he refused to comply. Clearly they were not following Allah's guidance and the validity of their continuing relationship is highly doubtful.

Whether the divorce is initiated by the husband or demanded by the wife, she must be given the opportunity to lawfully meet, be courted and loved by another man. Experiencing a new life is mandatory for honouring the depth of the *mithaq*. Only then can she make a more informed decision about whether she would like to remain with her new husband or return to her former mate. This imposition by Allah is phenomenal when you think about it. Not only must the husband honour all the conditions of *talaq* and *'idah*, but he must also do so knowing that his wife must wed another. Even if he hates it, even if she declines it, and even if society does not approve, Allah and His Messenger command it.

When Tamima Bint Wahb came to Prophet Muhammad ﷺ and said, "Oh Messenger of Allah, Rifa'ah divorced me irrevocably, and then I married Abdur-Rahman ibn Az-Zubair, but being with him is akin to [being with] a piece of cloth [no chemistry]." The Prophet ﷺ smiled and said, "Perhaps you want to return to Rifa'ah? No, not until you taste his [Abdur-Rahman's] sweetness, and he tastes your sweetness" (Sahih Bukhari). She, very candidly speaking, must share the bed of her new husband in order to make an informed decision about her future. If, after all is said and done, she wishes to return to her former mate and he of course is amenable, then no one has the right to obstruct their reunion. It is her choice if the couple reaches an amicable agreement (Al-Baqarah 2:232).

As there is no coercion in faith, in *the deen*, there is certainly no coercion in lesser matters including marriage. When Allah commanded Prophet Muhammad ﷺ to ask his wives whether they desired the life of this world or wished to remain with him, He was teaching us just that. "Oh Prophet say to your wives: if you desire the life of this world and its accoutrements so come, I will remunerate you and release you a beautiful release (*sarah jameel*). And if you desire Allah and His Messenger and the home of the Hereafter, then indeed, Allah has prepared for those who are doers of good among you a great reward" (Al-Ahzab 33:28-29). Every individual can choose to believe or not to believe and every individual can choose to stay in a marriage or to leave. If the wife chooses another life, she *must* be relieved of the marital bond and beautifully at that. The Prophet ﷺ, himself, was not given the right to hold anyone against their will, nor were they to be reproached if they chose to leave. Although all of his wives chose to stay, this act was precedent setting for the believers.

There is no explicit mention of wife-initiated divorce in the Quran because *this* is Allah's command: a woman who requests divorce *must* be obliged by her husband with all the rights and duties of divorce still in place. If there is any hesitancy on his part to agree because of material considerations, then as mentioned above there is no offense on either of them if she gives something of his gifts back. When Jamila, the wife of Thabit ibn Qays, sought the Prophet's ﷺ help when she longer wished to remain married, the Prophet ﷺ asked if Jamila was willing to return the garden that Thabit had given her as dowry to which she agreed. The Prophet then instructed Thabit to accept the garden and *give her a divorce* (Sahih Bukhari).

Islamic scholars and jurists would later consider this *khul'* – wife- initiated divorce – as opposed to *talaq* which they reserved for the husband. To be clear *khul'* was a device crafted by Muslim jurists to provide women with the ability to end their marriages when their husbands were obstinate. Bizarrely the jurists made *khul'* subject to the husbands consent and if that fails, which it inevitably always does, then the wife is to seek a judicial ruling which remains incredibly challenging if the husband withholds such consent. Moreover, they understood the return of dowry to be a form of ransom that the woman offered in exchange for her freedom, making it a condition of *khul'*. Yet Allah says in the Quran that the return of any gifts was subject to fears that His limits would not be upheld drawing the attention of believers to the higher ground of pardon and generosity. A woman's right to divorce upon request is not disputed in the Quran or Sunnah and is not contingent on the return of any gifts, particularly as such gifts may no longer exist – sold, consumed, lost, depreciated – at the time of separation.

For women living in non-predominantly Muslim societies and hence secular judicial systems the option of resorting to the courts is constrained by the common stipulation that the presiding judge must be Muslim. Calls by some contemporary scholars to permit any legitimate court to grant a woman divorce have been very challenging and tend to be marginalized by the more vocal members of *fatwa* councils. Although *fatwas* are non-binding legal opinions many believers seek them for guidance on matters around which they have doubt and fear contravening their faith. Discussions in the European and North American fatwa councils have been ongoing for years with published opinions either obscured by unclear language or removed from their websites completely, against the wishes and sometimes majority vote of their members. Abandoning women in legal limbo is irresponsible and immeasurably damaging to the families and communities of our Ummah.

Contrary to its face-value, *khul'* gave the impression – and eventually contributed to a widespread culture – that a husband could deny his wife a divorce. This is a blatant violation of Allah's commands. "And if you divorce women and they reach their term, so hold on to them with goodness or release them with goodness. And do not harmfully hold them to transgress and whoever does this has committed an injustice against himself. And do not take Allah's *ayat* in contempt and remember Allah's blessings on you and what He sent down on you of the Book and wisdom to advise you with it. And heed Allah and know that Allah is knowing of all things" (Al-Baqarah 2:231). A husband simply cannot hold his wife against her will. When the Prophet ﷺ intervened in the case of Jamila, he simply instructed Thabit to divorce her. Thabit did not have a choice. That is the culture that our scholars and legal systems ought to have nurtured for the sake of all parties involved.

Khul' also included the unwarranted condition that the wife demonstrate *valid* reasons for her pursuit of divorce even though no such requirement is enumerated in the Quran or in the case of Jamila. She was simply no longer in love with Thabit. Otherwise, she stated that she had no issues with him. Making the provision of valid reasons, however one might define that, a condition of *khul'* has only served to destroy any hope of reconciliation on a transcendental level. How do you find friendship after airing each other's faults and secrets? After striving to show how awful someone was to you, instead of struggling to forgive and move forward?

Khul' also altered the dynamics of the *'idah*. Although the *'idah* remains after the woman has obtained her divorce, its purpose its greatly altered because neither party is required to fulfill its duties other than for the woman to wait. She does not remain in the marital home so there is no chance of the couple possibly changing their minds without having to initiate another marital contract. Whether it is the woman or the man who initiates the divorce the purpose and need for the *'idah* as it is envisioned under *talaq* should not change. When the husband pronounces divorce even at the request of the wife, he still owes her kindness and support until the *'idah* is over. And she is tasked with patience, courtesy and an open heart during this period. The conditions of *khul'* diverted people, especially men but also women, from the truthful effort that the Quran was demanding of them before the final farewell.

Our Ummah is so far from the Quranic and Prophetic guidance on divorce that most believers would be forgiven for thinking it strange to discuss this matter in the middle of our expositions on connectivity. Divorce has become one of the most divisive social practices. Painful, time consuming, expensive, hurtful, humiliating, enraging, and frightening are just some of the words that come to mind based the experience of countless women. Unfortunately for many others, the situation is much worse. Divorce, more often than not, is ugly with few able to overcome the evil inclinations of their *nafs* paraded on by the cajoling of Shaytan.

She sat in the court of the Kaaba after performing *'umrah* – the lesser pilgrimage – tears streaming down her cheeks. "Ya Rab, you know why I've come. You are not in need of my words. You know the depth of my heart. To You I cannot say anything other than truth, for You see through me. You know what I've endured and how hard I've tried. You know what is best for me and my children, but I can't. I need your help. I want out." For three days she prayed in the most sacred place on earth, the House of Allah, pleading for Allah's guidance, for His approval and support of the decision she was about to finally make. These were some of the hardest days of her life and they were about to get much harder.

She was one of those women who had to resort to the courts to obtain *khul'* because her ex wanted to make it as difficult as possible for her. Living and working in a Muslim society governed by an Islamic judicial system at the time, she applied for *khul'* through the courts. Month after month she would appear in court to make her plea only to be given another date. It was exhausting, depressing and humiliating. When her ex finally showed up for a session, he told the judge that he did not want a divorce. This despite the fact that they had been living apart for months and that he had told her to get one if she wanted giving the false impression that he would consent. When the husband does not consent, the system in this state mandates the appointment of two arbitrators to attempt reconciliation within six months of the request by the judge. Her wishes, previous court appearances, and document presentations, were all dashed. She had to comply.

Two male arbitrators were assigned their case. She met with them first. She informed them of her wishes. Although she kept it short and respectful, they were not genuinely interested in anything she said. Their role was to pressure her to give in, to return to her husband and get on with life. The reality of *valid reasons* hit hard. What did these men think was valid? How much would she be forced to reveal? Did any of it matter in the face of their predetermined mission?

The challenge was that she did not wish to air her family's private affairs. She wanted to maintain that semblance of civility that she knew her faith demanded. One day, she thought, this would all be over, and they would have to replant the seeds of friendship. They were believers, they had three children between them. So, she remained as reserved as possible given their pushing and prodding. Two men was not exactly conducive to deep discussions or a fair arbitration. All they saw was a woman, a western bred and educated woman, who needed a lesson in humility, to yield – submit to her husband – as the report they produced would ultimately conclude.

They each received a copy of the report at their next court hearing. The first line sent her heart into the deepest black whole. *The marriage had failed because of the obstinacy of the wife.* After months, months, of wasting her time attending court, suppressing her sadness, speaking truth, trying to protect what she could of her family's privacy as Allah commanded her, she was found at fault. The judge ordered the couple to take the reports, reflect on them until several months later when he would give them his judgment. She left the court room and rushed down to a lawyer who had become a dear brother over the course of the preceding months. When he saw the report, he advised her to leave the country within 48 hours before her ex had the chance to ban their travel. He told her that with a report like that, she would not only have to pay a heavy financial price for the divorce, but she could lose the children. That was her red line. No one was going to take her children.

Within 24 hours she had booked the flights leaving behind everything – her home, furnishings, valuables, clothes, car and job. But her real everything was with her, the kids. Fortunately, she had a close relative living with her at the time, who could wrap up the loose ends that she was forced to leave unattended. She returned home tired, depressed, jobless, with three young children. But she was wiser. She hired the best lawyer that she could find, something that she had refused to do during the *khul'* process assuming the truth to be sufficient. But the truth sometimes needs stronger arms, someone to help carry it. Upon finding out that she had returned home, her ex made a pre-emptive move and finally divorced her – *in absentia*. A home divorce would have meant a potentially very different division of marital assets.

It is extremely disheartening how our misguided divorce culture and its religio-legal manifestations impelled this couple into so much discord. The circumstances that led to the divorce were painful enough without the need for so much negative pressure and grief, wasted time and resources. All of this made disciplining the *nafs* to focus on the higher objectives of faith and family even more challenging than they already were. Beyond the hardship of the separation, there was no *valid reason* why they could not maintain Allah's limits to treat each other with kindness and dignity – to honour *al-mithaq al-ghaleez* upon which Allah has bestowed an authoritative sultan.

Quranic guidance is not about unwarranted male privilege but rather order within family and society. Divine instructions are presented so that each party learns how to control their own behavior while providing the other with the greatest possible latitude for a dignified life. This is detectible not only in the language of the rulings in the Quran, but in its description of women in the narratives that reveal their magnanimity – a woman is commanded to and ultimately yields only to her Lord.

It is often stated that the relative ease of marriage and divorce in Islam are intended to prevent believers from being tempted to fornicate, entertain any kind of sexual promiscuity, or engage in extra-marital affairs. A believer has no excuse when it comes to these matters. They are unequivocally forbidden. But on a more refined plane, when we study the *ayat* concerning these life transforming events we find the sublime appeal to connection. In divorce no less than in marriage believers are called upon to recall Allah's favours, to recognize the dangers of division, and to have compassion for one another. We are called to put our trust in Allah, following His guidance and disavowing inclinations of greed. "And He will provide for him from where he did not anticipate and whoever puts their trust in Allah, He is his assurance. Indeed, Allah will achieve this affair. He made for everything a term appointed" (At-Talaq 65:3).

Divorce is among one of the hardest events in life. Those for whom this is not the case have missed the sanctity of the marital relationship. The Quran recognizes the likelihood that many believers may falter in the process, forgetting to honour what was, acknowledge the pain that is, and proceed with dignity. The culture that has emerged around divorce, unwarranted male privilege based on misreading of the Quran, and biased legal systems challenge the essence and word of revelation. Amidst all of that, we must struggle to recall our connection, *ba'dukum min ba'd*. Allah turns in forgiveness and mercy to those who try to put things right and remain heedful. "And if they [the couple] part, Allah will suffice each from His bounty, and Allah is ever Expansive, Wise" (An-Nisa' 4:130). The closing of one book, is the opening of another, a renewal of purposeful paths not intended to sever relations but to re-establish them once more within their original and immutable boundaries.

ꕥ The Time of Dandelions

And it is as such that We have made you a moderate [literally middle] ummah that you may be witnesses over the people and the Prophet be witness over you. And We did not make the qiblah [prayer direction] that you were on except to know who follows the Messenger from he who would turn on his heels. And it was ever great [difficult] except on those whom Allah had guided. And Allah would never cause your faith to be lost. Indeed, Allah is toward people Compassionate, Merciful. We have seen the turning of your [Muhammad] face in the sky, and We will turn you toward a qiblah with which you will be content. So, turn your face toward al-Masjid al-Haram. And wherever you [believers] are, turn your faces toward it [for prayers]. And indeed, those who were given the Book know that it is the truth from their Lord, and Allah is not unaware of what they do (Al-Baqarah 2:143-144).

I often wonder if this momentous event, the changing of the direction of the *qiblah*, was to happen today who would follow the Messenger ﷺ and who would flee in another direction. Before facing the Kaaba, we used to pray toward *Bayt Al-Maqdis* or Al-*Masjid Al-Aqsa*, in Al-Quds known as Jerusalem. Al-Quds with its eminent position in the lives of several of Allah's prophets including Ibrahim, Dawood, Sulaiman and 'Issa, was this Ummah's first *qiblah*, the direction toward which our beloved Prophet Muhammad ﷺ and the earliest Muslims turned in prayer.

The changing of the *qiblah* from Al-Quds to the Kaaba in Makkah occurred after Prophet Muhammad ﷺ had migrated to Madinah. During one of his prayers in Al-Masjid Al-Nabawi, he received revelation to redirect the community of believers toward the Kaaba. This was a predestined decree, a decisive command, to distinguish those who truly believed from those who were disguised among their ranks. If connection to people and place was to fulfill its purpose, it had to be genuine.

Change of the *qiblah* also revealed the genuineness of those who had previously received the Book, the Jews of Madinah, some of whom knew yet still unjustly concealed the truth of Prophet Muhammad ﷺ. The initial alignment of the *qiblah* with the People of the Book – *ahl al-Kitab* – had established common ground among the followers of Islam's different prophets. The change of direction was not so much about distinguishing Islam as it was about teaching people the importance of following the Messenger and honouring the message, not clinging to the worldly and prioritizing their designs over those of Allah. Connection did have a material element, but its divine essence was much more significant and worthy for believers.

Allah's command permitted the Prophet ﷺ to demonstrate that Islam had come to distill and refine the distortions that had occurred in the messages before it. Facing the Kaaba emphasized a return to the pure monotheism of Prophet Ibrahim ﷺ. The Jews of Madinah viewed it as a snub to their authority and religious precedence. Henceforth, they would not follow the Prophet's *qiblah*, he would not follow their *qiblah*, nor would they even follow the *qiblah* of each other (Al-Baqarah 2:145). The change of direction was a suggestive moment, opening the eyes of the Ummah as to who believed and who betrayed.

This change, however, never altered the sanctity or reverence that believers had for al-Quds, which remains one of the holiest cities in Islam along with Makkah and Madinah. Al-Masjid Al-Haram, Al-Masjid Al-Nabawi and Al-Aqsa are Islam's holiest sites. So many believers continue to journey to Al-Aqsa to pray and plead, perhaps to walk in the footsteps of the beloved and all the nobility that preceded him.

This was the site of the *Isra'* and *Mi'raj*, when the earth met the seven heavens in a two-part night journey of flight and ascension in which Prophet Muhammad ﷺ traveled from Al-Masjid Al-Haram to Al-Masjid Al-Aqsa upholding the sanctity of Al-Quds in believing hearts. Occurring approximately one year before *hijrah* – migration of Prophet Muhammad ﷺ and the believers to Madinah – during a time of extreme persecution of the Ummah and personal sorrow for the Messenger ﷺ. He had just lost his beloved wife Khadijah ﷺ and dear uncle Abu Talib. The *Isra'* and *Mi'raj* infused a new spirit of hope into the ailing community as it confirmed them into a greater, eternally truthful reality. "Glory to He who transported His Servant by night from Al-Masjid Al-Haram to Al-Masjid Al-Aqsa, whose surroundings We have blessed, to show him of our *ayat*. Indeed, He is the Hearing, the Seeing" (Al-Isra' 17:1). While the Quran gives us a glimpse into that night, establishing the truth of the affair, it is the narrations of hadith that give us the delightful details.

The hadith describe Prophet Muhammad's ﷺ travel to Al-Aqsa on a white-winged horse-like creature. Inside the masjid were 124,000 prophets, whom the Messenger proceeded to lead in prayers. They then praised Allah, exchanged greeting of peace, and had some discussion about 'the Hour'.

When the time for ascension, *mi'raj*, came, Jibril ؑ accompanied Prophet Muhammad ﷺ to *As-Sakhrah Al-Musharafah*, the noble rock at the centre of the mosque. From there, they journeyed together through the seven heavens. At the gate of every level Jibril ؑ would ask the gatekeeper to open the gate, to which the gatekeeper responded with three questions: who are you? who is with you? and has he been summoned? When Jibril ؑ responded, the gate opened, and the gatekeeper welcomed Prophet Muhammad ﷺ and expressed jubilation with his visit. In each heaven, the Messenger of Allah ﷺ met with its inhabitants and was welcomed by a different prophet. Adam ؑ, Yahya ؑ, Yusuf ؑ, Idris ؑ, Harun ؑ, Musa ؑ and Ibrahim ؑ in that order.

In the seventh heaven Prophet Muhammad ﷺ was shown *Al-Bayt Al-Ma'mur*, literally the House of Abundant Supply, where groups of seventy-thousand angels performed their daily prayers never to return again, as each day invited a new group. It is here that the Prophet ﷺ received the command for the five daily *salah*. Starting at fifty salah per day, the Prophet ﷺ was persuaded by Prophet Musa ؑ based on his experience with his followers, to request multiple reductions from Allah. At five, the Prophet ﷺ, felt obliged to accept Allah's command with the beautiful assurance that He would grant a ten-fold reward for every good deed making the value of the five daily prayers equal to fifty. He then ascended even further until he reached the Lote Tree of the outermost boundary – *Sidrat al-Muntaha* – beyond which no earthly creature could pass. It is said that this is where the Prophet ﷺ saw Jibril ؑ in his true form.

His journey from Al-Haram to Al-Aqsa was a remembrance, an implanting in the collective consciousness of the Ummah, of the connection between places, prophets, prayers, and people. It reminded the believers that with every hardship there is ease, and that their patience in the face of violence, marginalization, and isolation would be rewarded. Al-Quds would be forever venerated in Muslim hearts.

Al-Quds is the sacred land of Allah's prophets and messengers, a witness to their unity and the unity of their leadership and messages to all people. In *Surah Al-Anbiya'*, The Prophets, Allah recounts the stories of several prophets informing us that "We made them *imams* guiding by Our command. And We revealed to them the performance of [all things] good, and establishment of prayer, and giving of *zakah*. And they were, to Us, worshipers [servants]" (Al-Anbiya' 21:73). The foundational elements of all prophetic messages are the same including to do good, stand for justice, be patient, establish prayer, give in charity, and fast among many other commonalities. "Indeed, this is your Ummah, one Ummah, and I am your Lord, so worship Me" (Al-Anbiya' 21:92) and in another *ayah* it ends with "and I am your Lord, so heed Me" (Al-Mu'minun 23:52). The prophets are one Ummah.

People too were once a single Ummah. But over the course of time, with changing fortunes, geographic distance, and most importantly susceptibility to the cajoling of the Shaytan, they began to differ over fundamental matters, some choosing to believe and others to disbelieve. As the Quran explains it, "People were once one Ummah. So, Allah sent the prophets, givers of good tidings and warnings, and sent down with them the Book in Truth, to adjudicate among the people regarding that which they differed. And no one differed in it except those who received it, after expositions [clear proofs] had come to them, out of insubordination among themselves. So, Allah guided those who believed regarding what they differed in of the truth by His permission. And Allah guides whoever He wills to the Straight Path" (Al-Baqarah 2:213). The prophets were sent to encourage and warn, to judge among the people with equity and justice. Those who disbelieved continued to dispute even after indisputable evidence had been provided to them. In contrast, differences in conceptions of truth were settled among those who believed by Allah's grace.

There are two kinds of differing evident in this *ayat*. There is the differing about the truth that occurs among believers for which there is a remedy because Allah is the helper of His servants. There is always a higher ground that true believers can reach and agree upon, the highest being what the Quran describes as a common word – *kalimatin sawa'* – or the worship of Allah alone. Then there is the differing about the truth that occurs between believers and disbelievers or among disbelievers, and for that there is no remedy because the disbelievers have no Helper and cannot appeal to a common word. The lack of guardianship and vindication for the unjust, meant that the unity of the ummah was bound to collapse (Ash-Shura 42:8). Of the three things that Prophet Muhammad ﷺ invoked Allah to protect his Ummah against, including not to be exterminated by famine, an external enemy, or self-affliction due to disunity, the last was not granted (Sahih Muslim). Unity demands effort and purification of the self in its individual and collective forms. The key for that had already been provided: accept the invitation of Allah and His Messenger.

Yet everyone remains subject to the mercy of respite for the duration of their lives or until the Day of Judgement. "And people were not but one ummah, then they differed. And were it not for a preceding word from your Lord, judgement would have been delivered between them regarding what they differed" (Yunus 10:19). Allah has decreed a term for everything. There is no hastening of His command. Time is the justification of the ultimate destiny of people and their communities.

The Quran also points to the irreconcilability of those who only believe in the material reality of truth, exclusively attaching value to worldly possessions and accolades, incapable of grasping things as pervasive as Allah's mercy. Their worldliness blinds them to Allah's wisdom and honours. To the value of unity. They cannot appreciate that it is Allah who has divided their livelihoods among them, and elevated some above others so that they may commission each other in various works. We are told that He could have granted the disbelievers immense opulence, but that would have altered the wisdom and purpose of wealth disparities and labour capacities that move the human spirit and drive civilizations. In any case, all the wealth they amass has no value in the Hereafter. All of it is nothing more than the pleasures of this world while the Hereafter, the real bliss, remains for the heedful (Az-Zhukhruf 43:31-35).

For each people Allah made a way of life (*shir'ah*), a path to the water, and a regimen (*minhaj*), routines and rituals that infuse order in each's collective journey (Al-Ma'idah 5:48). He could indeed have made us all one ummah, with the same *shir'ah* and *minhaj*, but instead He sought to test each people with what they had been given. The expectation, the exhortation, is that we all race to do good, to demonstrate the beauty of our way and our regimen, not to the exclusive benefit of ourselves or the detriment of others but for the benefit of the whole, the ummah that could have been.

Al-Quds is both the start and the finish line of that sacred race between people with different ways and rituals to demonstrate their beneficence or depravity. The city has been conquered and reconquered, ruled by those who would guard its sanctity as a place of unity and those who would impose their superiority through the persecution of others. Its first acquisition by the Muslims was under the rule of Umar Ibn Al-Khattab ﷺ, the Ummah's second caliph. Its previous rulers the Persian Zoroastrians and Roman Christians had shown little regard for the city's sanctity as a place of pilgrimage and worship for Muslims, Christians, and Jews. For the Persians, Al-Quds had no spiritual value permitting desecration of its holy sites, while the Christians only revered their sites, intentionally desecrating sites revered by the Jews as they had allied themselves with the Persians. For the Muslims all sites held sacred value and so restoring the city to its foundation of unity was seen a religious obligation.

For four long months, the Muslim army camped outside Al-Quds not wanting to shed blood in this holy land, while negotiating for a peaceful surrender. As part of the deal, the Muslims guaranteed the city's Christian inhabitants that they could continue to live and worship in Al-Quds, that their churches would be secured and that they would be protected against invasions. In exchange they were to pay the *jizya*, a tax lower than *zakah*. The Christians had witnessed precedence to these guarantees in Egypt, where the Muslims had made good on a similar pact with the Christian population there. The Grand Patriarch Sophronius agreed to these terms on condition that Umar, himself, come to sign the agreement.

Now at this time, Umar, was ruling over a vast region from the caliphate's base in Madinah and was known not to travel much. But he obliged the Patriarch given the significance attached to securing the future of Al-Quds. It is narrated that Umar entered the holy city on foot, tattered and bareheaded, while his servant rode his camel. The three had journeyed alone from Madinah to Al-Quds with Umar and his servant taking turns riding, it just happened to be his servant's turn upon arrival. No less a humble servant of Allah, Umar was true to his word, "We are a people who Allah honoured with Islam." Islam was his crown and shield, his treasure and truth. While this surprised those who were anticipating the spectacle typical of regal visits, it fomented the power of Islam and Muslims in people's hearts – no embellishments were needed.

The agreement with the Grand Patriarch was thus signed and the keys to the Holy Sepulcher were handed over. Umar resettled a number of Jewish families who were permitted to return. The Muslims worked hard to restore the city to its former glory establishing it as a hub of scholarship, pilgrimage, trade, and beautiful structures including the Dome of the Rock. It is this faith that re-established the unity that Al-Quds demanded, a unity that embraced the city's pluralistic glory. For centuries Al-Quds thrived in peace and harmony. To this day the keys to the Holy Sepulcher are held by a Muslim family, a member of whom opens the church daily for Palestinian Christians and pilgrims to worship.

Over time, the unjust privileging of wealth and power, the exchange of guidance for misguidance, meant divisions were weakening Muslim unity and legitimacy. Al-Quds fell into the hands of the Fatimids, a heretic sect of Islam, that desecrated the Holy Sepulcher in their attempts to remove remnants of Umar ﵁. This deeply ruptured relations with the Christians and created alarm throughout Europe. Although the church was eventually reconstructed, and the site maintained, a thread of discord had been sewn into an otherwise beautiful tapestry. How convenient was it for the Europeans, who were reeling in the cultural and economic despair of their dark age, to tug at this thread unraveling the entire fabric and justifying for themselves the pillaging of another people's lives and land. This is how the Crusades were initiated against the Muslim world.

Pope Urban II took the lead to demonize the Muslims inciting Christian fighters to join the battle. Savagery and salvation in one swoop. His false tropes justified the torture and slaughter of tens of thousands of innocent people – people living on their lands. The ugliness of the Crusaders was unspeakable, boiling and roasting people and eating them. When they reached Al-Quds in 1099, it took five weeks and the murder of up to one-hundred thousand people to claim the city. In one account, the Crusaders waded in blood up to their knees sending those who had not been killed scurrying to other regions. All of this made the terms of surrender that Salahuddin Al-Ayyubi offered to the Crusaders upon reclaiming the city in 1187 very astonishing.

Born in Tikrit in 1137, Salahuddin was ethnically Kurd not Arab. He grew up in Damascus, as his father joined the service of the ruler of Northern Syria, in a world that vilified the Crusaders but had little hope of overcoming them. He was both a renowned scholar and formidable warrior, widely considered the greatest general of all time after Khaled Ibn Al-Waleed ﵁. Salahuddin was acutely aware that taking back Al-Quds demanded unity of the Ummah – this was not only a matter of pragmatism, but it was also a sacred condition. His approach was therefore very strategic. Unfolding over a span of ten years, Salahuddin thought and fought to consolidate power with patience in victory and defeat.

His eventual entry into Al-Quds defied everything the Europeans had expected. There would be no revenge. He offered the Crusaders incredibly generous terms including safe passage, restoration of their holy sites, and guarantees of secure worship. His magnanimity agitated the Crusaders even as it spared their lives, property, women, and children. The thought that the enemy could so benevolent, inclusive, righteous, exposed their lies, challenged whatever light still flickered in their wretched depths. They attacked again and lost, ultimately losing hope that Al-Quds could be recovered so long as Salahuddin was alive. He passed in 1193.

For a brief period from 1229 to 1244, the Crusaders regained control of the city but then were finally expelled by the Mamluks who united with a Sunni Persian dynasty to secure the city once and for all. The Mamluks fortified the city, established major infrastructure, defenses, schools, mosques, hospitals, charitable endowments, and markets. In 1516 rulership over Al-Quds passed to the Ottomans who continued to build on the legacy of their predecessors. Under the leadership of Sulaiman Al-Qanuni, also known as Sulaiman the Magnificent, the Ottomans continued to consolidate power through the introduction of new laws, notably to protect religious minorities, and the requisite legal structures for the functioning of a robust society. Muslims, Christians and Jews lived and worshiped together during a 400-year span of peaceful co-existence and enlightenment. No one was persecuted for their faith. People from all over the world were welcome.

By the mid-1800s the Ottoman Empire was in decline. Internal divisions and external pressures from a rapidly industrializing and modernizing Europe instigated a process that would see the Empire gradually lose territory and regional influence. Pillaging the lands of others fueled Europe's industries and economies. In 1882 British forces invaded and occupied Egypt, an Ottoman province, to secure its interests in the region while making way for the impending Zionist project to create a Jewish homeland in Palestine. But it was not until the Ottoman Empire lost in WWI that the British gained control of Palestine and were able to brazenly commit it to the Zionist cause through the Balfour Declaration. Israel declared independence in 1948 and occupied Al-Quds in 1967.

For the Zionists, Judaism was transformed from a religious covenant to an extremist nationalist identity. To many rabbis and truthful Jews, this was not acceptable, this was not their faith, nor was the displacement, ethnic cleansing, theft of land and property, torture, killing, and detention of Palestinian men, women, and children not to mention the violation of nature that all this injustice entailed. These Jews, based in and out of Palestine, acknowledged the peace and safety within which they had lived and traveled among the local Palestinian population. What the Zionists were doing was no more representative of the Jewish faith than the Crusaders were representative of the Christian faith, at least not the faith of the Torah and Gospel mentioned in the Quran.

The occupation of Al-Quds, the destruction of Palestine, the current genocide, mark a new era of suffering for our Ummah. We need to heed the lessons of the past, we need to heed Allah, if the sanctity and unity of Al-Aqsa are ever to be recovered, if the connection that this holy place was intended to evoke is to once more fill the hearts of believers – *all believers.*

The story of Al-Aqsa, and the current tragic chapter filling its pages with the blood of martyrs and innocent lives, have instigated new forms and intensities of human connection. Unlike any time in the past, the current crisis is being livestreamed for the whole world to witness. For over 500 days with a death toll that some have placed in the hundreds of thousands and still counting, we have witnessed the horrendous cruelty of the world in which we live, the one we permitted to emerge. Some people have lost all sense of connection.

The genocide has revealed the decay of global institutions that confirmed their deference to the states that first created them and not the rules they purport to uphold for the collective good. It showed us how democracies and authoritarian dictatorships are scarcely to be distinguished when it comes to Palestine. This is not an encounter of Muslims with the non-Muslim West but rather one of sound hearts and the depraved everywhere. And those with sound hearts have been searching for answers.

Stunned by the beauty and resilience of the Palestinian people, many are discovering Islam much like those who witnessed Salahuddin's amnesty to the Crusaders. They are reading about the history of Palestine, familiarizing themselves with the Quran and our beloved Prophet. These people are changing the Islamic landscape. They are discovering, articulating, and disseminating the primary sources within their cultural contexts and for their generation, one that is seeking the healing power of connection among themselves and across cultures. These developments must be embraced as difficult as that may be for some traditionalists who see rigidity as safety and continuity. These new entrants and their understandings are vital for weaving Islam in the fabric of their societies and the sustainability of future peace.

Their inclusion imposes new demands on the Ummah. We must work on ourselves. Only with free intellectual and cultural exchange, with gentle communications, can these new connections take root. The recognition of a changing landscape and the Ummah's growing membership must be nurtured inside us even before we can successfully engage with others, before they can feel the pull of our hearts welcoming them to the Ummah.

Changing technologies and social media have impacted individual and communal perceptions of the genocide, but this has not led to a mitigation of raw power and compromise as expected, at least not in the immediate term. Governments all over the world have been ignoring the demands of their people to stop the aggression, to sanction the occupier, to help defend the Palestinians. No one has so much as been able to enforce the provision of humanitarian aid or challenge the US veto in the UN Security Council. This will undoubtedly lead to self-harm. The unjust and unjustifiable state of affairs is unravelling itself. But it will require years if not decades for sound-hearted individuals and communities around the world to reform the institutions that either rejected or were impotent in the face of their demands. The lack of ethics of responsibility in government, academia, technology, business, and media has been laid bare.

Amidst the exposure of this widespread institutional corruption, a new global consciousness is emerging. This chapter is titled after the metaphor that Chinese netizens have used to represent Palestinian fighters. Dandelions, a flower that the Chinese online community chose in its search for an appropriately poetic and symbolic description of the Palestinian resistance. The term has gained traction since the escalation of Israel's aggression on Gaza and the incredibly valiant stand of its freedom fighters despite the odds.

Palestinian fighters, like the metaphor suggests, are the bitter-sweet scented blooms of the earth, rising and thriving in disturbed soil, in harsh conditions. They are the heralds of spring turning green fields into gold. Their roots, stems, and flowers are medicine for a sickly world. Those who have tried to cast them off as weeds have failed miserably. They have only drawn attention to their plight.

The world now knows how dandelions have been cheated of their rightful place, it knows their suffering – constantly plucked, crushed, and mowed. We have learned the value of their deep taproots in grounding and connection, and their airborne seeds that ensure the survival of their species and those of so many others who depend on them. We have learned of their resilience in the face of conditions that most other flowers could not bear. Dandelions remind us of the interconnectedness of all life, embodying Allah's *ayat* in the most sublime ways.

Through this metaphor, Chinese netizens demonstrate such a beautiful understanding, even admiration, for those who have faced the harshest criticism in defending the Palestinian cause. Wielding sticks or stones, these are a people accustomed to fighting for freedom till their last breath. This is a fight for justice everywhere, a call to unity for sound hearts.

Our Creator gifted us, all of us, dignity and light that consistently inspires us to redress the injustices of past and present, in this is there is hope. The connectivity of all creation propels us to act through mercy and equity. We were meant to know one another. Conscientious people around the world are seeking truth, looking to each other to restore a moral order that can help us deal with a tragedy the like of which we have not witnessed in our lifetimes. Our governments have taught us to look beyond politics, to re-educate ourselves with the aim of returning to the core values of our shared humanity. Only then can we hope to reform our political systems, restore moral order, and effectively address the economic and social crises we are facing, not by violating each other but by finding mutually beneficial alternatives. Every land has its bounties, we do not need to pillage, corrupt, and kill to enrich ourselves.

To speak of Al-Quds is to speak of the Amanah, the Trust, not to possess this or that land, it is all Allah's earth, but to hold to the unity that it represents and demands, unity among sound hearts of the past, present, and future. The truth of this city is one of sanctity, interconnection, and a resilience unparalleled anywhere on earth. It is here that we witness the *ayat* of Allah in their unfathomable complexity, the convergence of His Prophets beyond time, and the most intense struggles of His *'ebad* – the best of them and the worst of them.

Al-Quds has always held a special meaning for this Ummah, the Ummah of Muhammad ﷺ, from among whom is a party of guardians – those creating a path that extends to Paradise with their luminous yellow bloom, the dandelions. It is a city that was and will always remain the Ummah's test of unity. This is where we face our reckoning.

The Glorifiers

She danced. She danced like her life, everyone's life, depended on it. In this open competition she must persuade the others with the duration and tilts of her moves that she is the best choice. A few hundred among thousands are qualified, permitted to dance. When a dancer is convinced that another is better, she either ceases to dance or joins in by imitating the other contestant's moves. They do this for hours until all those still dancing follow the same routine. This is when everyone buzzes with excitement, there is a winner. It is time to go home.

I am of course talking about honeybees, nest-site scouts, and how they communicate during their search for a suitable nesting site. "And your Lord revealed to the bees, 'Take from the mountains houses, and from the trees, and what they [humans] lattice. Then eat from all the produce [of flowers], so pursue the ways of your Lord.' There emerges from her insides a syrup of different colours, in it is a healing for people. Indeed, in this is an *ayah* for a folk who [actively] think" (An-Nahl 16:68-69). We often think of honeybees in terms of their vital role in pollination and the delicious honey they give us, we are also discovering the anti-cancer properties of their venom and its major component melittin, but Allah points us to yet another gift of this incredible creature: how to make collective decisions that are also filled with sweetness, healing, and light.

In the Quran, Allah commands us to consult each other in mutual affairs, whether in public or private matters. This consultative process is referred to as *shura*, an advice seeking process. "And those who respond to their Lord, and establish prayer, and their affair is conducted by *shura* among themselves and out of what We provide them, they spend" (Ash-Shura 42:38). The literal meaning of *shura* is the extraction of honey from its source alluding to the best teachers we have concerning how to successfully make collective decisions.

Honeybees operate in a complex reality, very much like ours, that emphasizes the necessity for collaboration. Allah revealed numerous and complex survival criteria that the bees use to assess the suitability of nesting sites. He mandated the bees with a fascinating form of decision making that enables them to choose their new dwelling with extreme accuracy. Every scout bee participates directly in this process rather than through representatives. As described above, they dance to present their proposed choice. Each routine guides to the location of choice while simultaneously demonstrating the extent to which it meets divinely revealed criteria. Other scouts must make independent assessments having checked out the sites for themselves. They do not offer blind allegiance. As more bees coalesce over a certain site, support for weaker alternatives fade. Everyone is focused on survival, which demands collective success.

Our teachers gift us with several principles for effective group decision-making. It is indisputable that the bees follow the guidance revealed to them by Allah. They have strict references regarding what they need to achieve and how they can achieve it. Each scout is focused on the shared goal that benefits the swarm, not on gaining support for her specific proposal. This is how they remain flexible and bona fide participants. Not all bees are involved in this process, different groups have different roles in which they are expected to excel for the benefit of the collective. The queen bee has her role and does not intervene in the decision-making process. The scout bees seek diverse solutions that all approximate, to a greater or lesser extent, the criteria they were told leads to success. They then aggregate all this information and debate an optimal choice. A decision is ultimately made when quorum, not consensus, is reached to maintain efficiency while not compromising on accuracy. Quorum is a state whereby there are enough supporters for a choice that warrants the confidence required to make a decision.

If you think this process is just for bees, think again. Although scientists have focused on the brain, I believe certain decisions, the most important ones, emerge from our hearts, peculiarly shaped like a swarm of bees. Irrespective, we make decisions in much the same way as honeybee swarms except instead of individual bees we have neurons. When faced with the need to decide on two or more alternatives, different neuron groups will *vote* for one or the other alternative. No single neuron knows the full picture or is reliable due to random fluctuations in firing rates, but a coherent decision will eventually emerge. Neurons competing in our heart-minds or bees debating a new nest site, follow similar rules. This divine design achieves an optimal trade-off between decision accuracy and speed. The bees teach us how to translate this internal process into a successful decision-making model when neurons, like bees, are actually individual people.

To learn from our teachers we must reconnect, unlearning the language of human-centrism and relearning or remembering – bringing all members of creation back into the fold of unity – the language of connectivity, Allah-centrism. We need to believe, *really believe*.

This is a challenge that I used to present to my students in discussions concerning the necessity of establishing boundaries when dealing with governance and public policy. Whose interests count and whose do not? Do we only consider humans, or should non-human creatures enter our analysis and decisions? Allah tells us in no uncertain terms that all creatures form communities like ours. "And there is no animal (*dabba*) in the earth or flying creature flying with its wings, except that are communities like you (*ummanun amthalukum*). We have not overlooked anything in the Book. Then unto their Lord they will be gathered" (Al-An'am 6:38).

Ummamun amthalukum – communities, *ummahs*, like ours with everything significant that this entails, everything that Allah deemed sufficient for the validity of this comparison. I remind my students how Islam's second caliph, Umar ﷺ, grieved over the responsibility for a baby goat in a distant part of the caliphate. "If a baby goat (kid) perishes along the shores of the Euphrates," he lamented, "Umar will be held to account for her on the Day of Resurrection" (Ibn Abi Shaybah). Every ummah was created by and is cared for by its Creator, save human interventions for which we are responsible. The Trust is truly a delicate and unnerving covenant.

We are an unruly species having preferred to carry the Trust over submission to the perfection of divine decree through compulsion. Ignorant and unjust is how the Quran describes this choice. The skies, the earth, and the mountains were presented with this choice too, but they declined the responsibility. How could they carry what they could scarcely withstand together, let alone as individuals? We humans took on the covenant to carry the Trust, we ratified it, not wanting to be coerced into its implementation. But from the very start it proved too heavy, way beyond our capacity. How could we not sever what Allah commanded to be joined when all creation – seen and unseen – is connected? How could we not corrupt in the earth when even the best of our deeds intervenes in a such a complex reality that there is no way we could achieve the outcomes we hope for if Allah does not hold all parameters steady, if He does not rectify our deeds as the Quran promises the sincere believer? So, here we are, we must cope. We must demonstrate that if not in outcomes, then in intentions and efforts we did our best and for Allah is the determination of affairs.

We need help on this journey. Of course, Allah's prophets are our guides and teachers but there are other creatures who Allah inspired to live according to His guidance and to who He directed our attention. The bees are one example among so many presented in the Quran. "So Allah sent a raven [or crow] digging in the earth to show him [Qabil] to cover his brother's [Habil's] privates. He said, 'Oh woe to me, I have failed to be like this raven and hide the privates of my brother.' So he awakened [becoming] of the regretful" (Al-Ma'idah 5:31). From the earliest of times, animals were commissioned to teach us.

So many of our modern innovations can be traced to our observations of nature both plants and animals. From medicines to airplanes and ships to wind, solar, and hydro energy, all came about by learning *from* nature – though we like to frame it in terms of learning *about* nature. To learn from something engenders respect. It is to be taught by it, to admire its contributions, honour its genius, preserve its essence and proportions, and give gratitude for its role in our deliverance. These are practical lessons that support our lives and livelihoods. Non-human creatures also teach and gift us through the worship of Allah. These are the *glorifiers*.

Devotion to Allah through glorification and prayers is the greatest lesson that our non-human companions teach us. All creatures know and worship their Creator. "Do you not see that Allah is glorified by whoever is in the skies and earth and the birds in rows? All have known their *salah* and glorifications and Allah knows of what they do" (An-Nur 24:41). You may be thinking how can we *see* that? We can see it in the beauty, stability and coherence of nature. Allah is asking about our sight not understanding. Such an orderly reality must yield to a singular Truth performing acts of worship that harmonize its interactions, define the modality of its connections. By decree, revelation, and inspiration, nature submits to Allah's command, each element fulfilling its worldly purpose, which is something we can observe.

What we cannot see is the ritual aspect of their worship. The Quran tells us that everything in the skies and the earth prays to Allah and glorifies His praises. Glorification is especially singled out and emphasized in the opening *ayah* of each of the *suwar* known as *Al-Musabbihat*, the Glorifiers, including Al-Hadid, Al-Hashr, As-Saf, Al-Jumu'a and Al-Taghabun. Throughout the Quran we read about all the created matter including the angels, trees, sun, stars, moon, thunder, and so on that glorify His praises. The mountains and birds glorified Allah in a chorus echoing the glorifications of Prophet Dawood ﷺ (Saad 38:18-19; Saba' 34:10).

We also cannot perceive nature's prostration before Allah. "And to Him prostrates whoever is in the skies or the earth, voluntarily and by decree and their shadows [as well] in the mornings and in the afternoons" (Ar-Ra'd 13:15). Our shadows, who would have thought. "Do you not see that to Allah prostrate whoever is in the skies and whoever is in the earth and the sun and the moon and the stars and the mountains and the trees and the animals and many of the people. And for many the punishment is warranted. And whoever Allah slights, can have no bestower of honour. Indeed, Allah does what He wills" (Al-Hajj 22:18). To disbelieve in the truth that all creation prostrates to Allah is to say that there is only one way of doing things, that it is the human way, and that we must be able to observe it. This once more is human-centric or anthropocentric thinking, not theocentric.

Allah-centred being and becoming means that our relationship with nature, as it is with each other, remains vertical, not horizontal. Vertical does not mean hierarchical; it is actually quite antithetical to that. It means that we are consistently focused on our and nature's relationship with Allah. We are not fixated on horizontal relations, how things are equal or unequal with each other, comparing capabilities, complexity, and intelligence paradoxically from our limited perspectives and skills. Rather, our aim is to understand Allah's guidance and the teachings of Prophet Muhammad ﷺ as they apply to non-human creatures and how we must treat them, honouring their purposefulness. The glorification and praising of Allah by all created matter imbues each with intrinsic value. This is irrespective of our standards and valuations. Nature, everything created, is to be valued because it knows and worships – through its roles and rituals – the Creator and Sustainer.

Allah tells us that He does not disdain from giving the example of a gnat (Al-Baqarah 2:26). These small creatures that most people think of as a nuisance are pollinators, food sources for other animals, and decomposers of organic matter. They are critical contributors to the health and balance of the environment that we all rely upon. But as we have just learned, gnats are also choristers in a glorious hymn that praises their Creator. Prophet Muhammad ﷺ once relayed a story in which a prophet was stung by an ant, so he ordered the ant colony be burned. In response Allah revealed to him: "Because of an ant's bite you have burnt a community from amongst the communities which sing My glory" (Sahih Bukhari). All life is sacred.

This is a teaching that I tried hard to impart to my children. If you can take an insect out of the house rather than harming it, then do it, it is an obligation. This is a glorifier, its tiny voice contributes to the balance of our universe, it offers that bit of gratitude that may make up for your deficit. The way nature focalizes Allah elevates her value, perhaps even beyond that of humans. For many this is a humble pill to swallow.

Non-human creatures have submitted to their Creator. They are in a state of Islam. In the story of creation, Allah said to the sky and the earth "'Come, obediently or by decree,' they said, 'we come in obedience'" (Fussilat 41:11). They realized that there is no escaping Allah's will, expressing an intelligence that evades many people. "So, is it other than the *deen* of Allah that they desire and to Him have submitted (*aslama*) whoever is in the skies and the earth obediently or by decree and to Him they will return?" (Al-'Imran 3:83). Unlike the sky and the earth many people decline the command to 'come', but this can only ever be a temporary rejection. Everything returns to Allah.

Glorifiers, produce a steady lyrical hymn that calms the universe, allowing it to rebalance, to withstand the chaos of human life. The chirping of birds and crickets, the purring of cats, howling of wolves, croaking of frogs, rippling of water, splashing of waves, buzzing of bees, howling of wind, rustling of leaves, vibration of flowers, are all expressions of connection with Allah and the universe they sustain. We may not understand, and thankfully in most cases cannot hear, but their glorifications are constant. Praising the One who created and provides for them without fail. "Glorifying Him are the seven skies and the earth and whoever is in them. And there is not a thing except that glorifies with His praise, but you do not understand their glorifications. Indeed, He is ever Forbearing, Forgiving" (Al-Isra' 17:44). We have so much to learn from our non-human teachers, and so much gratitude to offer Allah for their presence and essence.

Lack of connection has dire consequences for nature and the balance of our universe. Every year tens of millions of animals are subjected to horrifying living environments and experiments, the victims of ruthless agribusiness and biomedical research. In government, academic, and corporate labs, they are subjected to toxins, induced diseases, extreme temperatures, drowning, electric shock, psychological trauma, isolation, confinement, unnatural breeding, restricted diets, and genetic manipulation. All their divine rights are violated by those who do not believe in their intrinsic value, or even their sentience. Anything considered of human value or resulting in human consumption from such activities is neither *halal* nor *tayyib*. Harming Allah's creation cannot be the solution to excessive human consumption and greed, poorly planned social organization, or to the ailments that inevitably afflict us because of our distorted behavior and beliefs.

Although some Muslim scholars have allowed animal testing based on vital human need, this does not conform to the inviolability of their lives for anything other than food – obtained in ways that are both *halal* and *tayyib* – in cases where their meat is permissible. Prophet Muhammad ﷺ had forbidden harmful experimentation with animals. A physician once approached him saying that he kills frogs for the extraction of some medicine, the Prophet disapproved and forbade the man (Sunan Abi Dawood). Even in the lawful slaughter of animals for food, he forbade believers to allow one animal to witness the slaughter of another, or to see the sharpening of the knife, stating "Do you wish to slaughter the animal twice: once by sharpening your blade in front of it and another time by cutting its throat?" (Musnad Ahmad). He taught us that there is reward for compassion toward all living things. This makes experimentation that is endlessly repeated for training purposes or performed for mere curiosity even more heinous. I am not even going to get into animal testing for cosmetics.

One of the saddest animated films that I have ever watched is the 1982 British drama *The Plague Dogs*. The plot revolves around two dogs, Rowf a large black labrador mix, and Snitter a black and white fox terrier, who escape from a government, possibly military, research facility where they were being subjected to awful torture. Rowf was subjected to repeated drownings, while Snitter had to endure brain experiments, leaving both severely traumatized. It was so heartbreaking to see the dogs struggle to avoid being recaptured by the authorities who believed them to be carriers of the bubonic plague due to a lab mix up.

During their adventures, Rowf and Snitter strike a deep and sweet friendship as they try to cope with their physical and psychological pain. In the end they are forced out to sea as the authorities, manning all kinds of weaponry, close in on them. The dogs swim toward an imaginary island, encouraging each other on until they disappear in the mist. Perhaps there was an island, but the likelihood that they would reach it was grim, especially as Snitter was starting to complain that he couldn't swim anymore.

I remember bawling my eyes out at the end of the film and remaining disturbed for months because of the reality that I knew underlay its narrative. I knew these torture labs existed, I knew that much of these experiments were performed to eventually subject humans to harm particularly in wartime, and

I knew that dogs were sentient beings with high levels of intelligence. The Quran highlights the role and status of dogs in the story of the Companions of the Cave that I shared in a previous chapter. These young men took their dog with them as they were escaping the persecution of their people. Allah preserved all of them, giving the dog an important role in appearing to guard the entry to the cave. It is unfortunate that so many Muslims today dismiss the Quranic narrative in favour a dim view of one of Allah's most talented and service-oriented creations.

In agribusiness intensive farming means that animals are kept in confined spaces not in their natural habitats or open farm environments. This subjects animals to unhealthy conditions both physically and psychologically. Limited space prevents normal movement affecting their physical and mental development. The isolation of animals from their natural environments prevents them from engaging in communal activities and forming the social bonds that Allah placed between them. Lack of exposure to the sun and other natural elements affects their sleep, feeding, hormone production and moods. In their confinement, they are denied foods they would rather eat in ways they are divinely inspired to eat. They cannot choose their mates as they would in nature, and the females are subjected to almost continuous pregnancies exhausting them prematurely. So many of their natural behaviors, the memories of their species, are lost in these sordid conditions. It alters them. It alters their behavior just as it would those of humans but when they change or react, they are further subjected to punitive measures like debeaking for birds or dehorning for cattle and sheep. Only profits matter.

The Quran and teachings of Prophet Muhammad ﷺ are serious about the protection of animals and their habitats. They teach us to respect the expectations of nature and its rights to safety and predictability. Prophet Muhammad ﷺ declared the Haram – sacred zones – of Makkah and Madinah off limits to hunting and cutting of trees. He was following in the tradition of Prophet Ibrahim ؑ who had previously banned hunting and the destruction of trees and plants in the vicinity of the Kaaba. The Messenger declared that Madinah's haram be a twelve-mile radius where weapons and hunting were not allowed. He also declared *hima* or protected zones for wildlife, forests, and grazing lands, setting precedent for communities and leaders that followed. He ﷺ taught us that animals are not to be harmed in any avoidable way.

Attributing the mutilation of animals and any changes to Allah's creation to the scheming of the Shaytan, the Quran warns of the great loss to those who succumb to his enticements (An-Nisa' 4:119). Allah curses those who make a target out of anything with a spirit and those who brand animals. Islam also prohibits hunting animals for sport. They are further not to be subject to superstitious practices (Al-Ma'idah 5:103; Al-An'am 6:144). Growing up, we were occasionally reminded of two Prophetic narrations, one concerning the evil fate of the person who confined a cat without food or water until it died, and the other of the blessed fate of the person who quenched the thirst of a dog by fetching it water from a well.

So many of us were moved by the images of the people of Gaza saving animals from under the rubble, digging gently with their bare hands to save a life. We saw horses, donkeys, dogs, cats starving to death, injured, scared. We saw the people of Gaza carrying their pets and any animal they could save on their constant journeys of displacement. They too were grieving, hungry, tired, scared, and injured, many had lost loved ones in front of their eyes. These are a people who value life, every life. Then there was Khaled Nabhan, may he be rejoicing in the highest level of Paradise, known around the world as the beloved grandfather of his 'soul of soul' granddaughter Reem, who amidst his anguish and the relentless bombings, still made the effort to feed the hordes of starving cats in Gaza. He understood their pain. They are all gone now. All these glorifiers, gone.

Her paint strokes, smooth and thoughtful, connect the sacred and the profane, telling stories about love, balance and connection, and stories about our earth's suffering. Those standing before her work hear a gentle voice coaxing them, *come, connect with oneness*. Salma Arastu listens into Allah's unity for her designs. Her paintings express the basest tendencies in human nature and the potential for beauty and illumination in connection with our Creator. Salma, a friend and dear sister, is an internationally exhibited artist based in California. She was born into the Sindhi and Hindu traditions of Rajasthan, India, and later embraced Islam. Through paintings, sculpture, calligraphy and poetry she uses her art to "break down barriers that divide to foster peace and understanding." To her, "all living beings are our unique and generous family."

Five years ago, I had the privilege of working on one of Salma's projects, *Our Earth: Embracing All Communities*. She had produced a spectacular series of paintings that drew inspiration from Quranic *ayat* and the teachings of Prophet Muhammad ﷺ, connecting them to different dimensions of our current environmental crisis. The themes she chose drew on Quranic guidance related to the earth, water, pasture, fire, animals, fish, people, birds, insects, flowers, stars and trees. Some works reflected the beauty and bounties of the earth, while others combined this with the pain and ugliness of pollution, waste, and violence. Her idea was to create a book out of these paintings including translations of the *ayat* that inspired the paintings with suitable commentary for each. These were my tasks, an honour I will always cherish.

Art is an experience that is inseparable from the observer, it is about connection, much like our understanding of the *ayat*. What we see reflects who we are, the expanse of our vision, what we believe. I appreciate Salma's art for its subtlety, for the quiet ways it seeks to educate about the connectivity of all creation and the impact of our choices on our beautiful earth and its non-human inhabitants. Once an element – a wave, a colour, a letter, an image – is introduced, it cannot be disentangled, it can only be connected to something else for better or worse. I respect her courage for incorporating Arabic calligraphy and Quranic guidance, bringing her expressions of the message to a global audience, though perhaps she would not think it courageous at all. What courage is there in declaring faith in the One, the True, the Sublime?

Every canvas in the series is a testament to the connectivity of revelation, nature and people. Salma understands vulnerability, the possibility of ruptures in the relationships that her art seeks to connect. She calls us to re-think, to awaken – through our faith – to the harm we inflict on other living creatures through cruelty, negligence and waste. But the earth, like Salma, is patient, embracing her inhabitants, gently persuading them through her generosity, through her wounds, that love must be reciprocal. Her palette reflects the softness of her style and philosophy, holding delicate but vibrant colours that come together in a performance of awe, of love for Allah and His creation, that expresses gratitude for our extended family and the beauty of life. "For me," she says, with a tender voice, "love is the only way to protect life's generous tapestry."

Communicating with others forms of consciousness, the glorifiers, including plants, animals and the forces of nature, is the purview of the prophets and the pious. "And gathered for Sulaiman were his soldiers of jinn and humans and birds and they were [spread in] divisions. Until they came upon a valley of ants, an ant said, 'Oh you ants enter your dwellings so as to not be destroyed by Sulaiman and his soldiers, while they do not sense it.' So he smiled, chuckling at her speech and said, 'My Lord, enable me to thank for

Your blessings that you bestowed upon me and upon my parents, and that I may work righteousness that You approve, and admit me by Your Mercy in [the company of] Your righteous servants" (An-Naml 27:17-19). It is said that Prophet Sulaiman ﷺ diverted the army's route in response to the ant's plea.

Prophet Muhammad ﷺ also understood and communicated with nature. He taught us about the sentience of the glorifiers, of their ability to feel fear and love. He once comforted Mount Uhud, telling it to remain calm when it was shaken by an earthquake. He also famously said, "It is a mountain that loves us, and we love it" (Sahih Bukhari). He is known to have comforted the tree trunk that became distressed because it missed his proximity when he abandoned her for a fabricated pulpit. He encouraged the planting of trees, saying, "Whoever plants a tree and diligently looks after it until it matures and bears fruit is rewarded" (Sahih Bukhari). I think that one of the greatest acts of human degeneracy is the destruction or cutting of mature trees. Standing witnesses, with unparalleled majesty among the plants of the earth, they have experienced so much, given so much. Our beloved Prophet ﷺ emphasized the gravity of such an act and its restitution in the Hereafter.

Our Prophet ﷺ understood and loved animals. His she-camel played an important role in his life and travels, sometimes helping him – through Allah's command – to make important decisions. Al-Qaswa, as she was named, actually chose the site where Prophet Muhammad ﷺ settled in Madinah. It is understandable that many families wanted to host him, but he gently indicated that he would let Al-Qaswa roam until she chose the spot. He informed the people that she was under Allah's command. She eventually knelt in an open space owned by two orphan boys. The Prophet ﷺ purchased the land with the desire to build a mosque and home. In the meantime, he stayed with Abu Ayyub Al-Ansari whose home was closest to the site. This became the location of Al-Masjid Al-Nabawi, chosen by a she-camel under orders from her Lord. It is difficult not care for all of Allah's creatures, hold them in high regard, when we actually believe that they have this potential.

Everything glorifies Allah and though we may not understand, sound hearts are capable of sensing and responding. For those who have pets, who live with animals on a daily basis, we know the bonds that form between people and animals. I was blessed with the gift of Oreo, my black and white tuxedo domestic shorthair cat, who lived with our family for a splendid decade. Through him, the children learned responsibility and compassion. We came to recognize elements of his language, expressions, and preferences and he reciprocated. He knew when I was sad and would try to comfort me by placing his paw on my hand, or rubbing his forehead on mine, or just sitting beside me. In his final days, Oreo became very clingy approaching me more than usual to seek comfort or perhaps to give me comfort. He knew how much I loved him. I asked, 'what is going on?' He continued to purr with that telling look in his eyes. We both knew his time was coming. The way he tried to spend every last moment with me was heart wrenching. Oreo is buried in our backyard under a beautiful bush of red roses surrounded by fragrant lilacs. We had thousands of tea-breaks together, wrote three books, and travelled overseas twice. While he will never be replaced, Seeko the most adorable grey and white tuxedo, has entered our lives once more bringing us the joy of connection with our non-human friends.

We must rekindle our connections to nature and all of its inhabitants. In her chorus of unification, we feel the greatest comfort. Nature speaks to the truth of everything that makes us human. It is why we feel at peace in her company, her glorification is the same as that performed by every cell in our bodies even as we do not recognize it, even as we do not honour it. Every heart finds peace when its possessor is silent long enough for it to reconnect with this hymn of healing, gratitude, and praise, the song of *the glorifiers*.

PART 4

Holism

Learning the Language of the Universe

A couple of years ago I was asked by the Islamic Institute for Development and Research (IIDR) to give a short course on one aspect of choice concerning the life of Prophet Muhammad ﷺ as part of their In Pursuit of Greatness series. Indeed, we know that those who follow Prophet Muhammad will prosper (Al-A'raf 7:157). The challenge was that they had already covered so many of the more obvious dimensions of his life and character, particularly those aspects where there were plentiful resources. So, I was asked to avoid his role as change-maker, counsellor, entrepreneur, husband, father, leader, mentor, and teacher! I thought on this for a few days before it occurred to me that Prophet Muhammad ﷺ had said that every single prophet had, at some stage in their lives, been a shepherd. In fact, he also said *all of you are shepherds, and each is responsible for their flocks* (Sahih Bukhari). Why? Why was shepherding a right-of-passage for every prophet? What is it about shepherding and sheep that made this kind of training a necessity – so much so that not a single prophet did not tend sheep at one point or another in their lives before receiving their missions. And why were we all of us, men and women, likened to shepherds responsible for our flocks? The lessons of shepherding must hold the keys to success in our private and public lives. Why else would Allah have willed the Prophet ﷺ to spend thirteen years as a shepherd, a period as long as his mission to Makkah and even longer than that in Madinah?

I soon discovered that nothing addresses every dimension of what it is to be human, to serve humanity and other creatures, more holistically than an episode in shepherding. No training can make us better leaders, spouses, parents, neighbours, teachers, bosses, employees, caregivers, and so on. Nothing encourages the kind of purposeful, connected, and holistic contemplation that is required to develop outstanding moral character. Or provides the kind of experience that drives home the inseparability of one's inner reality and ultimate destiny from that of the world. Shepherding brought to the prophets the recognition of fundamental truths, the unity of the universe, and its Creator. His infinite mercy. It taught them the language of the universe, an intimate, gentle, and infinitely connected grammar. A grammar that expressed the purposefulness, connectivity, and holism of creation. That permitted its possessor to "Read in the name of your Lord *who created*" (Al-'Alaq 96:1), a charge that Prophet Muhammad ﷺ would have been fully qualified to undertake.

Shepherding of course involves the tending of sheep – one category of what the Quran refers to as *al-an'am*, which also includes the family of cows, goats, and camels. There is an entire surah titled *Al-An'am* with several mentions in other *suwar*. "Indeed, there is a moral (*'ebrah*) for you in al-an'am..." (Al-Mu'minun 23:21). A *'ebrah* – or moral – is a lesson or collection of lessons in a narrative or real-life experience that holds profound wisdom. These lessons are both stated explicitly in the Quran and left for us to discover in our interactions with and observations of nature. The Quran explicitly tells us, for example, that we derive many benefits from *al-an'am* including beauty, food, drink, and transport. It also tells us that we owe our ability to survive and thrive in this world to their concurrent creation. They were placed on earth in the same instance as we were and Allah permitted us to command them (Ya Sin 36:71) as we command each other in various ways and for various purposes so that we may reach higher feats, collectively. Our reach and capabilities were literally extended by the creation of this class of animals and by children (Ash-Shu'ara 26:132), mentioned in that order. It should not then be surprising when Allah tells us that the sky and its flawless beauty with its sultry night and revealing daylight, the grandeur and expanse of the earth, its crystal waters and lush pasture, and steady majestic mountains, and the incredible varieties of edible produce for consumption, abundant replenishment of water, compliance of the soil for seeds, producing grapes and dates, and olives and palms and orchards, fruits and fodder are "pleasures for you and your *an'am*" (An-Nazi'at 79:33; 'Abasa 86:33). The earth and its pleasures are meant to be shared.

In fact, "there is no stomping creature on the earth or flying creature that flies with its wings except that form communities like yours," the Quran teaches us, "We have not overlooked anything from the Book and to Allah everything must return" (Al-An'am 6:38). Research has confirmed that the brains of sheep have much in common with our own and that we share many comparable abilities. Electrical activity and chemical responses in sheep are very similar to humans in terms of how different parts of the brain become activated when people are shown images of their loved ones. This means that they exhibit intelligence and ingenuity including the ability to problem solve and to reason. They know how to heal themselves by consuming certain herbs, knowledge that is passed down from ewe (female sheep) to lamb. They can recognise faces that differ by less than 5% as well as to react to expressions of happiness and anger. Like us they live in social communities with organized and deep relationships. Lambs recognise their mothers more than any other animal through voice and milk recognition even if she is found among thousands of other sheep. When lambs are weaned from ewes, both mothers and children cry for days. Their memories last for at least two years. Ewes fall in love with rams (male sheep), have best friends and feel desolate when those close to them die or are sent for slaughter.

Sheep work and live in groups. They maintain strong social hierarchies with every flock having its sheep leader. As in human communities, males or rams dominate other rams and ewes, resorting to aggression to maintain status. Ewes are also known to display aggression and will stomp and charge in threatening situations. As a prey animal, sheep succumb to the aggression of other animals as well as that of each other. Their susceptibility to harm tends to make sheep fearful of isolation from their flock. Their heart rates increase when they cannot see members of their flock and when approached by a dog or human. Most sheep are responsive to the leaders among themselves. If the leader follows the shepherd, the rest follow. Even then, however, there remains a keen sense of individuality and each has their unique personality.

The Quran indicates that the behavior of *al-an'am* is the basest possibility for humans, though many fall short of even that expectation. "Or do you think that most of them hear or comprehend? They are nothing but like *an'am*. No, they are more lost in their way" (Al-Furqan 25:44). When people are oblivious of the value of the guidance that Allah has sent, they render themselves no more – and potentially less – than this class of animals. That is not meant to degrade animals because their nature and the inspiration or revelation they have recieved is sufficient for their purposes, connections and contributions to the whole. The same cannot be said of people because we need guidance. Allah's proofs are in plain sight for everyone to see, furnished in a language that no human could deny having been expressed in every perfect detail of our creation, of nature. But those who have hearts with which they do not understand, eyes with which they do not see, and ears with which they do not hear are like the *an'am*, rather they are more astray, they are thoughtless (Al-A'raf 7:179).

We are all shepherds, but what does that actually mean? What mental and physical capabilities does that entail? If we cannot literally practice shepherding, what lessons can we draw from those who have, from observing the life of Prophet Muhammad ﷺ? As I did precisely this, four lessons gradually emerged. Solitude. Service. Sensibility. Security. These are the four stars – as

I came to think of them – of shepherding. Internalizing these lessons appears to alter the temperament of great leaders, understanding of their role, and future vision they harboured for themselves and their flock. Likewise, these lessons of, solitude, service, sensibility, and security, are indispensable for our lives as believers, in the way we conduct ourselves, engage with others and impact the world. We were likened to shepherds for a reason, it is a duty to find out why.

Solitude is a state of being alone in mind and occasionally in person to understand oneself, to face the expanse within that can only be satisfied or quenched with a recognition of ultimate truths – primarily the recognition of one's Creator and the nature of His creation, to cultivate a relationship with Him, and to reflect on and make peace with the purpose of life and one's role in its grand scheme. By definition, it is an intensely private affair, an aspect of success, *falah,* unlike service, sensibility, and security, that cannot be captured through observing its practitioner. Its benefits can only be reaped in the absence of others whether through removing oneself physically or mentally.

Prophet Muhammad ﷺ shepherded for 13 years. He continued to seek solitude thereafter through meditation in the cave of Hira in the Mount of Light, *Jabal An-Nur,* where he would eventually receive the first revelation. And even after receiving his mission, he would practice solitude or *i'tikaf* in the last ten days of Ramadan and 20 days in his final Ramadan in addition to other intermittent activities. Undoubtedly, shepherding gave him plenty of opportunity to reflect, to understand himself, family, friends and community, and most important his relationship to and qualities of his Lord. It is in solitude that Prophet Muhammad ﷺ likely situated himself in time and space, where he recognized the feebleness of all creation in relation to the Creator, where he implored Allah to guide him to Truth, to satisfy that hunger that can only be satiated by Allah's love and light.

Through solitude he was taught that it was okay to be away from people. We need occasional social distance even from our closest partner or friends to be okay, to recalibrate. For our beloved Prophet, genuine contentment was to be found only in the quiet of Allah's company and the extension of truthful affinities beyond the immediate material experience. Among sheep and other elements of nature, he would have felt at peace. That same feeling that we get when we go for a nature walk to find rest and calm. The beauty of the natural world has this effect on the human psyche not only because it is peaceful and beautiful, but because on a subconscious level we – as *'ebad Allah* – connect with all other creatures that glorify and sing His praises even as we do not understand exactly how they do this. "The seven skies glorify Him and the earth and what is in them, and there is not a thing except that it glorifies His praises, but you do not understand their glorifications. Indeed, He is ever Forbearing, Forgiving" (Al-Isra' 17:44). But though we do not understand, the receptive heart will take comfort in the unicity, *tawhid*, that this chorus of voices expresses. It will swell with gratitude and heal with the appreciation of the harmony that only this divine symphony could achieve. And this happens without us even being aware.

It almost goes without saying then that solitude for the heart is as important as clean air and nutrition are for the body. The quest for truth cannot be found in the company others though it can of course be supported and reinforced by kindred hearts. We must, each on their own, develop the capacity to be with Allah even as we live through different events and transition through life, just as sheep move among pastures. For that to happen we must practice consistency in being with ourselves, reflecting on nature and on the Quran. Prophet Muhammad ﷺ said, "Your Lord is pleased with a shepherd high in the mountains who calls the *adhan* for the prayer and prays. Allah says: 'Look at this servant of Mine; he calls *adhan* and *iqamah* for the prayer for reverence of Me. I have forgiven my servant and admitted him to Paradise" (Sahih Abi Dawud). Solitude is the space of the truly genuine. In it we reinforce our purpose, recognize our connection, and revive ourselves in the holistic form in which we were created.

Entering a state of solitude requires focus long enough to develop ideas about what we believe. What is our purpose? To whom are we connected and what is the nature of those connections? How does my purpose fit within the complex and grand scheme of all connections and how does it contribute to the holistic nature of life, of the universe? What about the purpose of others? These deep thoughts are critical dimensions comprising the mental models inherent to every mature individual. They are the beliefs that each of us holds, whether consciously or not, which inevitably manifest in the choices we make, our ability to be just, equitable and merciful. Prophet Muhammad ﷺ had taught that "the best among you are the best in character" and that nothing enables people to enter paradise more than "heedfulness (*taqwa*) and good character" (Al-Tirmidhi). Solitude exhorts the *nafs* towards honesty and purity in personal and private matters. Prophet Muhammad ﷺ advised believers to "never do in private what you would conceal from others in public" (Ibn Majah). Indeed, our ability to live dignified lives and afford dignity and rights to others is rooted in this practice. Solitude, first and foremost, involves the willingness to take a deep dive into this mindset or mental model with the aim of rectifying and aligning thought with the imperative of *tawhid*. It is a state and a process that allows us to think matters through for ourselves and to reach defensible conclusions potentially against the popular judgment of others.

The fruit of solitude is wisdom. In those moments of quiet, of distance from the hustle and bustle of life, of its show and pretensions, the *nafs* is permitted to mature. It is given a chance to turn inward discovering the depths that Allah has placed within it. There it will find endless wealth and wonders. It will experience the contentment of its Creator's company, of His light and love. This is a satisfaction so deep that one's hunger for such encounters only increases with time. Nothing in this ephemeral, transitory, existence could ever replace it. We were told by Prophet Muhammad ﷺ to hold on to those who have found this inner realm. "If you see a person who has been given *zuhd* (spiritual height of abstention) from the world, and has good speech, then draw close to them, for they have been taught wisdom" (Ibn Majah). This spiritual height, found in the deepest recess of one's inner being, allows its possessor to live in the world with a fairy's footprint, wanting little of material comforts but nevertheless appreciating all of Allah's blessings and freely sharing with all in need, even want. "A Muslim," tells us Prophet Mohammad ﷺ, "never gives a fellow Muslim a better gift than wisdom through which Allah increases him in guidance or turns him away from harmful behavior" (Al-Bayhaqi).

The truth is many people have a fear of being with themselves. Being alone is generally regarded negatively by modern society. Those who practice 'aloneness' may be identified as loners, odd, anti-social. Not surprisingly, many consider being alone a form of punishment, something to be avoided. Think of how children are often punished through quiet time or how they may be sent to be alone in a corner. Or even of academia where admissions criteria are always demanding more and more extracurriculars and social contributions. *Do you practice solitude? What have you learned from such experiences?* asked no one, ever. Freud viewed it negatively and linked it with anxiety. In line with this ridiculous posturing, today's pop culture regards solitude as abnormal, leading to evil or weirdness at the very least. This is only true to the extent that people deny their wholeness, their createdness, and thus, their dependence on a Creator.

In *Thus Spoke Zarathustra,* Nietzche claims: "It is what one takes in solitude that grows there, the beast within included." That perhaps is the condition of the superficial believer or the disbeliever. Those who deny their own light so that when they take the deep dive, if they even attempt it, only find a dark void. As the Quran confirms, "And if they encounter those who believe, they say, 'we believe'; and if they are alone with their devils, they say, 'we are with you; indeed, we are only scornful'" (Al-Baqarah 2:14). Solitude can indeed lead some to keep company with their devils, instilling fear in them and pre-empting any possibility of seeking light, of sensing Allah's warmth. The fear of being alone weakens the capacity to be the best version of oneself, to be a genuine individual, a shepherd. Our thoughts and actions no longer belong us but are dominated by others for better or worse.

Not any experience of solitude will suffice. Genuine solitude must fulfill important conditions. To start, it must be voluntary. It cannot be forced or imposed by external forces. We must be free to return to family, friends and community when we need or plan. We must be able to control, challenge and change our thoughts and emotions throughout its duration. And its benefits must be reflected in our lives in the form of positive relationships.

The second lesson that shepherding would have instilled in Prophet Muhammad ﷺ, and all those striving for success, was *service*. To be of service, invaluable service, is to provide ideas and to perform actions based on Allah's guidance that are needed by the recipient whether the recipient recognizes the need or not. Shepherding is service in the way of Allah. Prophet Muhammad ﷺ said: "The leader (*sayyid*) of a people (*al-qawm*) is their servant (*khadimuhum*)." *Sayyid*, however, is not just any leader; it is a station more akin to the most honoured. And *khadimuhum* is not their servant in the conventional sense, that is one who serves based on what the client demands, but rather one who serves in conformity with Allah's guidance. The service – *khidma* – that renders one *sayyid* over others is the willingness and ability to guide to what is right and beneficial and protect from what is wrong and harmful.

Sheep themselves cannot give thanks let alone remunerate the shepherd. Instead, they have an owner or master who rewards the shepherd. "And We have not sent you except as a deliverer of good tidings and a warner. Say: 'I do not ask you for it any payment - except whoever wills to forge a way toward his Lord' (Al-Furqan 25:56-57). Like his mission that followed, Prophet Muhammad ﷺ was accustomed to servicing a client who was not his commissioner. It is not the sheep that commissioned or rewarded the Prophet for his care and protection, it was their owner – and even then, it was the Owner of the owner or the Master of the master – to whom he was ultimately accountable. In the Quran, this lesson is clearly driven home for the believers. "And they feed [nutritious] food out of love for Him, to the needy, orphan and captive. Indeed, we feed you for the countenance of Allah. We do not want from you reward or thanks" (Al-Insan 76:8-9). Those who believe in Allah give to people, positively contribute to life, without any demand for any returns in this life. Instead, they hope for a day of peace and reconciliation in the beautiful company of their Lord.

Even when compensation is involved in exchange for a service, a believer's ultimate loyalty is to Allah. There is no obedience that involves the betrayal of Allah because that also means a betrayal of His creation or the very cause that we are aiming to serve. This focus on one ultimate master means that we remain stable in our personal and professional lives irrespective of the worldly manifestations of power and authority. "Allah gives the example of a person in whose [life] there are conflictual partners and a person who surrenders to one other person; are they equal in comparison? Praise be to Allah but most of them do not know," (Az-Zumar 39:29). To simplify matters, the Quran asks us to consider the predicament of a person who is managed by, or yields to, one master versus someone who is trying please everyone with no real focus, loyalty, or compass.

True service demands a knowledge of what is good and beneficial and what is wrong and harmful. In some cases this may require us to stand apart from the flock and accept the possible consequences. Having been put on an exemplary or higher law, the Shariah, Prophet Muhammad ﷺ was commanded to follow a certain path and to avoid the impulses that may have animated those around him (Al-Jathiyah 45:18). Thus, he was told "... So, if you were to follow their desires after what you received of knowledge, indeed, you would then be among the perpetrators of injustice" (Al-Baqarah 2:145). And the people were told, "And know that among you is the Messenger of Allah. If he were to obey you in much of the matter, you would be in difficulty, but Allah has endeared faith to you and beautified it in your hearts and has made hateful to you disbelief, immorality and disobedience. Those are the rightly guided (*rashidun*)" (Al-Hujuraat 49:7). The believers were told that the Prophet was on a special path and that it was not in their benefit for him to swerve from it in accordance with what they, with their limited perceptions, desired. This is the value, the very meaning of faith, to the believer. It compensates for our human limits, our inability to encompass sufficient truths to take the right course. Sheep know and trust the shepherd.

The duty to guide, to shepherd, is incumbent on all believing men and women. The Quran tells us "Believing men and believing women are guardians of one another; they command what is beneficial and forbid what is reprehensible..." (At-Tawbah 9:71). In this act of guardianship, men and women act to guide, to lead each other to what is best. Neither Quran nor sunnah show bias toward men or women, all are shepherds. The extent of our abilities being a matter of competence, not gender. Prophet Muhammad ﷺ said: "When a person is entrusted with authority over the affairs of the believers, and he, in turn, delegates this authority to another while he could find a more competent person for the task, he has betrayed Allah and His Messenger" (Sahih Bukhari). In those early days of Islam roles and responsibilities were based on merit and both men and women were subject to this principle.

The Prophet ﷺ chose Bilal to call to prayer, Abu Bakr ؓ to lead prayers, Asma ؓ to undertake covert operations, Umm Salama ؓ to advise in Hudaibia, Rufaida al-Aslamiyyah ؓ to open a clinic for the wounded, Fukahia bint Yassar ؓ to build a minbar, Nusaybah bint Ka'ab ؓ to defend him in Battle of Uhud, and the indefatigable Khalid ibn Al-Walid ؓ to lead the Muslim army. In line with this teaching, Umar ibn al-Khattab ؓ believed that "whoever delegates a public office to another for the sake of friendship or personal favour indeed betrays Allah and His Messenger and the believers." Merit was the key. It is notable that Khalid Ibn Al-Walid ؓ delegated to Khawla bint Al-Azwar ؓ the leadership of an expedition against the Romans, she, being the most competent to do so. Relatedly, Prophet Muhammad ﷺ said, "whoever advises his brother to take a certain course while knowing that a better course lies elsewhere, has in essence betrayed him" (Abi Dawud) this is because *ihsan* or excellence are prescribed by Allah in everything that we do (Sahih Muslim).

Service, and particularly that undertaken with *ihsan*, is not possible without keen *sensibility*. Sensibility is the state of empathizing, understanding, navigating, and responding to signals expressed, overtly or not, by those whom we come into contact with. Sensibility responds to feeling connection whether it is long term or just in passing. By heightening sensibilities, shepherding deeply impacts the faculties of hearing, seeing and heart-sense (*sam', absaar, af'ida*). Those immersed in this experience would have seen and known the *ayat* of Allah even before receiving revelation. They would see, as the Quran would later reveal, the nature of the sky and the balance that supports it (Ar-Rahman 55:7; Adh-Dhariyat 51:7), the seas and their separating barriers (Ar-Rahman 55:19-20), the majesty of the wind as it follows Allah's commands (Adh-Dhariyat 51:1-4). They would have learned that out of green trees we can kindle fire (Ya Sin 36:80), navigate according to the positioning of the stars (Al-Waqi'a 56:75), and make precise calculations because of the courses of the sun and moon (Ar-Rahman 55:5) among many other universal laws. Never a mechanical existence, but rather a sentient and unified creation that praises and prostrates to its Lord. This is the world in which we are intimately connected and which holds the keys to our reciprocal flourishing.

The Prophet's knowledge of his connection to Allah, family, companions, neighbours, Muslims that had passed, Muslims yet to be born, the natural world, the world of the unseen is unsurpassed. Prophet Muhammad ﷺ stated: "Gentleness never accompanies anything without enhancing it, nor is it ever removed from anything without diminishing it. We owe gentleness to ourselves and to everything around us. His sensibilities extended to all creatures. "Who is the owner of this camel?" the Prophet once asked. A young Ansari man said that it belonged to him. Prophet Muhammad ﷺ said, "Won't you fear Allah in your treatment of this animal which Allah as placed in your hand? The camel complained to me that you keep him hungry and overwork him" (Abi Dawud). He also said, "Do not treat animals as chairs to sit on. A mount may be better in glorifying Allah than its rider" (Musnad Ahmad). In these and many other teachings, the Prophet ﷺ demonstrated the importance of empathy and compassion, of the expansiveness of genuine sensibilities especially when it comes to the care of others but also to self-care. "Your Lord," he ﷺ said, "has a right over you, your body has one; your family another, and your guests have one – give each one their rights" (Sahih Bukhari).

Today, sensibilities tend to be shallow, fragmented, mechanistic, reductionist and distorted. The quest for unconstrained freedom and hyper-individualism has contributed to a multitude of social ills. Without the purposefulness that comes with duty and responsibility, connection that comes with knowing and prioritizing relations, and holism that comes with purpose and connection within a magnificent universe, people feel lost, lonely, and pointless. Loss of mind, meaning, life, reality, connection are all manifestations of weak or non-existent sensibilities. How common is it now to hear of or deal with loss of mind, all those mental health issues across the life spectrum from youth anxiety, depression, dishonesty, lewdness, confusion, suicide to dementia in later years.

Even more rampant is loss of meaning by way of a continuous challenge to our moral values through media, governance, educational curricula. Almost anything is acceptable in the world in which we live and very few people know what to do with the truth even when it is clear to see. Without mind and meaning, loss of life becomes inevitable. Wars, racism, extremism, environmental degradation, loss of biodiversity, species extinction, all symptoms of societies that are no longer sensible. And this is heightened by the loss of reality, or excessive interactions without physical and emotional connections, challenging our moral and physical nature, idolizing virtual worlds ultimately leading to a loss of connection.

How many people believe that the elements of creation are or can be separated and recombined or manipulated at will even as we scarcely understand their truthful purpose in the first place? How many people believe that scientific 'advancement', economic 'progress', and most hideously political objectives justify the destruction of certain ways of life both human and non-human? When we don't respect purpose, we don't understand or respect connection, and in turn we corrupt, wittingly or unwittingly, the holistic manifestations that this selfish mess produces.

Perhaps the highest priority in the mind of a shepherd is the security, *amn*, of his or her flock. To be secure is to be free from threats ad dangers. Prophet Muhammad ﷺ would have learned that ensuring this for his flock involved a knowledge of their strengths, weaknesses, ways of life, needs, and environment. He would have observed the dangers that come from within the flock based on the relationships among the sheep but also the state of their health and happiness. Likewise, he would have become familiar with external threats like those posed by the weather, availability of quality pastures, and the cunning of the wolf. He recognised the vulnerability of a lost sheep as reflected in his advice to "take refuge in congregation (*'alaikum bel jama'a*) for the wolf eats up a solitary sheep that strays from the flock" (Abi Dawud). In his observations of all these dynamics and the efforts he expended in keeping the flock safe from harm, he likely contemplated the majesty of the Lord that kept the universe safe, the Lord who held so many things constant so that life could proceed with some semblance of predictability, so that he ﷺ could keep his flock safe.

Leading from the rear, Prophet Muhammad ﷺ would have had his eye on every member of his flock, ensuring that no one strayed. Despite this, he knew that the safety of the sheep depended on more than his guidance. They also needed to be willing followers, they had to put their trust in him or those among them who followed him. There was only so much that he could do to keep them safe. "A wolf caught a sheep," the Prophet ﷺ once told his companions, "and when the shepherd chased it, the wolf said, 'Who will be its guard on the day of wild beasts, when there will be no shepherd for it except me?" (Sahih Muslim). The sheep themselves had to be attentive, to respond to his message.

It was this concern that would weigh most heavily on his mind when he finally received his mission and was commanded to call people to Islam. "If I told you that an enemy's cavalry was about to appear from behind this hill," stated Prophet Muhammad ﷺ when he first went out to warn his kin and inform them that he had received Revelation, "would you believe me?" To which they responded, "We have never heard you telling lies." "Behold, then," he continued, "I have been sent to warn you of a terrible punishment (if you do not follow me)." His first words were aimed at convincing people to change course, and to appreciate the imminent danger they faced if they refused.

Securing the *akhira*, the life to come, was his greatest concern because he knew that this could only be achieved if the life of this world, the *dunia*, was secured for all, believer and non-believer, human and non-human. "I do not want anyone of you to come to me on the Day of Resurrection, carrying over his neck a sheep that will be bleating. Such a person will (then) say, 'O Muhammad! (please intercede for me,) I will say to him. 'I can't help you, for I conveyed Allah's Message to you.'..." (Sahih Bukhari). It is only through heeding Allah's message in this life, a message that guarantees the pursuit of purposeful paths for all creation, that the *akhira* can be attained, that we can secure ourselves against its requite.

Today many people agree that human security includes the provision of income, food, shelter, health, safe environments, as well as personal, communal and political freedoms. Questions and disagreements, however, remain as to the nature of these provisions, how are they to be provided, and by whom. Many global treaties attempt to address these questions through the presentation of lists of demands, the right to this or that, entitlement for this or that. This is especially the case for human rights treaties like the Universal Declaration of Human Rights (UDHR). But rights and freedoms are listed in what is essentially a supply void. In fact, the wording is so meticulously chosen that responsibility for provision remains elusive more than seventy-five years after its proclamation. The same applies to the more recently promulgated UN Sustainable Development Goals (SDGs) that have been lauded by so many people, Muslim and non-Muslim alike. If human security was really at the heart of the SDGs we would not read "no poverty" but rather no excessive wealth and equitable distribution, we would not read "zero hunger" but rather protection of agricultural systems and rural societies, as well as no food waste and again, equitable distribution. The endless negotiations that go into the creation of these *agreements* almost inevitably focus on the obfuscation of who is responsible and can be held accountable for provision, with the effect that no real security is ever achieved.

The Quran sums up human security in one *ayah*. "And indeed, We have dignified the children of Adam and carried them in the land and the sea; and granted them from all that is good [and fair] (*tayyibat*); and favoured them over much of what We created with notable favour" (*Al Isra'* 17:70). Every aspect of this four-fold favour for the achievement of human security is two-dimensional – a provision by Allah and a call to effort by people. The very first condition then for human security is the provision and attainment of dignity. Dignity is not a given by mere coincidence of birth. Just like being carried on land and sea requires vessels, and the grant of all that is good and fair requires ingenuity and effort, dignity requires adherence to a moral code. True, the basics of that code are imprinted within us, but beyond that we need revelation to guide us in our treatment of each other and of all life systems more broadly.

Dignity is an achievement not a given as we are very capable of debasing ourselves and others when we neglect or ignore Allah's guidance. Dignity and heedfulness of Allah are inseparable. "…Truly the most dignified among you in the sight of Allah are the most heedful…" (Al-Hujuraat 49:13). Heedfulness, *taqwa*, guarantees our security and that of others through the regulation of our behaviours individually and collectively.

The grant of dignity through the provision of divine guidance creates an order in which we can all flourish in harmony with, not subjugation of one another and other living things. This guidance is prioritized because it is required to benefit from the opportunities for livelihood in land and sea, the second favour, that Allah has provided and to mitigate corruption that will inevitably arise. Guidance is necessary to recognize that it is Allah who has given humanity of all that good and wholesome, the third favour, with no one being deprived except to the extent that His order is betrayed. Yet even then, even by following such guidance, we are not definitively superior to the rest of creation since we are only favoured above much but not all. This qualification is intended to instil a sense of humility and striving to always be and do better.

The believer knows that the journey to Paradise, to *Jannah*, is all about heedfulness of Allah, about generosity and goodness toward all of His creation. "Those who spend in ease and hardship, and who supress [their] annoyance, and who pardon people, and Allah loves the doers of good" (Al-'Imran 3:134). For those who live as such there is security in the *akhira*. "And whoever performs good works, whether male or female, and they are a believer - those will enter Paradise and will not be wronged by as little as a date seed" (An-Nisa' 4:124). And in the life of this world, we may be granted Allah's reinforcements as those before us were granted (Al-'Imran 3:125) and we may be granted new friendships and alliances that lead to much desired victories. "And hold firmly to the rope of Allah all together and do not fragment. And remember the blessing of Allah on you as you were enemies, so He brought friendship between your hearts, so that you woke by His blessing as brethren. And you were on the edge of a pit of fire, so He saved you from it. It is as such that Allah expresses His *ayat* to you, that you may be guided" (Al-'Imran 3:103).

Yet like Allah's favouring of us, the sense of security regarding the attainment of the akhira is never absolute. The Quran asks us: "Are you secure from He who is in the heaven that He would not cause the earth to swallow you up as she quakes? Or are you secure that He who is in the heaven would not send against you a storm of stones? So you might know what My warning is like' (Al-Mulk 67:16-17). These challenges are intended to keep us eager in our pursuit of Allah's pleasure. That we may race toward all that is good and toward securing the good life for all creatures. "They fulfill their commitments [to Allah] and they fear a Day whose evil will be pervasive" (Al-Insan 76:7). To be clear, the idea is not to live in fear, but to avoid arrogance and injustice toward oneself and others, to accept responsibilities and fulfill duties. It is only then that *real* security can be achieved.

Shepherding is *the* training to discover and encounter the inner realm that defines what it means to be human, to surpass our likening to sheep, and cattle more broadly, and move us into the realm of shepherds. It is *the* training in the outer realm, conveying the language of the universe that unifies all creation, humans, and non-humans. And nothing more is required of the participant than a receptive heart. But how can we make it sunnah, the exemplary way of life set forth by Prophet Muhammad ﷺ? The answer lies not in literal replication, but in the conscious re-enactment guided by the principles of the Quran, hadith, and Seerah. Sunnah in its truest form, demands purposeful action rooted in understanding and alignment with the teachings of Prophet Muhammad ﷺ. While many of us can never shepherd in the literal sense, we can cultivate the virtues of solitude, service, sensibility and security within ourselves, families and communities. Through mindful practice and collective nurturing, we can illuminate the path of *falah*, greatness, for ourselves and for generations to come – a humble tribute to the timeless legacy of our Beloved.

Conquering the Shaytan

It is March in Malaysia, we are nearing the end of Ramadan 1446 AH, a month of fasting increased prayers and peace – at least here. The tropical weather is consistent throughout the year, with temperatures remaining in the same range of 22 to 32°C. There is stability and predictability in this kind of climate. The rains come almost on a daily basis to calm and cleanse, the earth is green and cheerful. Malaysia is a beautiful metaphor for the condition of a believer, living in heat but acclimatised to being temperate, taking the brilliant hue of a land blessed with water, green, and sun. Its mosques are beautiful and plentiful but so are its other temples as it embraces other faiths.

I have lived here for about a year and a half. Much of this book was written in Wolf and Turtle, a café in a retail strip called The Stories of Taman Tunku, the Prince's Garden in Malay, near my residence in Kuala Lumpur. It sounds more like a children's fairytale, *Wolf and Turtle in the Stories of Taman Tunku,* than an address. Though no fairytale, this book is one of those stories, occasionally weaving a human narrative symbolized by these two animals, at least as they are perceived in legend and the often-biased imaginations of people. Wolves and turtles may share a wetland habitat, they can and do live peacefully together, but wolves may take advantage of the turtles vulnerability and prey on hatchlings and eggs when conditions permit. In the folklore of many cultures, the wolf symbolizes danger, speed and strength while the turtle symbolizes patience, resilience and wisdom. Aesop's fable taught us from a very young age that the turtle should never be underestimated. Whether hare, as in the fable, or wolf in our case, the belittling of that which appears slower or weaker is undone in the end. We all know who won the race – the tortoise.

My stay in Malaysia has been slightly longer than the current duration of violence against Palestine. I found comfort in a country and community where right and wrong were clear from the very start, where government, media, academia and mosques – most of them anyway – recognized the depth of the tragedy and expressed their discontent. Prime Minister Anwar Ibrahim has been an unwavering supporter of the Palestinian cause, publicly and globally condemning Israel's aggression against Gaza. Malaysia does not recognise Israel and has advocated for a two-state solution based on pre-1967 borders. Multiple ceasefire violations, the intentional targeting of civilians including babies and children, unwarranted arrests and detentions, as well as the blocking of humanitarian aid by Israel have had widespread impact on Malaysians and the world.

Everyone is angry – everyone with a sound heart that is.

Malaysia is not alone, many countries have expressed support for Gaza through UN votes, humanitarian aid, diplomatic statements, recall of ambassadors, hosting negotiations, and legal backing. South Africa filed a case against Israel in the International Court of Justice alleging that Israel is violating the 1948 Genocide Convention by committing genocide against Palestinians in Gaza. Its actions were supported by human rights groups and many countries in the global South. It was also supported by hundreds of millions of ordinary citizens from all around the world including within Israel.

South Africa, like Malaysia has supported the Palestinian cause since its inception. Having itself suffered under the cruelty of apartheid, South Africans see support of the Palestinian struggle as a moral obligation. They know the pain. They believe in *ubuntu*. In a recent interview with President Cyril Ramaphosa the importance of this philosophy was clearly reiterated, it is what shapes South Africa's foreign policy. "This is who we are as South Africans, we promote human rights, solidarity, as well as respect for other nations… a foreign policy that seeks to prosper all other nations, to work with them in a multilateral fashion and support each other and to promote the values that are important to us as South Africans." He emphasized how their Truth and Reconciliation Commission and Constitution have become models for other nations seeking to heal the wounds of their pasts. "This is what ubuntu to us is all about."

Ubuntu is characterized by mutual understanding and striving for that understanding which demand respect of the other as a precondition to respecting oneself. It supports the idea that we are who we are as people because others are who they are. Ubuntu admits the diversity of the purposeful paths of others and their rights to pursue those paths, not only in peace and justice, but with cooperation from others through hospitality, generosity, care, and understanding. It is the epitome of interconnectedness and a holistic way of being in this world.

How do we gift ubuntu to the world? It is in historical moments such as this that the Shaytan appears to be winning. You can see his ugliness in the unspeakable amount of death and destruction, in the cruelty and greed that have wrapped their claws and dug their fangs in the neck of humanity.

The Shaytan is the mean creature who disobeyed Allah's command to prostrate to Adam, to humble himself before the human who had just received the divine breath. The brazenness of his arrogance led him to blame his Creator for his rebellion, and he vowed to capture as many humans as he could before the Day of Judgment to demonstrate the unworthiness of humans of divine blessings and favours (Al-A'raf 7:16-17). He is the one who tempted our parents out of Jannah, exposing their shame and introducing them to immorality.

You can hear his cajoling when strange thoughts enter your mind, encouraging you to neglect your relationship with Allah, to choose the less honourable path, to insult or harm others, to refuse to pardon and forgive – not because you love Allah but because you would rather wallow in anger. Prophet Muhammad ﷺ taught us that "anger is from the Shaytan, and Shaytan was created from fire. Fire is extinguished by water, so when you get angry perform ablution" (Sunan Abi Dawud). Performing ablution, *wudu'*, means returning to Allah, pronouncing His name as you run pure water over your face, clearing out your mouth, nose, and ears, and soothing your limbs. To perform *salah* after this is even better.

The Prophet ﷺ told us that he once saw the Shaytan while praying. He says, "I grabbed him and strangled him until I felt the coolness of his saliva on my hand. Were it not for the invocation of my brother Sulaiman, I would have tied him to a post for people to see" (Sahih Musim). His cold saliva true to his lifeless, uncompassionate, and deceitful nature. But scariest of all is that he can take a human-like form.

We are introduced to the Shaytan at a very young age. Do not do this or that so that the Shaytan does not catch you, cast a spell on you, and keep you in a perpetual state of whatever wrong that you were doing. It was a way to complement our love and fear of Allah. If you were not heedful enough of Allah, then at least fear the Shaytan, he was ugly and scary. Really, a misguided approach but I understand the logic. We were taught to seek refuge in Allah from the Shaytan's cajoling, those whispers that make their way into your chest without you even knowing.

> *Say, 'I seek refuge in the Lord of the people, the Sovereign of the people, the God of the people, from the evil of the cajoling shirker [Shaytan] who cajoles in the chests of people from among the jinn and humans.* (An-Nas 114:1-6)

We were taught about the Shaytan so that we may turn to Allah for help. It is only by seeking refuge in Him that we can conquer the Shaytan and his tribe.

The world of the unseen is complex and not detectable by ordinary people. There are *shayatin* (sg. *shaytan*) of humans and jinn. "And it is as such that We made for each prophet enemies, *shayatin* of the human and the jinn, some revealing to some others the adornment of speech to delude [seduce]. And if your Lord had willed, they would not have done it, so leave them and what they [deceptively] fabricate" (Al-An'am 6:112). The prophets are told not to concern themselves with the presence of *shayatin* among humans and jinn, the concern is to guard against them and their tactics. We must protect ourselves against their influence to ensure that their legions do not grow by our speech and actions or those of the people that we care for.

I care for peace loving sound hearts everywhere. In the Quran believers are described as a single Ummah (Al-Baqarah 2:213). I care for all believers. All prophets are described as one Ummah (Al-Anbiya' 21:92, Al-Mu'minun 23:52). I care about all the prophets and those who follow them with beauty, justice, and moderation. The Quran distinguishes between the disbelievers who are defined as those who do not believe in Allah and a Day of Judgement. On the one hand, there are among them those who are treacherous, vilifying and fighting or at the very least hating everyone who is not like them. On the other hand, there are those with whom the believers have a covenant of coexistence, those who are averse to enmity and fighting with the believers and others, desiring to live in peace with all (An-Nisa' 4:90). I care about them too. The Quran and teachings of Prophet Muhammad ﷺ command the prioritization of harmony. Allah even cautions believers about violating that last group telling believers that He could have given them the upper hand to fight us had He willed, so humble yourselves and accept their overtures of peace (An-Nisa' 4:90).

Division, however, is an inevitability among believers as it is among others. In reality I have much more in common with a kind and loving nonbeliever than with a harsh-hearted or divisive believer. Allah told Prophet Muhammad ﷺ to teach us to always speak what is best, to present what is better, so as to protect ourselves against the ability of the Shaytan to sow discord between us. He told him to remind us, that the Shaytan is an open and clear enemy to humans (Al-Isra' 17:53). Many Prophetic narrations emphasize the gravity of our speech for maintaining good relations. He ﷺ taught us to say only what is good or to keep silent (Sahih Bukhari). The fear of disunity, of falling prey to the violence of each other's tongues, is personified in the arrogance and disobedience of the Shaytan.

"My Lord," said the Shaytan, "Because you have ensnared me I will make allurements for them in the earth, and ensnare them altogether" (Al-Hijr 15:39). The Shaytan is out to get us – *all of us*. What he admits to one exclusion, "except, Your servants among them who are sincere" (Al-Hijr 15:40). Allah then says, "This is on my part a straight path. Indeed, you have no authority over My servants except thoso who follow you of the ensnared" (Al-Hijr 15:41-42). The Shaytan has no power over those who serve their creator, able to distinguish between the forces of good and evil and to follow the path of righteousness. The path to Allah is straight, clear, and decisive, it does not have the twists and turns, manipulations and seductions, of the Shaytan. Entering into the Shaytan's maze may be pleasurable and amusing at first, but he has designed it to lead to loss, confusion, frustration, and distraction. He has the runners ensnared.

Shaytan is real. His presentation in revelation is not legend or myth. He is not a false god, like Al-Lat, Al-Uzza, and Manat, the idols of pre-Islamic Arabia. He is a truthful force in the world of the unseen, and knowledge of him – both accurate and inaccurate – shapes the worldview of believers.

Until a time known only to Allah, the Shaytan and humanity have been granted reprieve. "He [Shaytan] said, 'Give me respite until the Day they are resurrected.' [Allah] said, 'Indeed, you are of the respited,'" (Al-A'raf 7:14-15). For the Shaytan it is a time to tempt as many of Allah's servants as possible into disbelief, to lure them in his maze, proving their ingratitude; for humanity it is a time to prove him wrong.

The Quran tells us that the Shaytan's respite will only bring him to perdition (Al-A'raf 7:18, Saad 38:85, Al-Isra' 17:63). Here the Shaytan will experience the pain of disobedience which led to the severance of family ties, famines, droughts, wars, disfiguration of the earth, pollution of the skies, and the misery and suffering of innocent creatures. Allah does not change His word, and there will be no injustice to His servants (Qaf 50:29). The Shaytan's word is the one not to be trusted. "And they will stand out [for judgment] before Allah altogether, then the weak will say to those who were arrogant, 'Indeed we were followers of you, so can you avail us anything of this torment?' They will say, 'If Allah had guided us, we would have guided you. Whether we are intolerant or we are patient, there is no escape'" (Ibrahim 14:21). They will use the same excuse as the Shaytan when he blamed

Allah for his disobedience. People will blame each other, and their leaders will place the blame on Allah.

All of this will be confirmed by the Shaytan himself now that his mission has come to the end. "And the Shaytan will say when the matter has been settled, 'Indeed Allah promised you the promise of Truth. And I promised you, but I betrayed you. And I had no authority over you except that I invited you, so you responded to me. So do not blame me and blame yourselves. I am not the answerer to your screams and you are not the answerer to my screams. I reject what you had previously associated me with.' Indeed, for the unjust is a painful torment" (Ibrahim 50:22). And with that, the Shaytan backtracks on all of his promises and seductions. No one is taking the blame for anyone on that Day. "The Day We [Allah] will say to Hell (*Jahanam*) are you full?' and she says, 'Are there some more?'" (Qaf 50: 30).

The tactics of the Shaytan are underhanded and multi-faceted. "Indeed, he [Shaytan] and his tribe see you from where you do not see them. Indeed, We have made the shayatin allies to those who do not believe" (Al-A'raf 7:27). In challenging Allah, he stated that he will wage the assault on humanity from in front and behind, from the right and the left, insisting that Allah will find most of us ingrateful (Al-A'raf 7:17). He will make promises and arouse in people deviant desires, promising nothing but delusion (An-Nisa' 4:120). He will instill a fear of poverty in people, and command immorality (Al-Baqarah 2:268). A fear of poverty can only breed poverty as it urges people to be greedy and stingy, thereby justifying all kinds of vice. Depravity can only increase its host in darkness.

Yet no one will take responsibility for this grim reality. The Shaytan's blaming of the other for his rebellion will become contagious. Those who commit injustices and all kinds of abominations will impute it to their predecessors and claim that it is Allah who commanded them to behave as such. But Allah does not command vice! (Al-A'raf 7:28).

Allah promises forgiveness and the provision of His bounties (Al-Baqarah 2:268). He grants all kinds of blessings so that we, in turn, may be good and generous to others. He gives, to enable us to give, so that He can give us even more. Not necessarily more in the material sense, but more in terms of contentment, joy, peace, and ultimately, forgiveness. These are things that all the wealth in the world cannot buy. "Oh you people, indeed the promise of Allah is Truth. So let not the life of this world delude you. And do not be deluded about Allah by the deluder. Indeed, the Shaytan is an enemy so take him as an enemy. He only invites his party that they may be companions of the Blaze" (Fatir 35:5-6). The more we direct ourselves toward Allah, toward Truth, the less prone we are to temptations. The possibility of sinful behavior is crowded out with kindness, love, generosity, and harmony.

Knowledge of the Shaytan is intended to strengthen our faith and direct our focus to the Merciful, not only to develop resistance against his insidious suggestions, but also to recognize his role in destroying nature and challenging our purpose and connection. We cannot be arrogant or complacent. The Shaytan can enter any of us, if we let down our guard.

I closed most of my social media accounts last summer, with few exceptions so that I could occasionally exchange funny clips with my mother, sister, and daughters. Like many other users, my voice was being stifled for sharing posts on what was happening in Gaza. It was not long before it was clear that I was basically talking to myself, or worse, providing information on my views without any benefits. There was no sharing, no social in social media, just social profiling.

We are now acutely aware of the algorithmic suppression, biased content moderation, and shadow-banning that is being implemented by social media platforms revealing a clear anti-Palestinian bias. Arabic key words are being flagged as violent or extremist, while pro-Israeli terms are left unobstructed. Pro-Palestinian posts are more likely to be removed or made less visible to others while those speaking out against the genocide are accused of hate speech and anti-Semitism even as their posts qualified as neither.

The heavy hand of powerful governments could also be felt. The US and EU are pressuring social media companies to remove content that they deem anti-Israeli under counterterrorism laws. Pro-Israel lobby groups pressure the platforms to moderate and censor pro-Palestinian content. The accounts of journalists and prominent social media influencers are also suspended. Videos from certain news outlets are demonetized or age restricted limiting access and reach. The list goes on. There is a clear and troubling trend in the digital world. The cajoling of the Shaytan.

It is indisputable. It is evident in the horror stories that have come out of Gaza. In the brutal murder of Dr. Adnan Al-Bursh, the Palestinian orthopedic surgeon and Head of Orthopedics at Al-Shifa hospital, while in Israeli custody; a death so horrendous I refuse to repeat any of its details out of dignity for our dead. It is evident in the airstrike that killed celebrated poet Refaat Alareer, whose last poem, 'If I Must Die,' demanded that 'you must live to tell my story.' It is clear in the detention and torture of children, and their targeting by snipers. There is a point when the Shaytan no longer needs to expend any effort, when his mission is complete and the *nafs* has graduated, it can now take over. The self has joined his tribe, incapable of exiting the maze, perhaps not even knowing it is in it.

We are not, as some may think of themselves, complicit. We have not allowed the *taghut* – anything or anyone worshiped or obeyed instead of Allah – to dictate our values so that morally bankrupt governments, media, and academic institutions, define our duty to command what is right and beneficial and prohibit what is harmful and reprehensible. When Prophet Muhammad ﷺ and the early believers witnessed the torture and killing of the weaker members of the nascent Muslim community, they were not complicit. There was only so much they could do with the resources they had. These early martyrs were actually not the weaker members, that is narrow a worldly perspective, which unjustly discounts the incomparable courage, patience, and sincerity that they had. We are not complicit we are bearing witness.

Despite all the censorship, social media has made us all real-time witnesses. Not just over the events in Gaza and events all over the world, but witnesses over ourselves. People are spending endless hours either exposing carefully selected and idealized details of their lives or observing those of others. It feeds the human urge to be known, to receive attention and praise. For some, it turns into an incessant drive for celebrity, wealth and power. Social media has made a good part of humanity crazed narcissists, barely able to do anything meaningful without sharing it on this or that platform and then checking every moment for comments and followership counts.

Addiction and delusion. It is not only through intoxicants and games of chance that the Shaytan strives to divide and create hatred among people while diverting them from the remembrance and worship of Allah (Al-Ma'idah 5:91) but it is also through all kinds of mediums that cause addiction. A 2022 Pew Research study found that close to sixty percent of American adults check their social media several times a day, with over a third checking several times an hour. Many either have a fear of missing out which produces anxiety or enjoy the thrill, dopamine effect, of notifications and new followers. Neither is conducive to healthy living, let alone being alive. Even in the millions, the followers that you may have beyond your *actual* circle of family, friends, and colleagues, are fragmented, diverse, and unknown – many may not even be real people, just traps luring people in. The closure of an account by any platform means the end of it all except for them, they continue to peddle in our profiles for profits and power. Ensnared.

It is time to find a way out of the maze. To return to our local streets, libraries, shops, townhalls, parks, forests – real communities. Time to go back to communication and sharing with our entire beings not just our thumbs. We have endangered our families, communities, and nations – and future generations – by giving up so much of ourselves by revealing what Allah meant to be protected, veiled. The Shaytan is wreaking havoc on our mental and physical health. We were made for a tangible world with all its natural glory, his is elusive and ugly.

Our propensity for vanity or laziness, I honestly do not know, has tricked us into believing that our online lives clothe, nourish, and connect us. Our predicament is reminiscent of Hans Christian Andersen's tale, 'The Emperor's New Clothes.' In the tale two weavers convince the Emperor that they can weave him an outfit so magnificent that the incompetent and ignorant would be incapable of seeing it. It would be invisible to them. When his officials checked on the progress of the outfit, they naturally could see nothing but refused to admit it not wanting to look stupid. Even the king could see nothing, but he refused to admit it. Finally, the weavers claim to have finished the outfit and fake dress the Emperor, fitting and adjusting the delusion to his undressed body. The townsfolk too all go along with the charade not wanting to be labeled as ignorant until an innocent child not encumbered by the delusions of the adults, points out the truth. Much of what happens on social media is as invisible as the emperor's new clothes. And in that we are complicit.

I am not saying that some measure of virtual communication is not useful. The global awakening to the Palestinian plight has been made possible through social media as mainstream media continues to justify and deny what is happening. But the price of its excesses has been too high. Anxiety, depression, low self-esteem, sleep disturbances, social isolation, attention deficits, and addiction mean that its potential benefits are greatly compromised. If this is the state of people on social media, what can realistically be expected of them when serious issues flood their screens? Too many people, especially young people, are not equipped to handle such tragedies whether in their personal or public lives. Building the necessary reinforcements for our personal and social wellbeing will not be found on social media. It must be nurtured in our hearts, homes and communities.

The easiest thing to do perhaps is to surrender to our lowest self, to curse and pray for evil, to want vengeance and let anger rule. But that leaves the door ajar for the Shaytan. Prophet Muhammad ﷺ did pray against specific oppressors, but he did so with sublime wisdom, not personal anger. When some of the companions cursed their persecutors, he gently asked them to refrain. "Do not curse them, for they may later do good deeds" (Sahih Muslim). In another narration he said, "a true believer does not taunt, curse, abuse, or talk indecently" (Sahih Muslim). He urged his followers to pray for the guidance of the wrong doers, not their destruction.

I remind myself that the deepest love for Allah is to encourage people to join the chorus of His glorification. It is to put what He would want for His servants first – to enter into His servitude and His *Jannah*. This is what Prophet Muhammad ﷺ prioritized and prayed for when he left Ta'if, and in the opening of Makkah, it is how Salahuddin acted as well when dealing with the Crusaders. We must settle our differences peacefully and with justice so that all creation, not just humans, can pursue their purposeful paths and connect as Allah willed. "Oh you who believe, stand out firmly for Allah, witnesses with equity (*qist*), and do not let hatred of a folk prevent you from being just (*ta'dilu*). Be just, it is closest to heedfulness (*taqwa*) and heed Allah for Allah is well acquainted with what you do," (Al-Ma'idah 5:8).

The call for ethnically cleansing Gaza to build resorts and luxury waterfront properties sadly invites Shaytan to the negotiation table.

A Beautiful Patience

> *By the era (al-'asr), indeed, the human is in loss, except those who believe and do good and counsel each other with truth and counsel each other with patience* (Al-'Asr 103:1-3).

Writing is not easy, at least not for me. It requires time and patience. The journey with this book in particular has been unlike any other that I have written. It started in January 2020, five years ago, when I felt the urge to write something which reflected the knowledge that I had gained since I completed my first book in 2006 on intellectual property and pharmaceuticals. I wanted to write something that demonstrated how much we, as humanity, were missing by discounting Allah's guidance in our public affairs. It was clear to me at the time that I needed to rethink the idea of intellectual property based on my knowledge of what the Quran and Sunnah taught us about the nature of knowledge and innovation. This, I felt, would be a useful contribution given the controversies that surfaced around intellectual property, vaccines, and therapeutics during the COVID-19 crisis. It would also allow us at the Maqasid Institute, a research and education organization that I had helped co-found in 2017, to demonstrate how our proposed research methodology and framework could be applied to real world phenomena.

In a previous work, I had presented a framework for public policy in Islam that I believed would be useful for this new project. The framework challenged the neoclassical economic and innovation systems frameworks that I had relied upon in my doctoral studies, which had also culminated in a book publication. I had always known that these frameworks were not up to the task of presenting humanity with suitable alternatives that preserved human dignity. Neither addressed issues of equity and justice, nor of course had any regard for divine guidance. A revelation-centred approach was unsurprisingly completely different. Here knowledge was truth, and truth cannot be owned, let alone monopolized only to be used by a small group of people. There were higher objectives like human dignity, saving lives, challenging intellects, sharing blessings, and collective wellbeing. When it came to ideas and innovation that necessarily depended on centuries of accumulated contributions from all over the world, the goal of obscene profits was nowhere to be found.

Everything was going well until I contracted COVID in April of that year. I was bedridden with a fever of forty for eighteen days, had a constant migraine, nausea, excruciating lower back pain, weak joints, and a swollen face. Then there was another ten days of much the same, but the fever was occasionally breaking which was a welcome sign that I might survive. There was a point midway through this ordeal when I informed my children, to their extreme horror, of my wishes should I not wake up. *Alhamdulillah*, He had other plans for me. But I ended up with what was later termed *long* COVID.

For me, because it seemed to have different symptoms for different people, long COVID meant that I would occasionally suffer weakness in my legs literally feeling like I was going to fall, back pain, and blurred vision. Worst of all I had brain fog. I was mentally sluggish. I could not focus or remember so many things. I could not remember what I had written. I could not remember the first sentence of a paragraph when I reached the last sentence of that same paragraph, not page, paragraph. I could not remember meetings or what I said in them. After four months I was still getting nowhere. The most I could do was administrative work and even then, I had to take so many notes to remember what I was doing. If it were not for my knowledge of the Quran I would have been shattered, my academic career seemed to be over.

One of the clear themes in the Quran is that people, all of us, are tested during our lifetimes in a number of ways, some more than others. We can see this in the many narratives about people's lives, but we are also informed about it directly. "And We will certainly try you with something of fear and hunger and diminution of wealth and lives and productive endeavors [literally fruits] and give good tidings to the patient (as-*sabireen*)" (Al-Baqarah 2:155). We will suffer a loss of material comforts, achievements, and lives, and we will suffer at the hands of some of those who do not share our way of life, *shir'ah*, and regimen, *minhaj* (Al-'Imran 3:186). The harm may be sent to us directly or it may be indirect, reaching us through a ripple initiated very far away.

All trials are ultimately imposed or permitted by Allah. "And if We let the human taste of a mercy from Us then seize it from him, he becomes hopeless, ungrateful. And if We let him taste a blessing after being touched with harm, he says, 'The hardship has left me.' Indeed, he becomes exultant, proud, except those who are patient and do good. These have forgiveness and a great recompense" (Hud 11:9-11). Patience is commanded in hardship and relief. Neither should divert the believer from the path of doing good, remaining beneficent to those around us. *Sabr* is not only concerned with the nature of a trial but also how we continue to manage our lives in its wake.

As-Sabireen is the name given to those special people who are patient, the ones who have the ability to withstand delay, loss, pain, and harm while remaining calm and content. They hold even tighter to righteousness (*birr*) in misery, harm, and terror, revealing the extent of their truthfulness and heedfulness (Al-Baqarah 2:177). Difficulties remind them that they belong to Allah and to Him they will return (Al-Baqarah 2:156). The depth of this belief inspires us to think and act with positivity, kindness and justice irrespective of our personal struggles. A beautiful patience, *sabrun jameel*, is how the Quran describes this higher level (Yusuf 12:18, 83; Al-Al-Ma'arij 70:5). Those who are capable of it are blessed with the prayers and mercy of Allah, they are the guided (Al-Baqarah 2:157).

The preparation that this forewarning provides the believer is invaluable. Not only are we told to expect trials and how to handle them, but we are also assured of the rewards that accompany patience. Good tidings for those who are patient (Al-Hajj 22:35). Exercising patience is so beneficial to our well-being in this world and the next that it is prioritized over taking legitimate punitive measures even when they are permissible (An-Nahl 16:126). All efforts of endurance, bearing suffering with faith and calm, are accounted for by Allah. Prophet Muhammad ﷺ told us that "No fatigue, nor disease, nor sorrow, nor sadness, nor hurt, nor distress befalls a Muslim, even if it were the prick he receives from a thorn, but that Allah expiates some of his sins for that" (Sahih Bukhari). The rewards for those who do good will never be lost, so be patient (Hud 11:115).

It is not only expectation of reward that should move the believer. Patience is also a divinely designed control mechanism. Together with heedfulness, patience leads to what the Quran calls *'azm al-umur*, or the binding of affairs. To bind an affair means to keep it within limits, not let it overwhelm you so that it gets out of hand, having consequences that could have been averted thereby harming you further or placing you in the wrong. The benefits of patience are truly endless.

Definitely easier said than done. Patience is challenging especially in the beginning of a trial. Prophet Muhammad ﷺ said, "Verily, patience is at the first strike" (Sahih Bukhari). This may be because we find ourselves scared and facing obscurity. In those moments self-management is tough. We may not understand what is happening or has happened, let alone how to react with dignity and grace. The Quran tells us to turn to Allah, redirecting our entire beings. "And avail yourselves with patience and prayer. And indeed, it is a great [charge] except for the humble. Those who presume that they will meet their Lord and to Him they will return" (Al-Baqarah 2:45-46). A trial thus becomes an investment in self, an invitation to rethink life and possibly death and who we are in relation to those realities.

Patience and prayer. Patience comes first, without it every other good becomes a challenge. The believers are first described as the patient, then truthful, obedient, charitable and atoning (Al-'Imran 3:17). None of these other dispositions can be satisfactorily attributed to an individual without the exercise of patience. Patience is not passivity; it is a way of being and a precursor to other commendable ways of being. It is to remain resolute with contentment, relying on Allah for outcomes and fully trusting that everything that happens is for the best. It's all good. The struggle with our wealth and persons continues so long as we are on this earth, so long as the covenant between us and Allah remains.

Ultimately, no one will enter *Jannah* without having had their patience tested. "Or did you think that you will enter Paradise while it had not been made known by Allah those who struggled among you and made known the patient?" (Al-'Imran 3:142). *As-sabireen* – "those who were patient, sought their Lord's Countenance and established prayer and spent from what We provided them secretly and manifestly and repelled with good that which was evil. For them is the ultimate home. They will enter perpetual gardens, and whoever was righteous of their parents and spouses and progeny. And the angels will enter upon them from every gate [saying], 'Peace be upon you for your patience.' So, how blessed is the ultimate home" (Ar-Ra'd 13:22-24). A double reward awaits the believer for their patience and how they exercised it, first through repelling evil with good and second for spending, being charitable, out of what Allah had provided them (Al-Qasas 28:54).

In March 2021 I was contacted by a researcher from the Alternative Policy Solutions project at the American University in Cairo, my *alma mater*, to contribute a commentary to a campaign that they were launching on access to medicines. It had almost been one year since my COVID episode, and at about the eight months mark my health had begun to notably improve including my mental abilities, which were gradually returning. After many months of private anguish and trying to hide my COVID-induced state of ignorance, I felt I could try to accomplish what seemed to be a simple request. For someone with my background it would have been very odd to decline. I also thought that it would be a good warm-up to return to the book that I had started the previous winter. I accepted, but not without much trepidation.

One month later I submitted a proposal to write a short piece titled, *Waiving IP Protections for COVID Vaccines: How America can Help Heal the World.* It seemed to strike a chord with those at the centre and we agreed to move forward. But long COVID would rear its ugly head a few days later and I had to give them a heads up that I may not be able to meet the deadline. At the end of May the researcher contacted me again to see if I would be able to write the piece. I responded in the negative. My head was just not working. I could not think. She accepted my apologies and wished me well. It felt devastating.

It was hard to give up. This mattered to me – the subject and the ability to write. How could I not be able to write 1500 words? So, I asked her for a deadline, and she said June 14. I told her that I would try my best. For about five weeks I struggled like an infant learning how to walk. The deadline passed. Then on June 17, she wrote me a follow-up message asking if I had completed the piece. Thankfully, I had. Five weeks to write three pages! *Alhamdulillah.* The article went live on June 24. The experience demonstrated that I was still clearly incapable of writing an article without extreme hardship let alone a book.

But something else had happened. I realized that this was not the book that I wanted to write in any case. Almost nothing had changed in the world in which I had finished my first study. Perhaps things had even gotten worse. The unbridled defense of intellectual property rights was as strong as ever, millions of people could still not afford needed treatments, many were dying from that situation, but no one seemed to be able or was willing to do anything about it. The economic and corporate forces driving innovation systems, and the governments that are pressured by or responding to them, were too strong to take on. Given this ongoing situation, my book would have fallen on deaf ears save for some amusing scholarly debate, if even that. It was unlikely to effect any real change. Another year would pass as I continued to heal and think of my book.

A*s-sabr* [patience] is illumination. Those who are patient and grateful are capable of discerning Allah's *ayat* (Ash-Shura 42:33). Patience is key to learning, understanding reality, and recognizing truth. I could have written another book on intellectual property and access to medicines, but the truth is already out there. It has been written about extensively. Perhaps no one had approached the subject in the way I would have liked, but sufficient, evidence-based, arguments have been made to prioritize human life over profits. There are even a number of institutions around the world dedicated to the cause. Still, nothing has changed.

I took comfort in Prophet Shu'aib's ؑ efforts with his people of Madyan. He advised them to worship Allah, there is no god other than Him. Worship meant belief in accountability, which included honouring weights and measures, not diminishing the commodities of people, nor spreading corruption in the earth after it has been rectified. All these things, he told them, were good for themselves not just others. He warned his people not to ensnare, opposing and obstructing, those who believed in the cause of Allah, by seeking to make it crooked. He reminded them how Allah had strengthened them, but how all that would be compromised by their corruption. Finally, Prophet Shu'aib ؑ addressed those who believed in his mission saying "And if a portion of you believe in what I have been sent with, and a portion do not believe, then be patient until Allah judges between us, and He is the best to adjudicate" (Al-A'raf 7:85-87). When all has been said and done, the best approach is to be patient and leave the final arbitration to Allah who is aware of absolutely everything (Luqman 31:16). *Sabrun jameel.*

In abandoning my strongest area of worldly expertise, shelving the subject matter I had studied so deeply and with it potentially my identity as a professor, I struggled to historicize who I once was. I had to persuade myself that there was so much more to life, my life, than to stay wedded to things that had clearly departed. "Say [Muhammad], "Oh My servants who believe, heed your Lord. For those who do good in this world there is goodness. And Allah's earth is expansive. Indeed, the rewards of those who are patient will be fulfilled without measure" (Az-Zumar 39:10). Yes indeed! Allah's earth is expansive. I knew that I could serve Allah in other ways, seek His Countenance through the pursuit of another path, I just did not know what that was. Patience was the key.

I had to completely, wholeheartedly, turn to the source of patience to gift me with patience in abundance and fortify me with its power as is promised in the Quran (Al-Baqarah 2:250; Al-A'raf 7:126). I knew that Allah intervenes with His own forces to support those who are patient and heedful (Al-'Imran 3:125). Prophet Muhammad ﷺ said, "Whoever persists in being patient, Allah will make him patient. Nobody can be given a blessing better and greater than patience" (Sahih Bukhari).

2022 was the year of women. Almost every event that I was invited to speak at was concerned with women and women issues. All of my Ramadan engagements were associated with women. I do not normally accept to do things in

Ramadan, preferring to turn inward and focus on faith, fasting, and family. But my health situation had really limited my activities and I needed to step out of my comfort zone. Also, it was incredibly humbling that so many people still remembered me, remember me at all. I decided to make exception that year and see where life would take me. Then a dear friend of mine and professor at the Doha Institute for Graduate Studies, Dr. Rabia Naguib, asked me to write a chapter for a book that she was editing on women's empowerment. It really did seem that the writing was on the wall.

I packed my bags and made my way to my sister's cottage in Prince Edward Island. There is no more an inspiring place to think and write than amidst the sandstone cliffs, blue skies, and gentle waves of the Northumberland Strait, a body of water connecting to the Gulf of the St. Lawrence which makes its way to the Atlantic Ocean. There I wrote the first draft of my chapter, *Re-Envisioning Women's Empowerment: A Maqasid Approach to Understanding Women's Status and Rights in Islam,* for Rabia's book and I did it in about two weeks. *Allahu Akbar*, Allah is Greater! My ability to write, by Allah's infinite generosity, had been restored.

Now, I was planning for the *new* book. It was clear to me from all the lectures that I had delivered, the questions that inevitably followed, and the research that I had done for Rabia's book, that there was a need for a book that took a fresh look at women in the Quran and Sunnah; a project that could not only answer women's questions but did so with the heart that such an effort required. I set out to examine every mention of everything female in the Quran. But first, I had to fulfill my commitment to teach an all-women's class in Singapore in the fall. *Maahaduna* – Our Institute – was being inaugurated as a flagship project of the Liyana Musfirah Network and I was invited to be a visiting scholar.

I had to design a full curriculum in a matter of weeks. I wanted my program to give the women a holistic experience; teaching fundamental knowledge that every believer must own within a loving framework of mutual exchange. The program was intended to bring each woman to a deeper love for Allah and His creation including herself. These were the keys to success (*falah*). Over the course of three modules, of which I taught one in person and two online, we explored three essential features of Islam and being Muslim including purposefulness, connectivity and holism – those presented in this book. Relevant revelational teachings were brought to bear on each element, with an emphasis on examples from the lives of women in the Quran and how these encouraged us to reflect on our own lives.

I returned home after the first module wondering if we would be able to maintain the warmth and intimacy that our in-person experience had given us. There is something very special about sharing immediate space, the ability to sense and communicate with heart. It is one of the most beautiful exchanges in a holistic learning environment. We had two remaining modules over the course of the coming year, and I was worried that the connection we had built would be lost. But the women in Maahaduna and I had developed a deep bond. We believed and were striving, each in her own way to do good in this world. Our class was all about truth and patience. *Insha'Allah* what we had built would withstand distance.

The voluminous research that I had done to create the curriculum for the Maahaduna program and the deep insights that I had gained convinced me that what was needed was a research institution not just a book. We needed a centre that could help women incorporate Quranic truths and Prophetic teachings in every aspect of their lives, clarify misconceptions, and encourage purposeful, connected, and holistic thinking and action. For the next year, Sanja Bilic, a dear friend and sister, and I put our minds to the task. She had the perfect combination of research and practical experience in contemporary issues related to gender, European Muslim communities and the negotiation of everyday, lived religious experiences of women. We agreed that women and girls are systematically discouraged from serious Islamic scholarship throughout their education and lives, limiting their knowledge, access, preparation, and opportunities to utilize and benefit from revelational teachings both in their lives and to contribute to communal and global challenges.

The idea for *Minhajuna* – our regimen – was born. We hoped to empower Muslim women with the knowledge and confidence that they needed to leverage revelational guidance in their personal and professional lives through focusing on research and teaching of the Quran and Sunnah using Maqasid Institute's methodology. The foundational pillars of purposefulness, connectivity and holism, understood and expressed as inseparable dimensions of our dependent, intradependent and interdependent relationships, would allow us to advance the position and rights of women while recognizing the complex relationships that define their lives. We prepared an excellent proposal and pitched it to relevant parties. But other than intellectually stimulating discussions and general agreement over the need for such a project, Minhajuna would remain an idea. I tell you this story as a form of solace and to release, once more, the energy of the heart effort that we wished would bear fruit. Ultimately, we resigned ourselves to Allah's better plan.

One of the strongest coping mechanisms for believers, the one that carries relief, ambitions and dreams, is invocation or *du'aa*. Calling upon Allah for help in everything, whether minor or major, is a form of worship. Prophet Muhammad ﷺ said, "Ask Allah for His favor. Indeed, Allah Almighty loves to be asked and among the best acts of worship is to wait in expectation of relief" (Sunan Al-Tirmidhi). As with so many other things in my life, I asked Allah to guide me in these women's projects, whether Maahaduna, Minhajuna, or the book that was well underway, to direct me to what would be of the most benefit to His servants, to humanity. My second *hajj* back in 2009 was actually dedicated to that singular du'aa. *Ya Allah exclusivize me for your service.*

A believer has complete faith that their invocations will be answered. Perhaps not in the exact way they wanted, but always in a way that helps them to achieve what they actually intended – even if that is not immediately evident. In the meantime, we cannot tire of asking nor of waiting for a response. Prophet Muhammad ﷺ said, "The servant will continue to have his invocations answered as long as he does not ask for sin or cutting family ties, and he is not impatient." The people said, "Oh Messenger of Allah, what is impatience?" He replied, "He [the invoker] says: I have invoked again and again, but I have not seen an answer. He becomes frustrated with that and gives up supplicating" (Sahih Bukhari). Sometimes it is not what we ask for, but when we ask for it that is the issue. Allah provides in due course so that our invocations achieve what we had hoped for while avoiding things we had not. Time and patience are inseparable.

In the surah that opens this chapter, *Al-'Asr* (the era or time) we are reminded that we are in loss. Time passes, it can never be retrieved, it can never be increased. People are generally in loss when it comes to time, except for those who believe and do good, and counsel each other with truth and patience. These are the keys that turn loss into gains. When we fill the finite time on this earth with all those things that upon our passing can be exchanged for what is infinite, we counter the loss. What an incredible deal.

Over the course of 2023, I reflected deeply on what the Quran taught us about women and how it did so. I compiled a 350-page document detailing all the *ayat* and relevant Prophetic narrations that had anything to do with women and female references, adding my commentary as I went along. Family and friends encouraged me on as I shared the manuscript's progress. But something serious was amiss. The Quran was not amenable to this artificial extraction of all things woman to the exclusion or subordination of all else. It was rejecting my approach, consistently demonstrating that our understanding of girls, women, and the feminine cannot be dealt with in detached terms. Nothing in creation can be, we can see that in our practical, daily lives. Any attempt at fragmentation contradicted the Quran and the realities within which it is necessarily embedded. It betrayed the Trust. The Quran was calling me to *holism,* to truth, and I had to heed. Nothing in Allah's magnificent universe is independent – individual yes, but never independent. Men and women, *ba'dukum min ba'd*, we are of each other, and we are of the earth. My book had to be rethought.

Content was not my only challenge, method and style were too. I questioned why I was writing the book in an inaccessible academic language – what my brother-in-law Garrett kindly calls *Basmalese* – when I wanted it to reach a wide audience. The Quran is tailored with knowledge, guidance, *and* mercy. It is lyrical, presenting its teachings with rhythm, rhyme, and repetition. Of course, no human can emulate its majesty but there were lessons to be learned in terms of how the text speaks to the heart. Why was I restricting myself to criteria that frankly could not serve the cause, while also betraying the infinite possibilities of how Quranic truths and Prophetic teachings could be, *must be*, presented? I was no longer interested in academic accolades, there was no need to be in the service of anything other than Allah if ever there was.

Then, in October of this major rethink came *Toofan Al-Aqsa*, the storm of Al-Aqsa. Storms are nature's way of clearing the earth. They are sent by the Almighty to rebalance the land and its inhabitants, bringing down temperatures, relieving drought, redistributing Allah's bounties, and altering the landscape. When Prophet Nuh ﷺ called out for Allah's help against his people, Allah sent an extraordinary storm. "So, We opened the gates of the sky with [causing a] downpour of water, and discharged springs from the earth so that the waters met for a well-measured command" (Al-Qamar 54:10-12). Destruction is not the end purpose of any storm, that goes against the ultimate goal of rectification, of setting things aright. "It is Allah who sends the winds, so as to excite clouds so He spreads them in the sky however He wills, and He makes them dense, so you see the rain come out from within them. So, when He visits it upon whoever He wills of His servants, they sense good tidings" (Ar-Rum 30:48). Storms are reminders that we need to wake, to fix something that has been broken. This is how Allah brings a dead land back to life; it is a mercy. I was now writing a *new new* book!

Patience now took on a whole new meaning, as did being beautiful. My book – my words – were now caught up in history. Big history. This was no longer about the events in my life, about a routine contribution that would hopefully have a positive impact. This was about bearing witness, about telling small stories in the context of a much bigger (really sad) story. Patience with this or that personal trial – even though as it turned out my COVID episode was to be the least painful during those years – was incomparable to the horror that was unleashed on this Ummah over the past year and half and counting. There was only one kind of patience that matched our current predicament: *the patience of prophets.*

In dealing with those who did not believe in meeting their Lord, Prophet Muhammad ﷺ was commanded to stay firm, do good, and remain patient – he was not to transgress under any circumstances. "So be resolute as you are commanded [Muhammad], and whoever atones (*taba*) with you. And do not transgress. Indeed, He is Seeing of what you do. And do not lean toward those who have been unjust so that the Fire touches you. And you do not have any protectors other than Allah, then you would not triumph. And establish prayer [Muhammad] at the edges of the day and in nearness of the night. Indeed, the good deeds extinguish the bad deeds. This is a reminder for the mindful. And be patient, for surely, Allah does not overlook [literally cause to be lost] the reward of those who do good" (Hud 11:112-115). Some *ayat* are self-explanatory, they need reflection and internalization not commentary.

Patience is a matter of time. The unjust, those who do not believe in the Day of Account, who destroy the lives of others and peace on earth have been deceived. "Rather, We have gratified these [disbelievers] and their fathers until life [seemed] prolonged for them. Do they not see that We take [back] the earth, diminishing it from its edges? Or are they the defeaters?" (Al-Anbiya' 21:44). On that Day, the one they so solemnly deny, they will recount how long they lived – and it will not seem that long at all. "He [Allah] said, 'How many years was your stay in the earth?' They said, 'We stayed a day or part of a day. So ask the counters.' He said, 'You stayed but a short while, if you only had known. Did you think that We created you in jest [without purpose] and that to Us you would not be returned?" (Al-Mu'minun 23:112-115). All creation has a purpose. Everything was created to worship Allah and in so doing to guard the precious life that was all along only His. To Allah we belong and to Him we will all return. "And the Day the Hour will unfold, the criminals will swear that they did not stay [live] other than an hour. It is as such that they were reckless" (Ar-Rum 30:55). An hour, that's it. It'll all be over in an hour.

In light of this reality, the prophets were not permitted to wish haste on the corrupters. It was all a matter of time, and time is not something that Allah betrays. "They challenge you [Muhammad] to hasten the torment. And Allah does not betray His promise. And indeed, a day with your Lord is like a thousand years by your counting" (Al-Hajj 22:47). The Shaytan himself was given respite. Everyone has an opportunity to change their ways, to repent, do better and become better. Everyone can choose to enter the servitude of Allah instead of that of the Shaytan.

We, all of us peace-loving folk, are also humbled by the Quran, for it is not only the disbelieving war-mongering corrupters that are at stake if the hour is hastened. We all are. "And if Allah were to reproach people for what they earned, He would not have left a single stomping creature (*dabba*) on the surface [of the earth]. Instead, He delays them to a determined end. So, when their end arrives, then indeed Allah is regarding His servants insightful (*baseera*)" (Fatir 35:45). If Allah were to take us to task for our misdeeds not a single person would be left on the earth, but He leaves us for an appointed term. He gives us reprieve so that hopefully through our belief, good works, confirmation of truth and practice of patience we can buy time.

"So," the Prophet ﷺ was told, "have patience as did the messengers of firm resolve and do not [wish] haste for them [disbelievers]. It will be as if, when they see what they had been promised, they had not stayed except for an hour of a day. [This is] A notification. So, will anyone be exhausted [destroyed] except the rebellious folk?" (Al-Ahqaf 46:35). Everyone – the best of us and the worst of us – has an expiration date. By the sheer mercy of Allah and His infinite generosity, we just do not share the same destination.

Patience is not a choice; it is a necessity. We must always choose the higher ground. "And not equal is a good deed and a bad deed. React with that which is better, then the one between whom you and they is enmity will be as if he is a warm (*hamim*) acquaintance. And this cannot be attained except by those who are patient, and none can attain this except those who possess great fortune" (Fussilat 41:34-35). Indeed, as Prophet Muhammad ﷺ taught us, "The best of faith is patience and clemency" (Musnad Ahmad). May Allah grant us the strength and wisdom to comply.

Rizq Mentality

And in the sky is your provision (rizqakum) and what you are promised (Adh-Dhariyat 51:22).

Almost every time my mom observes someone or something receiving what Allah has coming to them, she says "*arzaq*" – divine provisions – with a contented certainty. Birds eating left over rice, *arzaq*; a squirrel finding an acorn, *arzaq*; a student receiving a scholarship, *arzaq*; my sister finding deal at the grocery store, *arzaq*; running into a friend you have not seen in years, *arzaq*; the laughter of my grandniece, *arzaq*; your monthly salary, *arzaq*; catching the afternoon sun with my kitty and a perfect cup of tea, *arzaq*; all of these are divine provisions. To think that *rizq* (pl. *arzaq*) is material wealth alone is to miss the greater part of Allah's blessings. She is right.

In His infinite generosity, Allah grants *rizq* – provision – to everything He created. "And there is not a treading creature (*dabba*) in the earth except that its provision is on Allah. And He knows where it settles and [from] where it departs. All is in a clear Book" (Hud 11:6). *Rizq* not only enables survival, it allows us to live dignified lives, securing our livelihoods and granting ease and pleasure. "And We have sent down from the sky blessed water, so that We propagate gardens and harvest seed. And soaring palm trees with clustered produce. *Rizq* for the servants, and we vivified with it a dead region, as such is the bringing out [both in this world and the Resurrection]" (Qaf 50:9-11). Everything in nature and all the good things we are able to produce and how they relate to give us life, to enable us to satisfy our material and intellectual needs, is *rizq*.

The perfection of the earth and the sky, the beauty of the human form and everything kind and wholesome that sustain life are all divine provisions. "It is Allah who made the earth for you a [place of] settlement and the sky a structure and designed you (*sawwarakum*) so He beautified your design and provided you (*razaqakum*) with what is wholesome (*at-tayyibat*). That is Allah, your Lord. So blessed is Allah, Lord of the worlds" (Ghafir 40:64). The wholeness of our universe – its reliable interdependence and dynamism – is *rizq*. "And We made [diverse] livelihoods in her [the earth] for you and for those for whom you do not provide" (Al-Hijr15:20). Allah created the diversities of livelihoods, languages, and lands, for humans and non-humans so that we may all satisfy our needs, so that we may be grateful.

I grew up knowing that everything I had, all the good things were from Allah. My family, friends, home, schooling, neighbourhood, food, all material comforts were *rizq* from Allah. My abilities, skills, attitude, intelligence, were *rizq* from Allah. My face and all physical attributes, and health, all *rizq* from Allah. The same went for everyone around me. My sister and I were never allowed to speak negatively about anyone or anything because it was all divine provision. Everyone and everything had its beauty, valued with precise valuation to its Creator (Al-Furqan 25:2). If we thought otherwise, then we needed our hearts fixed.

I experienced the world then, as I do now, through a *rizq* mentality where Allah is the Proprietor and Provider of everything. Of course I understood how hard my parents worked to give us the life they did, but I was taught that anything that resulted from all that effort was still *rizq*, the ability to work was itself *rizq*.

The Quran clearly reinforces these truths. "And to Allah belongs whatever is in the skies and the earth and Allah is ever encompassing of everything" (An-Nisa' 4:126). "And to Allah belongs whatever is in the skies and the earth and Allah is sufficient as Trustee" (An-Nisa' 4:132). Because everything is owned by Allah, everything must be provided by Allah. "And how many of treading creatures (*dabba*) cannot carry their provision. Allah provides for them, and you, and He is the Hearing, the Knowing" (Al-'Ankabut 29:60). "Indeed, Allah is the Provider, Possessor of the Power, the Durable (*matin*)" (Adh-Dhariyat 51:58). The certainty that everything belongs to Allah and that it is only through His generosity that we receive blessings engenders humility and gratitude in the hearts of believers.

From a very early age we developed a recognition of Allah's blessings through the consistent remembrance of His name, *bismillah*. The deep appreciation for everything He provided through His praises and thanks, *alhamdulillah w'ash-shukrulillah*.

Rizq from Allah is granted in ways beyond our comprehension. There is rizq that we can quantify and rizq that is hidden or simply immeasurable to us. We cannot attach values to things like love, mercy, contentment, happiness, and so on. The value of *rizq* of this nature depends on the possessor. Whereas some of us may not care to be happy so long as we have material wealth, others would prefer contentment even if it meant simplicity. I remember the interview with Donatella Versace when I was still a teenager where she said that she'd rather be crying in a Ferrari than happy on a bicycle. Personally, I'd choose to be happy walking. Whatever kind of provision it is, and however it is valued by us, it remains that Allah is the one who extends and restricts it.

The Quran reminds us that the keys of the skies and the earth belong to Allah (Ash-Shura 42:12). Only He has access to the stores of all bounties, all things, which He releases in due measure (Al-Hijr15:21). "Allah extends the provisions (*rizq*) for whom He wills of His servants and restricts [it] for them. Indeed, Allah is Knowing of all things" (Al-'Ankabut 29:62). What He gives or withholds is based on insight and a truthful acquaintance with His servants (Al-Isra' 17:30). Allah endears whom He wills and demeans whom You wills (Al-'Imran 3:26). If He withholds there is no one to provide (Al-Mulk 67:21).

In a world of *rizq* nothing that is meant for you is going to pass you by, and nothing that passes you was meant for you. This is a very comforting thought. Whatever I am given in this life – whether plenty or restricted – is for the best, my best. It keeps me contented. Sure, and obviously, I must strive, I must aim to be the best version of myself and satisfy my purpose, then I must accept the results with a beautiful patience. "So, when you have concluded the prayer, disperse in the land and seek from Allah's bounty. And remember Allah plentifully that you may succeed" (Al-Jumu'a 62:10). We must exert effort even as we know that outcomes are the purview of Allah.

We must be grateful for all the blessings that we have in our lives even if the ones we think we want, need or expect are missing. At any given moment we still have incalculable blessings. "And if you should count the blessings of Allah, you could not calculate them. Indeed, Allah is the Giver of Forgiveness, Grantor of Mercy" (An-Nahl 16:18). We certainly need forgiveness and mercy given our shortcomings, our inability to be as grateful as we ought to be under all circumstances.

This is a great lesson for homo economicus – the fictional human in neo-classical economics that has perfect knowledge and can always act to maximize his self-interest. It turns out we cannot even account for or properly value the blessings that fill our lives, let alone have perfect knowledge. The sheer arrogance of using such a theoretical model for understanding economic behavior, has led to a whole host of other theoretical constructs that are just as divorced from reality as homo economicus.

It is interesting how the *rizq* mentality changes the way we perceive of all the blessings in our lives. When we believe in *rizq*, in divine provision, we feel grateful. Allah has either given us something directly, like our own persons, parents, and children, or managed the universe so that it could deliver the provision whether it's the warm rays of the sun or a sweater. Those who believe reflect on the extent of Allah's bounties in their lives. It engenders humility, gratitude and generosity. The connection to Allah is strengthened, as it is with all the intervening elements that made the final version of that *rizq* possible. Allah tells us "if you thank, I will increase you" (Ibrahim 14:7). And Prophet Muhammad ﷺ taught us that 'He is not thankful to Allah who does not thank the people." The *rizq* mentality is inclusive, holistic.

Those who do not have this mentality tend to attribute everything they have to their own efforts. There is no connection to the Provider, and their reliance on others for what they achieve is downplayed or denied. There is no duty to anyone, only pride and self-gratitude. The Quran informs us about such people. "So if harm touches the human, he invokes Us. Then, when We consign blessings to him from Us, he says, 'Indeed, I attained this based on [my] knowledge.' Rather, it is a trial but most of them do not know. Those before them had already said this, but they were not availed by what they used to earn. So they were afflicted by the evil of what they earned and those who committed injustice of these [people] will be afflicted by the evil of what they earned, and they cannot avoid it. Do they not know that Allah extends provision for whom He wills and restricts [it]? Indeed, in this are *ayat* for a folk who believe" (Az-Zumar 39:49-52).

There are people who call on Allah when they believe that they need help, not realizing that Allah's help is needed in every moment of life. When a crisis arises, they call on their Maker, pleading with the only One who can really aid them. But when He comes to their rescue and they are saved, their tune changes and they attribute success to their exclusive efforts. The relief turns out to be a test. A test in humility, gratitude, and giving. Your efforts are obligatory, but they in no way command outcomes. Just think of how often you have worked hard for something only to be overjoyed or disappointed by the results. It is Allah who extends provision, allowing it to reach you, or He restricts it, preventing all or some supply.

Rizq is the province and providence of Allah. We are expected to receive it with gratitude and generosity. We must share His bounties upon us with those near and far, to accept our duty and its attendant responsibilities. The currencies of *rizq*, are gratitude (*shukr*) and giving *(infaq)*. To give is to acknowledge the intended flow of Allah's bounties on His creation. Everyone is granted blessings, *infaq* is the act of sharing with the confidence that it increases bounties. Prophet Muhammad ﷺ told us that charity does not decrease wealth (Sahih Muslim).

The Quran tells us to spend, encourages us to have minds of plenty not scarcity. "The example of those who spend their wealth in the way of Allah is like a seed that produces seven spikelets. In each spikelet is a hundred seeds. And Allah multiplies for whom He wills, and Allah is Expansive, Knowing" (Al-Baqarah 2:261). The believer knows that to spend in the way of Allah, on all things good, to help others – both human and non-human – can only lead to an increase in their provision, *rizq* (Saba' 34:39).

Scarcity, a core concept mainstreamed by secular economic thinking, has poisoned humanity. Defining individuals as consumers that have unlimited wants and needs in a world with limited resources, it gave rise to distorted ways of living and being. That same homo economicus who allegedly has perfect knowledge accepts this dishonest state of affairs. He somehow knows everything but still has unlimited wants. Having his way means depleting the earth, hoarding, and willingness to duel to the death. The mentality of scarcity has unleashed unbridled greed. Greed that breeds poverty, violence, and a molestation of nature to feed insatiable appetites.

Scarcity is a fabricated phenomenon, a fear implanted by the Shaytan. "If you were to rely upon Allah with the reliance He is due," taught us Prophet Muhammad ﷺ, "He would provide for you as He provides for the birds—they go out hungry in the morning and return full in the evening" (Sunan At-Tirmidhi). But that requires a different worldview, different beliefs. "Here you are, being invited to spend for Allah's sake, but among you are those who are miserly. And whoever is miserly is only miserly toward himself. And Allah is sufficient, and you are the impoverished. And if you turn away, He can exchange one folk for another, then they will not be like you" (Muhammad 47:38). Prophet Muhammad ﷺ told us that everyday two angels come down from the heavens and one of them says, "Oh Allah, compensate every person who spends in your cause" and the other says "Oh Allah, destroy every miser" (Sahih Bukhari).

What sense is there in Allah inviting us to be generous, to spend of our persons and wealth, to guard others, to facilitate their purposeful paths along with ours, if there was scarcity? Scarcity only results from greed, waste, excess, and hoarding; it is not a divine condition. "So," the Quran tells us, "heed Allah as much as you are able and listen and obey and spend for that is better for yourselves and whoever is guarded against the covetousness of his self – it is those who are the successful" (At-Taghabun 64:16).

There will always be those who are stingy and invite others to be like them (Al-Hadid 57:24). The Quran gives the specific example of those who are not even compassionate enough to so much as feed the needy. They rhetorically ask, "should we feed those whom if Allah willed He would have fed?" (Ya Sin 36:47). They see those who are generous as misguided, but it is they who are the heartless, misguided ones. It is they who deny Allah's favours upon them.

Yet, they are willing to spend their wealth to divert, distract, and disable those who have the *rizq* mentality, who believe that we all rise together. "Indeed, those who disbelieve spend their wealth to obstruct [others] from the path of Allah (*sabeel-illah*). So, they will continue to spend it until it is a source of [great] sorrow. Then they will be *defeated*. And those who disbelieved will be crowded into Hell" (Al-Anfal 8:36). I used to think that *ayat* such as this one were rather harsh. I never took lightly to Quranic presentations of torment and Hell. I now know better. How many creatures – human and non-human – were tormented in this life both directly and indirectly by those who did not believe in the Day of Account? How many died or needlessly suffered of thirst, hunger, and violence in a world of plenty?

In the days of Prophet Muhammad ﷺ, the hypocrites believed that if they did not support the early Muslims that they would abandon the faith. "They are the ones who say, 'Do not spend on those who are with the Messenger of Allah until they disband.' And for Allah are the stores [treasures] of the skies and the earth, but the hypocrites do not comprehend" (Al-Munafiqun 63:7). Their hearts could only understand *rizq* in the narrow material sense. The Muslims had been given something much – much – more valuable. Their material blessings were now crowned with the beauty of faith, contentment, and above all, the mercy and guardianship of *the* Proprietor and Provider.

The crown of the deniers, those who withheld what Allah had given them exclusively for themselves, will be of quite a different sort on the Day of Account. "And those who are covetous with what Allah has given them of His favours must not consider it good for them. Rather, it is evil for them. They will be crowned with what they coveted on the Day of Resurrection. And for Allah is the inheritance of the skies and the earth. And Allah is with what you do aware" (Al-'Imran 3:180). It will be a heavy, cumbersome crown, preventing its bearer from lifting his head if he is even able to stand. So, loosen your attachments to the material pleasures of this world. Live lightly and share generously, what Allah has in store is worthy of your efforts. "And whatever you are given of something, it is the pleasure of this life and its beautification and what is with Allah is better and more lasting, so will you not reason?" (Al-Qasas 28:60).

Allah gifts us in so many ways by allowing us to distribute His blessings. *Infaq* is an integral dimension of *taqwa*, which is the key to benefiting from the guidance of the Quran. "This Book, no doubt in it, is guidance for the heedful (*mutaqeen*). Those who believe in the unseen, establish prayer, and of what We provide them (*razaqnahum*) they spend (*yunfiqun*). And who believe in what was sent down to you [Muhammad] and what was sent before you, and of the Hereafter they are certain" (Al-Baqarah 2:2-4). *Taqwa* demands the recognition that all blessings are from Allah, and that they are meant to be shared.

We are expected to share what we really value. "You will never achieve righteousness (*birr*) until you spend some of what you love. And whatever you give is certainly well known to Allah" (Al-'Imran 3:92). You must be able and willing to share what you hold dear, not just what you would happily dispense with. This is the test of true faith. Allah distinguishes the believers by degrees in this regard and has prepared for His truthful servants forgiveness and an honourable provision (Al-Anfal 8:3). Prophet Muhammad ﷺ told us that "The believer's shade on the Day of Resurrection will be his charity" (Sunan Al-Tirmidhi).

Perhaps one of my favourite *suwar* in the Quran is *Al-Insan*, The Human. Its opening is humbling, confronting the human with his original obscurity. Was there not a time, it asks, when the human was not even a mention? But We created the human to test him and gave him the means with which he could rise. We guided him to the way, and he is either thankful or ingrateful. Those who are thankful "feed the needy and orphan and captive out of love for Him; [saying] 'We feed you for the Countenance of Allah, we do not desire from you reward or thanks; We fear from our Lord a day of anger and distress'" (Al-Insan 76:8-10). Believers know that there is a known share or right in their wealth for the one who asks and the one who is deprived (Al-Ma'arij 70:24-25; Adh-Dhariyat 51:19). In loving response, Allah protects them from the evils of the Day of Account, gifting them radiance and happiness.

The Prophet ﷺ was commanded to take from the wealth of the believers and to redistribute it, thereby purifying them. "Take charity (*sadaqah*) from their wealth purifying them and sanctifying them and pray for them. Indeed, your prayers are a calm (*sakanun*) for them. And Allah is Hearing, Knowing" (At-Tawbah 9:103). He ﷺ taught us to protect ourselves from the Fire even by giving half a date (Sahih Bukhari). All *infaq* is welcome but that done in secret is considered of greater value as there is no chance for us to contaminate our intentions, as what may happen if there is an element of show or haughtiness or if we hope to attain worldly gains by the act. "If you disclose your *sadaqat*, they are still a blessing [good]; and if you conceal them and give them to the poor, it is better for you, and He will absolve you of some of your sins. And Allah is aware of what you do" (Al-Baqarah 2:271).

Expectedly, the expiation of sins in the Quran almost always involves benefitting – spending on, feeding, freeing – others, teaching us to be generous (Al-Ma'idah 5:89). When these are not possible the alternative is always fasting for a certain duration, which is also a benefit to others as it restrains the believer and conserves some of the blessings that they may otherwise have consumed. "Do they not know that it is Allah who alone accepts repentance of His servants and takes the charities (*sadaqat*). And indeed, Allah is the Accepter of Repentance (*Tawab*), the Giver of Mercy" (At-Tawbah 9:104).

When we accept that everything we have, including everything we are, is *rizq* – divine provision – our connection to the Provider and to what is provided changes. It is belief that makes everything *rizq*. When we view reality in this way, our personal and collective lives are transformed. Humility, gratitude and giving can immeasurably improve our human lot and our impact on our non-human friends and neighbours. "Believe in Allah and His Messenger and spend from that in which He made you successors. So those who believe among you and spend will have an immense reward" (Al-Hadid 57:7).

When Prophet Muhammad ﷺ was asked by the believers about what to spend, he was told by Allah to say "Whatever you spend of [what is] good for parents (*walidayn*), and close relatives, and orphans, and the poor, and the wayfarer. And Allah is surely knowing of whatever good you do" (Al-Baqarah 2:215). The Quran also presents eight categories for which *zakat* funds referred to as *sadaqat* are due including the poor, needy, those administering funds for these purposes, reconciled hearts towards Islam, captives, debtors, the cause of Allah, and the wayfarer; all constituting duty from Allah (At-Tawbah 9:60).

All *rizq* belongs to Allah. We accept and benefit from it without even knowing. We try to give thanks, thanks for what we do recognize, thanks for what we take for granted, and thanks for a universe we scarcely know anything about except that it sustains and awes us. In gratitude, we also try to give all sorts of gifts, ensuring that the blessings that we have been blessed with are shared. This makes us content, happy, healthy, it fortifies connections and friendships. Giving has that effect. We acknowledge that we are custodians, everything is really on loan.

There was a time, when wealthy Muslims set up charitable endowments or *awaqf*, as a way of giving in perpetuity. Some still do but it is not as common as it was historically. A *waqf* (pl. *awqaf*) involves setting aside or *habs*, literally sequestering, an amount of money or other asset so that target beneficiaries can be cared for through its financial or other forms of returns. Over the course of Islamic history, *waqf* has been used to support charitable projects in education, health, agriculture, water provision, mosques, soup kitchens, and other projects involving human and animal welfare. These projects served important religious, cultural, social and economic purposes, strengthening connections between those whom Allah had amply endowed with those of lesser means. Through the provision of employment, improvement of infra structure, generation of knowledge, and enhancement of compassion, the awqaf reminded people of the source of *rizq*.

Prophet Muhammad ﷺ created the first *waqf* when he endowed the orchards of Mukhairiq, a Jewish rabbi who fought with the Muslim army in the Battle of Uhud where he was martyred. Mukhairiq had willed his orchards to be given to the Prophet ﷺ that he may commit them to charity. Prophet Muhammad ﷺ took the land and gave its produce in charity. In another instance, He ﷺ kept the principal of prized lands that had been acquired and donated by Umar Ibn al-Khattab ﵁, giving its profits – fruits – in charity to relatives, the poor, slaves, in Allah's way (*sabeel*), guests and travelers. As a *waqf*, the land was not to be sold, gifted, or inherited.

Awqaf experienced a period of strong growth under the Ottoman Empire during the 14th to 19th Centuries. The Ottomans developed the needed legal, judicial, and administrative systems that encouraged confidence in this form of giving. High level government officials and wealthy families established notable endowments serving many specialties. Bird and animal sanctuaries were often part of broader endowments for mosques, schools, and hospitals. Unfortunately, the seizure of *waqf* properties during the colonial period by British and French forces betrayed the trust upon which this institution was based, greatly weakening it and threatening its future prospects. Modern efforts in several Muslim countries to revive the *awqaf* for purposes of social solidarity are commendable but progress remains slow. The *rizq* mentality needs patience.

Allah does not ask for anything in return for the *rizq* He gifts us – *it is all His*. "Oh you people, remember the blessings of Allah on you. Is there a creator other than Allah providing for you from the sky and the earth? There is no deity except Him, so how are you deluded?" (Fatir 35:3). He wants nothing of His servants. "I do not want from them of provision (*rizq*) and I do not want them to feed Me" (Adh-Dhariyat 51:57). *Infaq* – spending from *rizq* – is solely for our benefit.

This is the fundamental essence of *infaq*. The more we give, the more we receive from Allah. Our worthiness increases when we show mercy and compassion toward His creatures. This may be difficult for those who view this worldly life as play and distraction, as the final destination. It is hard to comprehend for people absorbed in a mentality of scarcity and systems feeding off of self-interest and greed.

This is why *riba*, whether we think of it broadly as economic rents – unearned revenue – or more narrowly as interest both monetary and in kind, is so heinous in Islam. It is to charge for something that Allah gave without return. It is to accept *rizq* from Allah, then without His permission, ask someone in need to pay for it because the original recipient did not have a real or immediate need for it. The giver cannot charge for the divine provision that they, themselves, were gifted without charge. If they do undertake this prohibited act, they are still prohibited from utilizing those funds to satisfy the legitimate rights of others. It is a double prohibition.

> *And if We let people taste mercy, they rejoice in it. And if bad afflicts them for what their hands have put forth, they become seriously depressed (yaqnutun). Do they not see that Allah extends provision for whom He wills and restricts [it]. Surely in this are ayat for a folk who believe. So, give the relatives their right and the needy and the wayfarer [traveler], this is better for those who seek the Countenance of Allah and these are the successful. And whatever you give of riba [usury] to grow in people's wealth will not grow with Allah and what you give of zakat, seeking the Countenance of Allah, so it is those who are the multipliers. Allah, who created you, then provided for you,*

> *then deceases you, then revives you. Are there any of your partners who can do any of that? Glory to Him and High-above what they associate [with Him]* (Ar-Rum 30:36-40).

Most of us know what it is like to taste Allah's Mercy. To have enough and then some. And we know what it feels like to suffer misfortune, to struggle to make ends meet. To dream of a better life for ourselves and our loved ones but not have the means to make it come true. We are expected to share, to spend, in good times and in hard times (Al-'Imran 3:134). We are reminded that people's situations are not necessarily of their own doing. It is Allah that extends and restricts *rizq*. It is not for us to question and judge, but to give, to support, to relieve.

What we give has to be pure and legitimate. It cannot be obtained at the expense of others, giving from the proceeds extracted by charging for Allah's *rizq*. The surplus He gifted is not a means for exhausting others, it is an opportunity to extend help. I am not even accounting for the fact that interest bearing loans are not based on this surplus, they are based on the creation of money out of nothing and then lending that nothing for a fee. This is another level of deception. How can people relieve the crises of others by creating worse crises elsewhere? Using *riba* to augment people's wealth has no value with Allah, only *zakat* does. Giving from what is legitimately owned and earned, is the only kind of giving that has a multiplier effect.

The Quran asks, "Who is it that will loan Allah a beautiful loan (*qard hassan*), that He may multiply it for him, and he will have an honourable reward?" (Al-Hadid 57:11). Cognizant of our human failings, Allah eases the challenge that some face in giving others by framing the exchange as a beautiful loan to none other than Himself. You are lending Him His *rizq*! And He will repay it manifold (At-Taghabun 64:17). Think about that for a moment. The magnanimity of this offer is so intense that it is hard to hold back the tears.

The beautiful loan is not limited to monetary or material wealth because commerce in the Quran is a very different enterprise than that in our material world. In addition to material wealth, such a loan can take the form of giving through ourselves, personal effort. This may include all kinds of voluntary activities including gifting your skills once a week pro bono.

Then there are some extremely special people who do not loan Allah their persons and wealth but choose to sell altogether. "Indeed, Allah has purchased from the believers their selves (*anfusihum*) and their wealth with [the promise] of Paradise. They fight in Allah's way, so they kill or are killed. [It is] a true promise on Him in the Torah, the Gospel, and the Quran. And who is truer to his promise than Allah? So, delight in the sale that you have transacted. And it is that which is the great win" (At-Tawbah 9:111). Defending oneself and others against evil forces, those who refuse to let people live in peace, requires the highest level of sincerity and sacrifice. The giving is ultimate, and the reward is ultimate. A reward found in previous scriptures as well.

The *rizq* mentality cautions people about the life of this world. "Know that the life of this world is play and distraction and adornment and pride among yourselves and accumulation in wealth and children, [which is] like rain whose produce pleases the tillers then it dehydrates so you see it turn yellow then it becomes ruined. And in the Hereafter is severe torment and forgiveness from Allah and acceptance. And what is the life of this world except the pleasures of seduction (*mata3-ul-ghurur*)" (Al-Hadid 57:20). This may well be the nature of this life but "... if you believe and are heedful, He [Allah] will give you your recompense and He will not ask for your wealth. If He should ask you for it and press you, you would be miserly, and He would bring out your worst" (Muhammad 47:36-38). The *rizq* mentality is gentle, it is voluntary. Not adopting it, however, is detrimental.

The Quran tells us why Allah created life and death in a clear and simple ayah. "[He] who created death and life to test you [as to] which of you is best in deeds. And He is the Dear, the Giver of Forgiveness" (Al-Mulk 67:2). The skies and the earth were created to test us likewise (Hud 11: 7). They all belong to Him that He may reward those who did wrong according to their wrongs and those who did good with good (An-Najm 53:31).

So let us adopt the *rizq* mentality, acknowledge the source of all blessings and share with generosity what was gifted to us with generosity. It is not what we keep for ourselves that lasts but what we give. Prophet Muhammad ﷺ taught us that "When a person dies, only three deeds will survive him: continuing charities, profitable knowledge and a child praying for him" (Sahih Muslim). Let us not be among those who failed to give enough. "Spend from what We have provided for you before death comes to one of you so he says, 'My Lord, if only You would delay me for a brief term so I could give charity and be among the righteous" (Al-Munafiqun 63:10). Allah forbid.

The Deepest Recess of the Heart

Our Ummah was a single body, filled with mutual love, mercy, and friendship. Until we allowed them to lead us. Until we yielded to their artificial god abandoning the centrality of a sound heart for the soundness of the body. Our Ummah was a building, interdependent with supporting parts. We congregated in mosques, joined in rows with no gaps between our shoulders. It was a sanctuary for unity, sharing, learning, healing, and resolving our differences in the company of angels. Until we adopted their individualism, delusions of independence and false equalities over our communalism, collective thinking, and merciful equities. We shared a language with which we understood the Word of our Creator, and united across continents, until we were enamoured with their languages and lost our meaning. It was a sound body until the heart became corrupted. But Allah is the turner of hearts. He is At-Tawwab, inviting and facilitating our return.

A while back I had a dream where I saw my heart presented in front of me in its natural form and size except for an inscription written on its lowest portion, where the left ventricle extends to form the apex, "*tawhid*". The most profound statement. The location of the inscription struck me. It seemed to be knowingly positioned. Why had *tawhid* been written in what appeared to be the deepest recess of the heart, and not the top or centre? At the time I had not reflected deeply on the different references to the heart in the Quran, though I understood its centrality in the life of a believer.

The Quran tells us that Allah writes – *kataba* – faith in the hearts of true believers and reinforces them with a spirit from Him (Al-Mujadilah 58:22). These reinforcements ensure that believers can properly discern between good and evil, even among their closest relatives. The heart is where Allah endears and beautifies faith while making lewdness and disobedience hateful (Al-Hujuraat 49:7). A sound heart loves everything pure and beneficial and rejects everything corrupt and harmful.

Love is a very serious choice with implications in this life and the next. Who and what we love influences our choices, moods, behaviors, motivations, preferences and aspirations. The ability to exercise good judgement by prioritizing divine guidance particularly when we love is critical. Allah tells us in the Quran that we might love something that is harmful to us and dislike something that is beneficial (Al-Baqarah 2:216). The same applies to people. We may dislike certain individuals who actually bring great blessings to our lives (An-Nisa' 4:19). Questioning why we love what we love or conversely dislike what we dislike is important for the development and maintenance of a sound heart.

A man once asked Prophet Muhammad ﷺ his opinion of someone who loved a people but never had the opportunity to live among them. The Prophet ﷺ responded: "A person is with whom he loves." And in another narration, he responded: "You are with who you love" (Sahih Bukhari). I can imagine that the man was referring to himself and his love for the Prophet ﷺ. That he had wished to live among the Muslims who were close to the Prophet ﷺ, so he could more fully express his love for him in words and actions. It is also a message for us, a glad tiding – *bushra* – that we will eventually be united with our beloved Prophet ﷺ even as we did not live among his immediate companions.

The heart is a powerful thing, carnal and transcendental, it is not only the central organ in our bodies, but it also determines who we are and where we are heading – the final destination. Prophet Muhammad ﷺ, whose heart was purer than pure, consistently asked Allah to keep his heart firm on His *deen*. He ﷺ taught us to focus on the quality of our hearts and deeds as these are what concern Allah, not our appearance or wealth. Nothing will be of benefit to you on the Day of Account except the state of your heart. "The Day when wealth and children will not be of benefit, except he who comes to Allah with a sound heart (*qalb salim*)" (Ash-Shu'ara 26:88-89).

Sufi master, Al-Hakim Al-Tirmidhi (d.912), in his *A Treatise on the Heart* discussed four dimensions of the heart – chest (*sadr*), heart (*qalb*), inner heart (*fuad*), and intellect (*lubb*) – that are elaborated upon in the Quran. He associated each of these dimensions with different stations or levels of illumination. The chest is associated with the *light of Islam*. The heart proper is associated with the *light of iman* (faith). The inner heart is associated with the *light of ma'rifah* (knowing). And the intellect, the deepest recess of the heart, is associated with the light of *tawhid*!

The chest is the cavity that encases and protects your heart. It is its home. Think of your home with its structure, windows, doors, rooms, furnishings, conveniences and inconveniences. Think of how it makes you feel when you walk in after a long day or journey. Are you at ease? Do you find comfort? Or are you disturbed, wishing you had not returned? Is it cluttered, overcrowded with useless things, making it feel small and preventing enjoyment of its finer qualities? Is it clean, disinfected from things that may make you sick?

A home is intended to be a shelter. It is a protection against the weather, a nosy neighbour, potential violence from relatives and strangers, noise, and contagion from all things harmful. A home is where you refresh, rebalance, reflect. And if something, like a leaky faucet or broken window need fixing, you fix it so that it can continue to satisfy your needs. Your chest is exactly that home for your heart. In it you have either cultivated a sanctuary or a trap.

The chest, *sadr*, is the place of entry for inner and outer signals that lead it to expand or contract. You experience this when you think certain thoughts or receive certain news. When you think bad thoughts, your chest tightens, and you become anxious. Your heart begins to race as its environment is imbalanced. The opposite is also true, when you think good thoughts your chest calms and your heart beats normally. Outer signals have a similar effect. When we receive exciting news we feel fluttering or pounding in our chests again because our heart is reacting to a change in its environment.

The chest is associated with the light of Islam. Here rests the acknowledgement of Islam as truth, as a declaration of faith. "Therefore, whomsoever Allah desires to guide, He makes his chest (*sadr*) welcoming to Islam. And when He desires to misguide someone, He constricts his chest, narrowed, as if he were rising into [outer] space" (Al-An'am 6:125). It is the chest that welcomes Islam by opening up for the receipt of guidance or closing itself off in rejection. This is the light switch that you turn on when you walk into your home on a dark evening. The light fills the room and perhaps illuminates the areas around when there are no walls to prevent its energy. The expansion of one's chest is a gift from Allah. The Quran asks "Have We not expanded for you your chest?" (Al-Inshirah 94:1) meaning made it inviting to Islam.

The light of Islam begins the believer's journey to clean up or refine the chest so as to commence its expansion, to accommodate the growth of heart that is sure to follow. Everything truthful, beautiful, peaceful, and pure expands the chest while all kinds of disobedience to Allah, the evil cajoling (*waswasa*) of the Shaytan, and worldly distractions contract it. Some guests will come uninvited, we may not even notice their entrance as they speak gently and dress deceptively to please our ears and eyes obscuring their true nature; guests like jealousy, passion, arrogance and greed. They make their way in unnoticed, and then settle and grow, pressuring the heart to yield to their commands. Switching on the light helps us to recognize them and commence the struggle of eviction – *jihad an-nafs*.

Temptations presented to the heart must be filtered by the chest. If the chest is prone to accept and immerse itself in evil, or if it cannot recognize unwanted guests, it compromises the heart and the entirety of its possessor. "…He who invites disbelief into his chest, on them is the wrath of Allah…" (An-Nahl 16:106). There is no hiding what we harbour of good or evil, it will eventually make its way to our hearts and then reflect in our thoughts and actions. Prophet Muhammad ﷺ taught us that every take-up of evil by the heart warrants a black dot. If its possessor does not repent, the heart eventually becomes covered in black. Its possessor no longer recognizing what is good or how to avoid the reprehensible, it only knows its desires.

Keeping the chest pure is very important. The Quran tells us that Allah tests what is in our chests to eliminate any untruthful residue that may taint our hearts (Al-'Imran 3:154). He has sent down divine guidance to protect our hearts from any smears by filling our chests and crowding out any chance for the entry of evil. "Oh people, there has come to you an admonition (*maw'izaton*) from your Lord and healing for what is in the chests and guidance and mercy for the believers" (Yunus 10:57). The chest is home to the Quran. "Rather, it [the Quran] is clear *ayat* in the chests of those given knowledge and none except the unjust do not cultivate our *ayat*" (Al-'Ankabut 49:29). Again, Prophet Muhammad ﷺ taught us that every time the heart takes up what is truthful and good in obedience to its Creator, it warrants a white dot. Those white dots continue to increase until the heart becomes as white as the tip of the mount of Safa which is made of smooth white stone.

Open the doors and windows of your chest to the light of Islam. Cultivate the ayat when you invite them in. If you do not, they will escape you. Like any guest, the retention of truth, of knowledge – the *ayat* – demands effort and complementary actions. They will not stay in the company of unsuitable invitees, so stop the entry of that which will debase you, which will make you lose your most honoured guest – the Quran – the VVIP of all guests. Be cognizant of what you consume.

The heart is within the chest, as the Quran makes clear, a point I am compelled to emphasize given that not too long ago someone tried to convince me that the heart was actually in the head. Of course he did not mean physically in the head, but figuratively. Either way, his view does not conform to the Quran or teachings of Prophet Muhammad ﷺ. Faith is written in the hearts of believers, which are in their chests. The heart is where faith is adorned, where it takes its beauty. "It is He who sent down serenity into the hearts of the believers" (Al-Fath 48:4). Our hearts are tranquil in faith.

The heart – *qalb* –is associated with the light of *iman* or true faith. When Islam enters and settles in the heart, a believer becomes a *mu'min* not merely a *muslim*. "The Bedouins say, 'We believe.' Say [Muhammad], 'You do not [yet] believe, but say we have submitted (*aslamna*),' for faith (*iman*) has not yet entered your hearts. And if you obey Allah and His Messenger, He will not diminish anything from your deeds. Indeed, Allah is Forgiving, Merciful" (Al-Hujuraat 49:14). It is one thing to switch on the light, and another to acknowledge and act according to what it has revealed. This takes time and practice.

With the light on, the heart has a better chance to understand. The internal and external signals it receives can, more or less, be interpreted correctly. This is why the Quran questions those who have hearts but appear not to understand. "So, have they not travelled in the land so that they develop hearts with which to understand or ears with which to hear? For surely it is not the vision that becomes blind, but rather the hearts which are in the chests" (Al-Hajj 22:46). Unjust people have so much clutter, impurities, in their chests that the capacity of their hearts to see are greatly obscured. The black dots fuse into bigger and bigger veils.

It reminds me of an upsetting experience I had in an airport in Doha many moons ago. For the first time in my life, I was hiring a live-in housekeeper and nanny for my three young children. I stood at the arrival gate waiting for my guest. Two planes seemed to have disembarked but not a sign of her. So, I approached the information desk and informed them that I was waiting for a person, *shakhs* in Arabic, who had not yet turned up. Had the plane fully disembarked? They said it had and advised me to wait patiently. I waited for another hour, then approached them again. I asked if they were sure. The man then said, "Who exactly are you waiting for?" I pulled out her employment contract which I thought I might need to clear her arrival. He took a quick look it and blurted, "You said *shakhs*! She's a maid." My heart sank. He then told me that all the maids were directed to another part of the arrival hall – they were not considered persons. This story still pains me. Umm Mohamed, the mother of Mohamed, as we called her out of respect, was the sweetest, kindest, most generous person. She was our savior. Some hearts have no understanding whatsoever.

Prophet Muhammad ﷺ taught that "It is through the health of the heart that the body is healthy, physically as well as morally" (Sahih Bukhari). An unhealthy heart cannot play one of its most important roles, which is to advise its keeper especially when they face challenging decisions. The Prophet ﷺ said "Ask your heart, consult your conscience; good is what gives peace to the self and the heart; evil is that which troubles the self and makes the heart palpitate, irrespective of the advice of those who give religious opinion (*muftun*)" (Musnad Ahmad). I have so often seen people ask for religious opinions that actually betray their hearts. This has always perplexed me. Although their hearts push them to be generous or to make amends or to remain silent, appearing to know what is good for their keepers, their *anfus* command greed and conflict and they seek religious justification for the latter!

Unfortunately for them, the heart is not only the centre of understanding, but also where intention (*niyah*) is formulated. What is the intention behind seeking a religious opinion? Is it that you truly do not know how to be good or better, kinder, more generous, purer, or are you seeking the pretext to commit a wrong disguised as a right or to take the path of lesser good?

Any action you take cannot be divorced from the intention in your heart. It is intention that gives any act its value. The Quran emphasizes that the intentions of the heart and expressions of the body go together, but it elevates the intentions of the heart. The truths of the Quran tell us about the importance of purity for the heart (Al-Ahzab 33:53), the need for refinement of the heart (Al-'Imran 3:154), and the humility and fear in the rightly guided heart (Al-Mu'minun 23:60). Ultimately, as Prophet Muhammad ﷺ taught us, actions are by intention and for each is what they intended (Sahih Bukhari).

It is our hearts that will be held to account. The Quran tell us, "Allah does not reproach you for the drivel in your oaths, but He does reproach you for what your hearts have earned. And Allah is Forgiving, Forbearing" (Al-Baqarah 2:225). It also states, "… there is no blame on you in what you have mistaken, but instead what your hearts have purposefully committed, and Allah is ever Forgiving, Merciful" (Al-Ahzab 33:5). Understanding, intention, and accountability, demand heedfulness, *taqwa*, which Prophet Muhammad ﷺ confirmed when he pointed to his heart three times repeating "*taqwa is here*." Here, in the heart, the inner heart and the intellect with their unique stations and degrees of illumination.

I sat to the side on the Day of 'Arafat pleading with Allah to exclusivize me for His service. My tears flowed like a river knowing the weight of what I was asking. I quickly ran out of tissues and had to resort to my hijab. My face, despite an olive complexion, was puffy and red from the heat and emotion. It was a special day, in a special place, with special people but not all of them. Amidst my solitude, I could hear chattering and laughter. Then a young woman interrupted me. She was one of my former students who had come on the same tour package.

"Do you want to know why we were laughing?" she asked. I actually did not, but my silence misled her, and she informed me that they found my intensity funny. A person among the group had pointed me out with ridicule. They were laughing at me. To their minds nothing warranted this torrent of emotions. I turned away from her and continued to pray and invoke Allah. If they wished to waste this Day that was their choice.

A few nights later, after completing the rites of Hajj but still in Makkah, I made my way across a path, scattered with what I would later discover were symbols of events that would transpire in my life. The path ended with a massive black iron gate that was guarded by poor people who scrambled to open it for me as I approached. On the other side was a highway, with fast moving vehicles, all going in the same direction. I could only cross if I jumped on a vehicle and got off on the other side. I did that and despite the speed and direction of the vehicle, I landed on the other side without having traveled an inch. There, I entered a room that had three blue chairs, and three men that I recognized to be angels. One immediately got up gesturing me to sit, and then another took my right hand, but I pulled it away.

I was grasping a precious keychain-like holder with three interlocked rings each adorned with a precious jewel. The chain was held by another ring that was hanging on the first joint of my middle finger. But he indicated that he did not seek the chain, he wanted to see my palm. So, he took my hand again, and divided my palm in four quadrants. He said nothing about the first quadrant as if it had already passed. He said very little about the second as if it too was about to pass. He told me something about the third that I cannot recall. Then he turned to the fourth and said, "you will live as an honest, loyal and truthful person and you will die as an honest, loyal and truthful person. And when you die you will live in 467 [or 472] *Al-Fuad* street." Anxious that I would forget, I asked for a for a paper and pen to write down my address. But the other angel said to me, "No matter, it the street of *al-fuad*," – Fidelity St.! – like that was all I needed to remember.

The *fuad* or inner heart is associated with the light of *ma'rifah* or knowing. When the heart knows it alters the power of vision guiding its keeper to maintain faithfulness to Allah with unyielding loyalty and consistency. Knowing gives us a whole new perspective on reality, we see something deeper. We no longer just see the external manifestation of things but can experience something of their truth. It is to have insight not merely sight. "Indeed," the Quran tells us, "there has come to you clear insights from your Lord, so whoever sees it is for themselves and whoever is blinded it is against themselves and I [Muhammad] am not a preserver over you" (Al-An'am 6:104). It then warns us about the pursuit of things of which we have no knowledge, no insight, reminding us that the hearing, the sight, and the *fuad* will be questioned (Al-Isra' 17:36).

When the mother of baby Musa ﷺ received revelation to place him in the basket in the river to save him from Pharaoh's murderous rampage, her heart was naturally pained. The Quran tells us that her *fuad* woke to emptiness. Her *inner heart*, the space where we carry our loved ones, was as if it had been hollowed with a corer. In her desperation, she almost revealed what had happened, but Allah secured her heart that she may be of the believers (Al-Qaṣas 28:10). Because the *fuad* carries such precious cargo, we must consistently invoke Allah to help us guard and strengthen its casing.

The heart sees through the strength and truthfulness of the *fuad*. After Prophet Muhammad ﷺ received the first revelation in the Cave of Hira, there was a distressing absence of similar episodes. The Prophet ﷺ thought that something had gone wrong. Was Allah upset with him? That is when he saw Jibreel ﷺ in his true form filling the sky's horizon. It was a fearsome sight. He rushed back to his beloved wife Khadija ﷺ filled with fear, asking her to cover him. Surah An-Najm confirms this incident and the truthfulness of the *fuad*. "The *fuad* did not lie about what it saw" (An-Najm 53:10). The *fuad* does not lie.

Like every station of the heart, development of the *fuad* demands guidance and patience. The light strengthens with effort, it takes time to illuminate the depths of the heart. It is like a light switch that has a dimmer, the light is gradually increased giving our senses time to adjust and allowing us to address what the light has revealed before illuminating us further. Allah does not want us to be overwhelmed. If the true brightness of the Quran was switched on all at once, we would be dazed, incapable of applying it in any worthy sense. When Prophet Muhammad ﷺ was challenged by the disbelievers on this very point, he was told by Allah to say, "It is so that We may secure your *fuad* by it" (Al-Furqan 25:32). Truth is gradually anchored in the heart of a believer out of Allah's infinite mercy.

This brings us to the highest station of the heart, the intellect or *lubb*. Here in the deepest recess, we find the light of *tawhid* – unicity. *Tawhid* is belief in the Oneness of Allah, and the oneness of His creation. This station only admits holism, the integration of the seen and unseen, whose purposeful components interact through a seamless web of connections. It is the essence of the Trust that we covenanted to carry. The light of *tawhid* reveals *the* whole to its keeper. We no longer see the parts as forming wholes that are in turn only parts of bigger wholes, but *the* whole as commanding all of its parts.

In the Quran, those who kindle and emit this light are called *ulul albab*, the possessors of intellect. Their hearts are pure, free from distortions. They are certain about divine guidance and accountability, fearing the betrayal of any of Allah's limits thereby demonstrating the deepest respect for His laws. The Quran tells us that the possessors of intellect are those who are devoutly obedient, spending parts of the night prostrating and standing, cautious of the Hereafter and pleading for the mercy of their Lord. The Quran urges us to ponder, "... 'Are they who know equal to they who do not know?' Only those possessing intellect will remember" (Az-Zumar 39:9). *Ulul albab* do not step out of their comfort zone to approach Allah; His company *is* their comfort zone.

They practice consistent remembrance and reflection; their hearts having been trained to avoid frivolous thought and talk. Whether contemplating the Quran or observing nature, their finest moments are defined by reflecting on the *ayat*. "A Blessed Book sent down to you [Muhammad], that they may reflect on its *ayat*, and that those who possess intellect may be reminded" (Saad 38:29). The Quran also tells us, "Indeed, in the creation of the skies and the earth and the alternation of the night and the day are *ayat* for the possessors of intellect" (Al-'Imran 3:190-191). The *ayat* are always whole, inseparable.

There is no choice but the beauty of followership for *ulul albab*. The balance of life is too delicate while human injustice and ignorance are too rampant. Only the best of their understandings of the Quran and Sunnah are reflected in their speech and actions. The Quran tells us that even in the most difficult situations, *ulul albab* take the higher road. "And there is life in *qisas* oh you possessors of intellect, that you may be heedful" (Al-Baqarah 2:179). *Qisas* is the law of retribution in the Quran in cases of involuntary manslaughter. It is based on the reasonable determination of blood money for the loss of life, instead of the taking of another life, and encouragement of pardoning some of the agreed amount to ease the burden on the debtor. Those who possess intellect know that there is a saving of life in this law while having the capacity to honour it.

By this light, the light of *tawhid*, *ulul albab* have found their way to the water and generously invite others to join them, to share in its blessings. They recall that the Quran is a notification for people and that it may be used to warn, so that they may all know that He is One God (Ibrahim 14:52).

Intelligence is uniquely human. It can take many forms but artificial is not one of them. It is called artificial because this type of *intelligence* is part of machines and software not actual intellects. Its name, artificial intelligence – AI – betrays its true essence. Do not misunderstand my point, I am not passing judgement on the potential benefits of this field of knowledge. I am flagging its deceptive appropriation of a definitive feature of our species.

AI was not and cannot start from the whole. It is being built from parts, known parts. Its strength is based on working with the greatest amount of available data, what already exists. Correction, what has been observed and inputted. It can never account for the unseen. It can never know the Creator. So, while it can do wonderful things in many areas of human need, it cannot be characterized as *intelligent*.

We are told that human-like AI will soon be a possibility, convincing people that a machine can think and learn like a human. This seriously discounts what it means to be human, to have purpose and connection. Even for those who accept that the brain is the centre of intelligence and not the heart, we are more than our brains, which is the focus of AI research and machine learning. Neural networks are also characteristic of our hearts and research is showing that the heart communicates more with the brain than the other way around. The future ability of any machine to self-generate or perform tasks that humans cannot, will only be possible based on some original human instructions. Its abilities will not surpass true human intelligence but may instead demonstrate its serious limits.

For Muslims eagerly jumping on the bandwagon, not wanting to miss out, I urge caution. AI may be useful in supporting Quran recitation and memorization, it may help with translation and linguistic tasks, speed up *fatwa*, classify and verify hadith, serve pilgrims, create educational programs and provide virtual teachers but it will never satisfy the holism that defines our faith and fortifies our community. Convenience, immediacy, personalized learning – all pushing people into the abyss of isolation. Human connection is not an inconvenience, it is a divine *sunnah* that has a right to our time. We communicate with our hearts, not just with our tongues and bodies. Our eyes need to look *upon the world* so that our hearts can see and understand.

Our Ummah was established on heart. The heart of our beloved Prophet Muhammad ﷺ. "So, by mercy from Allah, you [Muhammad] were lenient with them. And if you were ill-tempered, harsh hearted, they would have dispersed from around you. So pardon them and ask forgiveness for them and consult them in the affair. And when you have decided, then place your trust in Allah, Allah loves the placers of trust [in Him]" (Al-'Imran 3:159). It was his heart that drew the multitudes to him, and still does centuries later.

Prophet Muhammad ﷺ understood the value of heart and protecting the hearts of believers. His very first project in Madinah, the construction of Al-Masjid An-Nabawi, is testament to his efforts to provide those hearts with a special house. To ensure that their hearts were properly nourished, purified, and connected. This was the chest that embraced and shielded the believers and their hearts from all kinds of evils. It reminded the young community of is purpose, enjoining them to seek faith, knowledge and unity. It brought them together to connect. This is the role of all of Allah's houses. "Indeed, those who plenish Allah's *masajid* are those who believe in Allah and the Last Day and establish prayer and giving *zakat* and do not revere except Allah. So, that perhaps these will be of the guided" (At-Tawbah 9:18).

Concerns over AI range from challenges to authority, authenticity, and respect for the sacredness of our texts and how they must be handled, to hyper-surveillance of Muslims. Two Microsoft programmers recently resigned after calling out the company for complicity in the genocide. During Microsoft's fiftieth anniversary, Ibtihal Abu Al-Saad and Vaniyal Agrawal, stood up to reveal how Microsoft was providing AI to the Israeli army, facilitating the ongoing aggression against the Palestinians. Ibtihal also sent a message to all employees informing them of the betrayal. May Allah protect them both and all the courageous individuals and groups struggling to make this a safer and fairer world for us all. Those living and working with heart.

Our Ummah would do good to recognize that there is nothing intelligent in things that have no capacity to believe. Useful…potentially. Intelligent… never. That which has no heart is not worthy of followership or careless adoption. A reminder for *ulul albab*.

Eye on the Prize

Indeed, for the heedful is a prize!
Orchards and grapevines
And [beautiful] earthenware
And full goblets
They will not hear in it [any] drivel or lies
A reward from your Lord, a giving of account
(An-Naba' 78:31-36)

It is only befitting to close this book with some words concerning my favourite *ayah* in the Quran – *ina lilmutaqeena mafaza* – indeed, for the heedful is a prize. This is the rightful reward for those who pursued the way to the water. Heedfulness, *taqwa*, keeps us firmly on this way and promises us an opportunity to attain that prize. "And those who are guided, He [Allah] increases them in guidance and gives them their heedfulness" (Muhammad 47:17). Out of Allah's Mercy many streams pour into this divine river or well as reflected in the diversity of His creation. "And those who strive for Us, We will guide them to our passages. And indeed, Allah is with the do gooders" (Al-'Ankabut 29:69). Those who believe and strive with their persons and wealth to satisfy their purpose and support others in the pursuit of theirs. "Indeed, those who believe and perform good deeds, are guided by their Lord through their faith. Beneath them are running rivers in gardens of bliss" (Yunus 10:9). In this world and the next, the believer is calmed, charmed, and rewarded by water.

Virtue ethics asserts that good actions and character are valuable in and of themselves irrespective of consequences. Those who take this view argue that an action must be good and obligatory in and of itself without regard for outcomes. Similarly, Kantian ethics asserts that moral principles are self-created and imposed, without God. Thus, people are not to expect any reward from an external power for doing good. Utilitarians base their ideas of consequentialism completely on worldly outcomes. They focus on the happiness, pleasure or wellness inducing effects of moral behavior dismissing divine command and intentions, as well as actions that may indeed be good but do not result in these consequences.

All of these are secular, mundane, approaches that seek the beginning and ending of good deeds in this life without their necessary and inescapable consequences both in this life and the next. A good action must not only be inherently good, but it must also be commanded by Allah, embody the spirit of good intention, and attain the approval of divine sanction, which completely overlaps with or overrides moral sanction. All worldly approaches make us doubt our sincerity when we perform good with our eye on the prize, not the ephemeral prize but the real prize, they shame or ridicule us for looking beyond immediate goodness to the infinite goodness that is held and can only be rewarded by the Creator.

In doing so, the pretext is crafted for those who argue that belief is not required for the commission of good. This may be so to a limited extent but in depriving virtue of its divine essence, it is also denies the blessings that are necessary for its rectification and extension beyond our capabilities. "Oh you who believe, heed Allah and talk with succinct speech. He will rectify your deeds for you and forgive you your sins. And whoever obeys Allah and His Messenger has won a great winning" (Al-Ahzab 33:70-71). Good intentions and actions demanded by the Quran and Sunnah are never for their own sake. They are to please our Creator, save ourselves and guard others against our excesses. There is always wisdom – *hikmah* – that underlays everything demanded or encouraged by the Quran and Sunnah, a *hikmah* that while encompassing the life of the world also and necessarily extends beyond it, a *hikmah* that does not centralize the *nafs* but rather its Lord and Creator.

The association of knowledge of the Quran with wisdom is often repeated throughout the Quran. Wisdom allows its possessor to go beyond basic understandings to exercise correct judgement, have confidence in the rationale of Allah's guidance and its implications in any given context thereby providing foresight. Prophet Ibrahim ﷺ invoked Allah to send a messenger from among the Arabs to teach His *ayat* and the Book and Wisdom and to purify them (Al-Baqarah 2:129). Allah responded to this prayer by sending Prophet Muhammad ﷺ who recited His ayat, purifying his followers, teaching them the Book and wisdom, as well as what they were previously unaware of (Al-Baqarah 2:151).

The Quran underscores the importance of wisdom especially when it comes to political power. When Prophet Dawood ﷺ defeated Jalut, Allah gave him dominion and wisdom, teaching him of what He willed (Al-Baqarah 2:251). The checking of one people by another is best achieved through such wisdom. Our affairs can be settled much more wisely than through the confrontation and conflict that we are witnessing today. "He gives wisdom to whom He wills and whoever is given wisdom, then he has been given much good. And none but those with intellect remember" (Al-Baqarah 2:269). It is through wisdom that those with sound hearts seek the higher ground.

Knowledge of the Book and wisdom is the surest defense against those who would mislead the believers (An-Nisa' 4:113). Sound hearts know that Allah's guidance of a certainty leads to greater prosperity, virtue and victory in this world and the one to come. An important dimension of this wisdom is to recognize and accept that the outcomes we hope for may not be evident in our lifetimes, but that through our efforts the necessary forces have been unleashed. So, as the Quran tells us, "Invite to the way of your Lord with wisdom and good [beautiful] advice. And argue with them with what is better. Indeed, Allah is most knowing of he who has strayed from His Way and is most knowing of the guided" (An-Nahl 16:125). Invite to Allah with humility, kindness, and patience, exclusively for His sake not for some personal desire or agenda. It may be that he who you are inviting becomes a better, more welcome guest, than you, even as you cannot perceive their worth.

During my tenure as a policy analyst in the Canadian Federal Government, I had a pleasant conversation with a colleague on this exact issue. He took the position that belief was not a necessity for being good. He argued that I may be good as a believer, but he was equally good as a disbeliever. We both, for practical purposes, did the same good things. I thought about it, then explained that the difference between us was that I was always conscious that Allah sees me. Sees everything that I do, and keeps account, whereas he did not believe in any kind of oversight. I explained that oversight, pretty much like that in government, ensures accountability which is necessary for the exercise of justice. How is it that we accept accountability in man-made systems of governance, but we do not accept oversight and accountability when it comes to Allah's dominion?

I also explained that his standards of good and lawfulness depended on some kind of social consensus which in addition to changing according to social pressures and norms, was nowhere near as comprehensive as the standards exacted from me by my Creator. Allah's guidance is pervasive, in private as it is in public, ensuring consistency and reliability in all dimensions of my life for myself and those around me. It does this while granting wide latitude for the expression of diversity but not to the extent that my path destructs those of others. Allah's guidance is based on knowledge of the whole, something humans are simply not capable of, allowing each of us to live our lives while respecting the rights of others – human and non-human – to live theirs.

As Muslims, everything good that we do is accounted for, down to a simple greeting. "And if you are greeted, so greet [back] with better than it or return it. Indeed, Allah is ever accounting of all things" (An-Nisa' 4:86). When I receive a greeting, I do not respond back because it is intrinsically polite, but rather because I know it would please Allah if I responded with something kinder. Perhaps something that would make my greeter smile.

Allah wants us to be happy, to care for each other, to live harmoniously and He wants to reward us for it. I do not expect any reward from my greeter or anyone for whom I perform a service. I hope for a reward from Allah. To want that reward is not a defect in my efforts or intentions, nor does it diminish anything of my virtue, it is part of Allah's divine *sunan* and is encouraged by Him. This is how He relieves His servants of the debts that they would otherwise owe to each other. I choose to live free of expectations from others by transferring the debt to the One who owns the skies, the earth and everything in between. The One who encouraged me to give *sadaqah* and to loan Him a beautiful loan, so that He may multiply it and grant me a noble reward (Al-Hadid 57:18).

The Quran tells us that if there is to be a race, a competition among people, then let it be for our Lord's forgiveness and a *Jannah* that is as wide as the skies and the earth, prepared for the heedful (Al-'Imran 3:133). "Tell My servants who believe," He commanded Prophet Muhammad ﷺ, "to establish prayer and spend from what We have provided for them, secretly and manifestly, before the coming of a Day in which there will be no trade and no friendships" (Ibrahim 14:31). Now is the time, in this life, to make the trades and the friendships that we can bank for the future. It is the time to exchange everything cruel, harmful and unjust for kindness, benefits, and equity. It is time to make amends and embrace others in a circle of kinship and love.

Truth is the currency and unit of account on the Day of Judgement. The Quran tells us that "The weight on that Day is the Truth. So, whosoever's weights are heavy – it is they who will be the successful. And whosoever's weights are light – they are those who lost themselves for the injustices they perpetrated against Our *ayat*" (Al-A'raf 7:8-9). The *ayat* are His Truth in the universe and in our very selves. We are a microcosm of the macrocosm; a Truth that with our human limits we are scarcely able to grasp. Those whose weights are light betrayed the interconnectedness of this reality and were too arrogant to accept guidance.

Our knowledge of Truth is inseparable from Allah's guidance. It is His Truth irrespective of our bias because it is His creation. His Truth is the standard, and it applies to everything. "Oh you who believe, be reinforcers (*qawamina*) with equity, witnesses for Allah, even if it is against yourselves, or your parents and close relatives, be they rich or poor. It is Allah who is worthier of [of your truthfulness regarding] them. So do not follow whims that you may be just. And if you twist or reject [this command] then be sure that Allah is ever aware with what you do" (An-Nisa' 4:133). How many legal systems protect against self-incrimination and afford alleged criminals the *right* to remain silent? And here, the Quran is telling us *speak the truth even against yourself.*

To be heedful is to be truthful. "Oh you who believe, be heedful of Allah and be with the truthful" (At-Tawbah 9:119). Being conscious of Allah means upholding the truth (*haq*) as well as the rights (*huquq*) of others. The heedful counsel each other with truth and intervene wherever they can to ensure the establishment of truth. "Whoever intercedes a goodly [truthful] intercession will have a share in it, and whoever intercedes an evil [false] intercession will have a portion of it. And Allah is ever timely over all things" (An-Nisa' 4:85). We have a dire shortage of truth in our world today, and the consequences have been devastating.

The magnitude of our world's loss-of-truth crisis is colossal. Any corrective measure will require a complex, multifaceted, and global strategy that integrates an equally colossal dose of patience. Sound hearts will have to work together from their different and dispersed points to bring truth back to the centre of our policies and institutions, back to the centre of our lives. There is a clear awakening all over the world permitting people from all walks of life to distinguish between good and evil, truth and falsehood. That is the good news. Rectification, however, will not be easy. Not with all the new tools and technologies that are being unleashed on a humanity just seeing daybreak, struggling to make the transition from darkness to light.

In a presentation on Parliament Hill in 2023, I, along with my friends and colleagues, urged Canadian universities, colleges, and educational institutions to demand that our government call for a ceasefire, that it condemn the targeted destruction of places of learning at all levels and the targeted assassination of Palestinian academics and intellectuals, that it honours their legacy through commitments to rebuild infrastructure, initiate collaborations, provide scholarships, and demand the protection of Palestinian intellectuals, educators, students, and their institutions. By focusing on intellectuals, I did not intend – in any way – to diminish the value of any life. As a beautiful Indian proverb says, "All the flowers of all the tomorrows are in the seeds of today."

I shared with them three truths that Muslims hold sacred. First, that "Knowledge is the inheritance of humanity" – this is a deep-rooted Islamic belief based on the teachings of Prophet Muhammad ﷺ. It is a universal law that we all benefit from shared ideas and build on each other's discoveries and innovations. Knowledge from the past, the present and as yet to be discovered in the future. The killing of intellectuals and the destruction of educational institutions robs humanity of this inheritance and its invaluable truths. It robs you and me of invaluable wealth, of cures, technologies, literature, language, of ways of knowing and being that contribute to our collective resilience.

Second, I told them that seeking knowledge is an obligation on all Muslims. Knowledge is the key to uncovering and verifying truth. This is a tenet of our faith and so the targeted destruction of schools, universities, public libraries, museums, and centres for learning, the disruption of and perilous access to them, for tens of thousands of individuals is extremely disconcerting and heartbreaking.

And finally, I reminded them that repositories of knowledge are to be protected and not jeopardized by hostilities in times of conflict so that their knowledge can be preserved and utilized for the benefit of those returning from war and to rebuild society as it recalibrates and returns to normalcy. Targeting intellectuals and other educational personnel is clearly intended to silence dissent, undermine the future of Palestinian people and their ability to rebuild their communities, to innovate, engage in trade, participate in scientific and cultural exchanges, and connect globally with like-minded peers.

I drew their attention to a document that a group of Canadian university presidents agreed to in September 2021. *The Role of Canadian Universities in Society* outlines the significant role that universities play in dealing with issues that endanger society. It noted the special privilege that these institutions have in employing their resources – people, programs, policies, finances, research, relationships – to influence social, political and economic systems. The presidents were clearly cognizant of the power of universities to amplify student voices or alternatively to supress them. They were acutely aware that their collective impact went beyond national borders and our current lifetimes. But the student agency and the better future they alluded to was nowhere to be found when it came to Gaza. I said to those presidents that in their silence, which actually turned into the active suppression of staff, faculty and students, their integrity and our humanity as Canadians was seriously at stake. When truth is lost, however, such calls fall on deaf ears.

The Quran tells us that Allah checks some people by means of another, had this not been the case "the earth would have been corrupted, but Allah is full of bounty to the worlds" (Al-Baqarah 2:251). We must not lose heart. Prophet Muhammad ﷺ taught us that the best struggle is a word of truth to a tyrannical ruler. Truth be told to tyranny in all its forms! The truth will prevail if we stay the course, if we maintain the soundness of our hearts, the purity of our intentions, and the best of means. It will prevail if those who live have the courage to tell the story.

We have a beautiful example in the life of our beloved Prophet Muhammad ﷺ. He and the believers with him strove with their wealth and persons in the way of Allah seeking mercy, equity, justice, balance, and everything beautiful that Allah ordained. He embodied the way to the water for those around him and for all succeeding generations. This is how that early generation of believers succeeded. "So, their Lord responded to them, 'I will never cause to be lost the work of any doer among you whether male or female, you are one of another. So, whoever emigrated and were evicted from their homes and were harmed in My way and fought and were killed, I will expiate their sins and I will surely admit them to gardens beneath which rivers flow, reward (*thawab*) from Allah and Allah has with Him the best reward" (Al-'Imran 3:195). In these gardens they will dwell in eternal bliss, that is the great prize (At-Tawbah 9:88-89).

The rewards of heedfulness enrich the believer in this life as well. "Whoever is heedful of Allah, He will give him an outlet and provide for him from where he had not contemplated" (At-Talaq 65:2-3). So put your trust in Allah. When you do good, Allah ensures the provision of openings for you. If you have thought of all the possible outcomes, know that you have not thought of the one that Allah has in store for you. "And whoever is heedful of Allah—He will make ease of his affairs for him" (At-Talaq 65:4). When you are heedful, life will seem that bit easier. So turn to Allah and ask for forgiveness, trust in Him and He will please you with something special, and reward you for the good you do unto others (Hud 11:3). All the beautiful things (*zina*) and wholesome provisions (*tayyibat*) are for the servants of Allah in the life of this world, and exclusively theirs in the Hereafter (Al-A'raf 7:32).

Glimpses of the life to come – the prize – for the heedful are sprinkled throughout the Quran. A constant reminder of the impending reward for our efforts, gratitude, truthfulness, humility, and patience. I have always loved the description presented in Surah Al-Insan (76:11-22). The Quran tells us that Allah will protect the believers from the evils and fears of the Day of Judgement. Instead, He will grant them radiance and happiness. Placing them in gardens and adorning them with green brocaded silk and beautiful accessories. They will recline comfortably on splendid sofas and enjoy perfect weather. Access to delicious fruits and drinks served by beautiful attendants in refined crystal crockery, will be abundant and within perpetual reach. And, it will be said, "Indeed, this is for you a reward and your strivings were appreciated" (Al-Insan 76:22).

May Allah have mercy on us and our loved ones, and on all those with sound hearts who struggled for the triumph of Truth. May He forgive us all, enter us collectively into peace, and grant us a magnificent reunion in His gardens of bliss, underneath which rivers flow. May we all be winners in the best and most worthwhile race on earth and then share in the bounties of our Generous Lord. My dear brothers and sisters, my beloved Ummah, let us heed the way to the water and keep our eye on the prize.